THE STORRINGS BROTHERS

75 YEARS IN CANADIAN FOSTER HOMES AND PRISONS

Glen D. Storrings
Murray K. Storrings
Dennis R. Storrings

 FriesenPress

Suite 300 - 990 Fort St
Victoria, BC, V8V 3K2
Canada

www.friesenpress.com

Additional Contributers:
Donald E Waite (Author & Photographer & Ex -RCMP), Foreword

ISBN
978-1-5255-5868-9 (Hardcover)
978-1-5255-5869-6 (Paperback)
978-1-5255-5870-2 (eBook)

1. BIOGRAPHY & AUTOBIOGRAPHY, PERSONAL MEMOIRS

Distributed to the trade by The Ingram Book Company

FOREWORD

Aposting to RCMP Haney Detachment as a rookie constable introduced me to the three Storrings brothers in Canada's 1967 Centennial year. The reputation of the oldest brother, Glen, as a street fighter was well known to senior members since thugs would come from near and far to go one on one with him. He rarely lost a fight. My first encounters with the brothers were no doubt while doing prison escorts by cruiser between court and jail. One night I was in hot pursuit in a car chase after brothers Dennis and Murray. They ran in the back door of a house in Hammond and turned off the hall lights, with me right on their heels. By the time backup arrived, they had escaped out the front door, leaving me scaring the daylights out of the homeowners in their bedroom. When backup finally did arrive, we found thirty-plus packages of cigarettes underneath the floorboards of the car's front seat. They had broken into a gas station and forced open the cigarette machine to steal the cigarettes and coins.

After my buy out on my contract from the police force to open a camera store in 1971, my travels took me to Yale to collect history for the writing of a book on the Fraser Canyon. My very first contact was Gladys Chrane, the grandmother of the three brothers. Gladys was the daughter of William Teague, the first gold commissioner of Yale. She told me a little bit about her daughter Eleanor and her three sons. Initially, I didn't make the connection between Gladys grandsons and the Storrings brothers from my policing days in Haney. A short time later, a newly married couple who lived adjacent to the Teague home helped Gladys turn her parents' place into a museum. He was from Haney and told me a little about the Storrings brothers being in foster care and being in trouble with the police.

In the early 1980s Murray opened a storefront just to the east of my portrait studio on the main drag of Haney. His shop was called "The House of Stained Glass," and he made stained-glass windows, lamps and ornaments. He used to cut glass for my photo frames. Sometimes we shared stories about playing "cops and robbers."

In the late 1990s Murray and his spouse moved into an apartment that my wife managed in Maple Ridge's downtown core. At that time, he had just retired from working two jobs simultaneously for the school board and municipality. He had started as a custodian with the school board and worked his way up to supervisor for the custodial department. He did maintenance at the leisure centre for the municipality. He was very involved in collecting family history, and I gave him some copy negatives from Gladys old albums. One time when he was at work his wife cleaned out their apartment and left him with only a TV and a chair. The police arrived at a very confrontational situation and sent the wife away.

In 2007 an author contacted me wanting an aerial photograph of Oakalla Prison Farm in Burnaby for a story, and I told him about the three brothers who had collectively spent a hundred years in foster care and jails in BC. The brothers agreed to a taped interview with the idea of a book or documentary on their experiences. They came to my home and we did a two-hour taping session. That evening Dennis and I took in the just-released 3D movie *Avatar*. It was the first time Dennis saw a movie in twenty years, and wearing the glasses, he recoiled during many of the scenes.

Over the next few days Dennis told me a lot of stories about his youth in foster care and jail, and it occurred to me that the brothers didn't have a chance from the get-go. Their parents and family let them down, social services let them down, and the police, courts and prison systems locked them up and threw away the keys. This book promises to be a good read.

Donald E. Waite
Maple Ridge, B.C.

MURRAY FAMILY HISTORY
PART 1

Grandmother Gladys Teague (Chrane) on far right with sisters on horseback trip near Yale, BC.

Backyard of the Teague/Chrane home in Yale, 1930. This was the front yard then, as the road was there.

The Teague sisters and a friend (Grandmother sitting) taken at Yale, early 1900.

Uncles Walter and Glenn Chrane, 1940s, WW2.

The Chrane sisters in Yale: Norma, June, Eleanor (our mother).

Our mother with a crow in Vancouver, 1950s.

William Teague, our great-grandfather, in Yale.

William Teague was from the St Day Area, Cornwall, England.

Great-Aunt Alice Teague (William and Alice Teague's daughter).

Gladys Chrane in her lovely flower garden in her home in Yale.

Bernard Savage was working in BC as a surveyor from England on a working visa. He was my grandmother Gladys Teague's boyfriend while in BC. She was nineteen at the time, but she wanted to get married but they split up. The story was that as a young man, he went off to some war in the US in the early 1900s and was never heard from again. Grandmother kept in contact with Bernard's mother in Leicester England the parish of Loughborough area over the years, and she also kept photos of him and her for over seventy-five years until her death in 1981 in Hope, BC. He was her first love.

Bernard Savage, left, and friend in Yale on a break at work.

All Hallows School class picture next door to Grandmother's home around the late 1800s in Yale where the Teague girls attended.

Chelsey Storrings (Murray's granddaughter) at Grandmother's home in Yale in deep thought.

Auntie Babe with her new Buick in Yale in the 1950s. House in back was Uncle Glen's, which he built in the late 1930s on Grandmother's property for his wife and his daughter Dawn before he left for the war when he returned his wife left him for another man his daughter Dawn lives in Agassiz.

School picture of the three Teague girls, Grandmother to the right of the teacher and her sister on the left. Another sister is in the back row, third from the left. Early 1900s.

The Teague home in Yale, BC. This article was Quoted by Susan and Darwin Baerg of Yale BC

This house is known locally as the "Teague House." As this brief history shows, the house has passed through many owners, some rather colourful characters from early British Columbia.

Lots 10 and 11 were bought at public auction from the Colony of British Columbia in 1865 by John Alway for the sum of about twenty pounds sterling each. It seems unlikely that the old house on the property was built by him soon afterwards, probably in 1866.

Alway was quite the local entrepreneur. An advertisement that appeared in the British Columbia Tribune *newspaper, published briefly in Yale in 1868, shows he was in partnership in a shipping and freighting firm:*

Alway & Bailey
shipping & freight fireproof warehouse
own teams of horses for Big Bend or Cariboo
Front Street, Yale

John Alway also advertised around the same time as an auctioneer and commission merchant. He made the headlines in a few papers in the colony after he reported that his India guide tried to murder him on a trip down the river in 1869.

In 1869 the old house passed into the possession of Helen Sutton, possibly the wife of W.H. Sutton, a well-known Yale merchant specializing in wines, liquors and cigars in addition to a wide assortment of stock, including billiard tables and coal oil. He also ran one of Yale's Livery stables.

In 1874 Isaac Oppenheim bought the house. He was one of the five Oppenheimer brothers who opened one of the province's largest mercantile chains, with stores in Yale, Barkerville and several other centres. One of Isaac's brothers, David, became Vancouver's second mayor.

During the height of railway construction in 1884, Isaac Oppenheimer sold the house to John Trutch. He was born in Antigua but was educated in England where he became a civil engineer and surveyor. He and his brother, Joseph, came out to the west coast in the early 1850s and eventually found their way to British Columbia where they were engaged in the early 1960s on construction of the first Alexandria Suspension Bridge. John married Zoe Musgrave, sister of Governor Sir Anthony Musgrave. Trutch moved in the highest social circles and it is likely that he wanted the house because it was right next door to Andrew Onderdonk's home, the centre of Yale's upper crust.

John Trutch was not as famous as Joseph, who was British Columbia's first lieutenant governor and became Sir Joseph Trutch. The reason John bought the house in 1884 was because he had been appointed as an inspector of construction along the railway. This was a contro-versial position because he was accused of neglecting his duties and allowing station house roofs to be put on the wrong way, with only half of the required nails.

Trutch did not stay in the house for more than a year and after CPR construction was finished, he and his wife moved to Victoria. He retained ownership, however, until 1985 when it was sold to Elsie O'Connor (who had likely been living there). She immediately sold it to Alice Teague. It remained in the Teague family for almost a hundred years. In 1990 the house was purchased from Walter Chrane, grandson of Alice and William Teague, by Susan and Darwin Baerg.

William Teague, with white beard, sitting on the right in the front row with some politicians in Yale, early 1900, below.

William Teague and fellow members of the government, taken in Yale.

The Teague family in Yale.
1895

The Teague family in Yale. My grandmother on the left of her father, holding a doll. Photo taken around 1893. Two other children, Cundy, born 1871, and his sister, Charlotte, born 1877, died within a week of each other when the flu epidemic hit in 1881. Grandmother Gladys was the youngest holding the doll, born in 1889 in Yale. She had four sisters, Elizabeth, Alice, in back row and sisters Nannie and Minnie Teague. William Teague was a miner, a government agent in Yale and a magistrate as well.

Our great-grandmother came from St Day in England. Her trip to Canada lasted fifty-three days with her husband at her side, and they moved to Yale. Later they moved into the home of Lieutenant Governor Sir Joseph Trutch in Yale. On warm summer nights she would sit looking over the Fraser River below their home. Mrs. Teague came from England with Judge and Mrs. Saunders. It took two months to round the horn, and she brought her daughter Alice and a piano—a wedding present from friends in England—then came up the Fraser river to Yale on a William Irving's steamer.

She had a sweet smile and a gentle voice, as one writer would say when he interviewed her in the 1920s. She had witnessed so many life-changing scenes, like the CPR being constructed through British Columbia when Yale was a busy town full of life.

The late Henry J. Cambie, pioneer railway builder and explorer, and Judge F. W. Howay were among her friends, and she was invited to unveiling ceremonies in Yale. The Teague home was next to All Hallows elaborate Church of England school, and all her daughters went there.

All Hallows Girls School in Yale.

She attended a gathering in Stanley Park to honour the pioneers that had been in the province for fifty years or more. We three brothers never had a chance to meet her, of course, but it seemed like we knew her. She died in 1927 at the home of her daughter and her son-in-law, Gladys and Robert Chrane (Ray). He changed his name from Robert to Raymond when he came to Canada.

William Teague was a hard-working miner, Indian agent and clerk of the court and the JP (Justices of the Peace). The old courthouse where Justice Bigbie used to officiate, which is now surrounded by trees, is where he and his wife lived for years before moving to the old Trutch house, now called the Teague house, as it still stands today as a B&B .William was born in St Day, England, July 18, 1835. He came to Virginia City at nineteen during the California gold rush and worked in Yale at a mine he and Shila Flint found on Siwash Creek, building a cable to cross the water and access the mine.

William Teague invented the cable car to cross the Fraser River in Yale. Kipp Reece and Teague then bought up most of the farmland that is now Chilliwack. He later had a mine at Barkerville near Gulph Flats and had an interest in the Blue Ribbon Mine and the Queens Mine in Yale, among others. He also had 800 acres across the river in Yale, but let it go for taxes owed. Our grandmother told us stories of him climbing the mountains around Yale; he would light a fire to show her he made it and was safe. Great-Grandfather took in a wayward young man, Leroy, to help him mine years later. Leroy was shot and killed in a gunfight on the street in Virginia City (Carson City). William Teague died May 27, 1916, with his daughter by his side in Seattle when he was there to visit.

Ray (Robert) Chrane and family, left to right, Walter Chrane, Glenn Chrane, June Chrane Doren, Norma Chrane (Dalstrom). Taken in the Chrane home, late 1930s.

Leroy and William Teague at mine.

Leroy worked by Teague's side for many years, but we never knew his last name or where he was from.

A Yale schoolmate from the early years, Raymond Sakowsky, and his friends Jackie and Murray.

A Yale schoolmate from the early years, Raymond Sakowsky, and his friends Jackie and Murray.

Taken in Yale several years ago next to Barry's store. Raymond delivered papers in Yale and to our grandmother's house in the late 1950s. Murray went to school with Raymond, who lives in Port Moody now. Grandmother always said she liked Raymond.

Uncle Walter Chrane and Auntie Babe (Norma Dalstrom) in Yale, 1992, taken on a summer day.

From left, our cousin Lynnette (Dalstrom) Deaton and her aunt June in Yale, 1992.

Our Uncle Glenn and his sister, our Aunt June.

SPORTS

2 Rivers Boxing Club inducted into B.C. Amateur Boxing Hall of Fame

MELANIE LAW
Observer Reporter

Quesnel's 2 Rivers Boxing Club has won yet another accolade – it has just been inducted into the B.C. Amateur Boxing Hall of Fame.

The club also celebrates its 20th anniversary this year.

Wally Doern, who started the club in 1998, says he was happy and surprised when he heard the club had been inducted.

"We have had many great boxers come through the ranks. We've always had a large membership and portrayed good sportsmanship, and we've put on several shows here," says Doern.

Brian Zelley, one of the founders of the B.C. Amateur Boxing Hall of Fame, says he has been a supporter of 2 Rivers since its inception.

"They are truly a positive force in the sport of amateur boxing, with the coaches and boxers always a first-class act."

Doern has coached a handful of boxers up to the provincial and national level, including Olin Lee

Above: Quesnel's 2 Rivers Boxing Club has been inducted into the B.C. Amateur Boxing Hall of Fame. Club owner Wally Doern is celebrating the club's 20th year in 2018. Right: Memorabilia from 2 Rivers' 20 years line the walls at the club in West Quesnel.

MELANIE LAW PHOTO

Wally Doern, our cousin, a boxing instructor in Quesnel, BC, for over twenty years.

Gary Doern in his singing days.

Cousin Wally with his 1957 ford at Yale Bc.

Cousins Gary Doern, Glen Storrings and Wally Doern

Taken in Yale. Left to right is Lynnette, her dad, Victor Dalstrom, and her mother, Norma Alice Dalstrom.

Shelly, Chelsey, and Marie Storrings and
D.H. Williams (Shane Doiron Hartle) our nephew, sister Penny's son.

LAUDERDALE HERALD

NTY, FLORIDA. "THE GATEWAY TO THE EVERGLADES"; ON THE DIXIE HIGHWAY; FINE ROADS; NO TOLL BRIDGES; IDEAL CLIMATE

CELLENT ADVERTISING MEDIUM, AS IT REACHES EVERY STATE IN THE UNION. OFFICIAL PAPER FOR BOTH CITY AND COUNTY

Our Hotels, Cafes, Apartments and rental cottages are first-class and the prices are reasonable.— Welcome to our city.

FORT LAUDERDALE, FLORIDA, SEPTEMBER 22, 1922.

Suscription $2.00 Per Year

FATHER OF THIS CITY TO AGAIN SEE SON WHO WAS REPORTED TO HAVE BEEN KILLED IN WAR

LAUDERDALE LAUNDRY READY TO OPERATE OCT. FIFTEENTH

Work of installing the machinery in the Fort Lauderdale Steam Laundry is progressing rapidly and the laundry will be in operation by the fifteenth of October, according to G. W. Hibbard, president of the concern when seen by a Herald representative Wednesday.

Mr. Hibbard said that at the present the washers and flat work ironer were installed and that the balance of the machinery had been shipped and would doubtless arrive in the near future.

A steam laundry is an industry that has long been needed in this city and the advent of the Fort Lauderdale Laundry is hailed with satisfaction on the part of the people of the city.

TEACHERS' MEETING HELD LAST SATURDAY

Most of the teachers were present on Saturday morning to attend the first teachers' meeting of the year, and to meet the new principal Mr. Robertson. There were several new members in the faculty as well: Mr. Hanson, Miss Lois Jackson, Miss Button are some who have recently come to Lauderdale. Miss Hiller who will teach kindergarten is accompanied by her mother and has taken rooms in the Wallace apartments; Miss Marcia Duncan has her mother with her and they have rooms at Prof. Henderson's home; Miss Lyndesmyer, Miss Mary Francis Dawson and Miss Montgomery are domiciled in the Smith apartments.

SARASOTA MOTORCADE TO BE ENTERTAINED HERE

The Sarasota Motorcade passed through Lauderdale Wednesday...

Robert (Ray) Chrane

"Your son was killed in line of duty" was the wording of the telegram from Washington back in the early part of 1919, after A. G. Chrane, 70 years old of this city, besieched government agencies for months in an effort to learn the whereabouts of his son, Lyndell Chrane, who enlisted during the early part of the war and was sent overseas. This result of the old man's tireless search staggered him like the sharp thrust of a bayonet. His son dead! And fourteen long, weary years have passed without a sight of the boy who went to a distant city to gain his education and stayed there. And now he was even torn out of the secret folds of cherished memory. The old man prayed earnestly and with great fervor that he may retain faith in Heaven's scheme. But he could not regain contentment. The child of long ago squeezed into his dreams little, pudgy hands embracing his gray head and big, moist brown eye laughing at him. Providence was piling it on heavy, he thought.

But, there exists in the Scheme of Life a remarkable balancing medium—Chance. And as chance would have it the scales of the old man's misery long weighted down, swung clear of its burden and revealed the gold, untarnished surface. Last week a letter came from a daughter of Mr. Chrane now Mrs. W. R. Oliver of Johnstown, Pa., who has lost track of her father in the mazes of her own life and burden. It was a rather hastily written affair. Seemingly penned under great stress or great excitement. But the contents! The old man's eyes ran over with tears of happiness after he read the first line. He could see no more of the writing. The entire world blurred. Nearby objects fade into thin air. What mattered the world and all its petty schemes. His son lived! What else mattered? What a Providence! The Fates were kind...

...of the daughter. He enlisted with the Canadians and after the war went back to Canada to live. But this year he had an arbing for his kinfolk. After a long search he located his sister. And now he is coming to Fort Lauderdale to see his dad. They have not seen each other for seventeen years. And, oh, what a meeting that's going to be!

1922 Newspaper clipping from the Fort Lauderdale Herald of our great-grandfather in Fort Lauderdale concerning his son, our grandfather R.L Chrane, who he thought was killed in a war but was in Canada. Our grandfather Robert (Ray) Chrane changed his first name to Raymond when he came to Canada to avoid detection and also added over ten years to his age.

```
                    murray history
American Revolution:
Also known as the American War of Independence. Lasting from 1775 to 1783,
Revolution was founded on discontent in the Thirteen Colonies regarding tax
representation in government and limitations on growth set by British treat
After war broke out, two armies invaded the province of Québec, but were
defeated. Most French Canadians remained neutral, while most in Nova Scotia
St. John (now Prince Edward Island) and Newfoundland were loyal to the Crow
1781, British forces were defeated and, in 1783, Britain recognized the
independence of the United States in the Treaty of Paris. After the war, 40
Loyalist refugees moved north into what is now Ontario, Québec, Nova Scotia
New Brunswick. This formed the nucleus of what would later become Canada.
Visit the Library of Congress: American Memory collections for more informa
Visit the PBS: Liberty! The American Revolution site for more information.
```

Information below on the Storrings history, connection to the Loyalists and the American Revolution.

Murray and Grandmother in Yale, 1950.

Murray at age three in Yale.

Murray's wife Betty, Grandmother and Betty Nicholson, Murray's mother-in law, in Yale in the 1970s.

Murray and daughter Shelly in Grand Forks.

*Murray's daughter Charlene Sloan
at my mother's gravesite in Chilliwack.*

Murrays dog Queenie on the Grand Forks River.

Dennis, Murray ,and Glen in picture

Looking from Grandmother's house down the Fraser River towards Yale.

Photo of Karla Conrad, schoolmate who often went to see our grandmother, as she lived across the highway above Grandmother's home. Karla's mother was Grandmother's best friend and phoned her every night to make sure she was okay.

1950s Café and hotel in Yale. Murray was in this café when we heard about the Buddy Holly plane crash. It had a juke box and was a nice place to go for a pop in the 1950s.

Uncle Elmer and Aunt Doris Storrings, 1916, in Saskatoon (our father's sister and brother).

Great-Aunt Maria from the Storrings side of the family.

MURRAY'S FAMILY HISTORY PART TWO: CHRANE, STORRINGS, TEAGUE, MICHELL, RUGG, DOERN, DALSTROM

Above, our great-grandfather William Teague, second from left, spinning a story about a gold mine to some men from the US and his friend Reece from Chilliwack. Late 1800s or early 1900s.

The original Teague home, which burned in a fire and was later rebuilt in or near the same spot in Yale.

Uncle Walter Chrane with friends in Lytton, BC, late 1930s

Uncle Eddie with his boy and wife Maria, in 1958. She is our GG aunt Maria and GG Uncle Eddie and a second cousin

Great-Grandmother Alice (Michell) Teague and cousin Stephen Michell of England, inventor of the Clack Valve who has a book on this subject printed in England.

William Teague at courthouse with his wife and his children Cundy and Charlotte sitting on a step, with the children's sister in Alice Teague's arms. Alice Teague's face is scratched out because she did not like her picture, as told by her daughter Gladys Teague, our grandmother.

*A male friend with Auntie June Chrane Doern, Gladys Chrane, our grandmother,
our mother Eleanor (Chrane) Storrings and a nice old car. Around 1940 in the Yale area.*

East Yale in 1955. Mt. Linky in the background.

Both Uncle Glen and Uncle Walter were in the Second World War in France and returned safe to Yale after the war was over. Glenn Chrane, Walter Chrane and Gladys Chrane our lovely grandmother, are in this photo. Gladys died in 1981 at Hope Hospital on Sept 2. Murray had just gone to see her and he was the last to see her alive. She was born June 24, 1889, in Yale and spent all her life in her beloved home there. She always said she wanted the heritage home kept in the family. She was captain of the Girl Guides and was active in the Women's Auxiliary at St. John's Divine Anglican church in Yale. Grandmother enjoyed hiking, horseback riding and going to the Queens Mine above Yale and collecting First Nations artifacts. She was survived by two daughters, June Doern and Norma Dalstrom, two sons, Walter and Glenn, nine grandchildren and seven great-grand-children. She was predeceased by her husband, Raymond Chrane, in 1955 and daughter Eleanor, our mother, in 1961.

Glenn Chrane, born September 23, 1918. Died Oct 14, 1995.

Walter Chrane, born April 05, 1921, died Oct 30, 2005.

Murray in Missouri, where he found his great-grandparents' gravesite below
Francis Rugg (Chrane and A.G Chrane).

Grandmother Gladys Teague (Chrane) at nineteen
years old on an outing at Gordon Creek in Yale.

Grandmother's niece Doris Mackenrot
Nannie Teague's daughter in Yale home.

Family and a friend on an outing in Yale.

Murray with Grandmothers' cat in Yale around 1949.

Murray as a teen at Iris and Robert Morse's home on St. Anne Street in Haney, 1963-64. One of few pictures of him as a teen.

Grandmother Gladys Teague Chrane.

The Storrings homestead in Ontario where it all began. One Storrings brother came over to Canada from the New York area and started a family in this homestead.

Aunt June and family.

Our Chrane family in Missouri, where our grandfather came from (R.L. Chrane). Other families were the Rugg's, Gaw, and Michell's from England, and many more I have found in my over twenty years of searching for family.

Auntie Babe with her dog in Yale.

Grandmother and her daughter Norma (Auntie Babe).

First-cousin Lynette (Dalstrom) Deaton wearing Grandmother's sister's (Charlotte) dress.
Also, in the picture is Lynette's mom and grandmother in Grandmothers' yard in Yale.

*Murray and friend Nelly in Romania, 2003, when he travelled to see her
and stay a month in that interesting part of the world.*

*Aunt June Chrane with her father
on a boat, 1940s.*

*Sandra Macpherson, Glen's girlfriend,
in Haney, BC, around 1959-60.*

Mother in Stanley Park, 1950s.

Glen, Murray and Dennis in Yale. 1950s

Murray's handmade stained-glass window.

Aunt Norma (Babe), B 1926 to D 2016, June and Eleanor Chrane our mother in Yale.

THE CHILLIWACK PROGRESS, Thur., Dec. 28, 1961

MRS. MARGARET TERESA STORRINGS

Requiem Mass was celebrated yesterday morning in St. Mary's Catholic church with Father G. McKinnon celebrant for Mrs. Margaret Teresa Storrings who died Friday at her residence, 465½ Vedder road.

Interment was in St. Mary's cemetery.

Mrs. Storrings is survived by her husband, Alex; three daughters, Mrs. A. (Doris) Pasacreta, Merritt; Mrs. W. (Phyllis) Sterritt, Hazelton; Mrs. J. (Joyce) Tolmie, Vedder Crossing; two sons, Aylmer, Vancouver; Douglas, Hazelton; 15 grandchildren; four sisters and one brother in Vancouver.

Mrs. Storrings was born in Arthur, Ont., in 1892 and had lived in the district for 12 years.

Henderson's Funeral Homes were in charge of arrangements.

Grandmother Storrings' obituary.   *Marie Eleanor Storrings, Murray's daughter.*

Marie with her first car in Maple Ridge.

Raymond (Robert) Chrane was born on June 26, 1891 and passed away March 12, 1955 from heart failure in Vancouver. He came from Salisbury, Missouri, and married our grandmother in the early 1900s but had a roving eye for other women which caused him problems later in his marriage Newspaper clippings were uncovered with the help of Janice

Wilkin from Campbell River, who was okay with using her name in this book. Janice will uncover family information for people in which she has done for me .

Below are the newspaper reports from 1929 about Raymond Chrane (originally Robert) who came to Canada to get a job with the railway in Boston Bar. He added years to his age, which makes him sixty-four when he died, not seventy-eight as his obituary stated. I found this out from a Rugg descendant's book (*The Descendants of John Rugg*) a family member sent me from Missouri.

THE VANCOUVER PROVINCE,

MONDAY, MARCH 14, 1955

CHRANE — Passed away March 12, 1955, Raymond Lindell Chrane o' 5541 Elm St., in his 78th year. Survived by his loving wife, Gladys; 2 sons, Glen and Walter; 3 daughters, Mrs. E. Storrings, Mrs. M. Doeren, Mrs. V. Dalstrom. Funeral service Wednesday at 3 p.m., in Simmons & McBride Funeral Chapel, Broadway at Maple St., Rev. Gordon E. Bratt officiating. Cremation. No flowers by request.

Court charges. In 1929 Grandfather got a young lady pregnant, and she was under the age of consent, as the story was told. She was the daughter of a policeman from the Laidlaw area. Grandmother left him after he was released from a prison farm in 1930.

THE DAILY PROVINCE, VANCOUVER

THURSDAY, MAY 23, 1929.

To Impose Sentences In Royal City on Saturday

NEW WESTMINSTER, May 23.—Sentences will be imposed in the Assize Court at 10 a.m. Saturday.

In the final case of the present sessions, Raymond L. Chrane, of Agassiz, who had been convicted on a statutory charge, was found not guilty on a second charge of that nature. The jury was out only about five minutes.

THE VANCOUVER SUN

FRIDAY EVENING, MAY 17, 1929

Agassiz Man Found Guilty at Assizes

NEW WESTMINSTER, May 17.— Raymond L. Chrane, chiropractor, Agassiz, was found guilty of a statutory charge by New Westminster assize jury, Thursday. The jury was out two hours.

For the second time during the assizes, Mr. Justice Murphy ruled out police evidence regarding admissions alleged to have been made by the accused following arrest.

Evidence of this nature was rejected in the case against James Wallace, Indian, found guilty of manslaughter.

In both instances the judge ruled that accused were not properly warned.

Found guilty in court, 1929, sent to Oakalla Prison Farm.

THE DAILY PROVINCE, VANCOUVER,
SATURDAY, MAY 25, 1929.

FIVE-YEAR TERM FOR FOUR MEN

Imposed at Royal City On Bell and Three Chinese.

YEAR FOR CHRANE

NEW WESTMINSTER, May 25.—Concluding a nine-day session, sentences in the Assize Court were pronounced today by Mr. Justice Denis Murphy. They were:

William Bell, Tacoma, convicted of the theft of $12,000 worth of jewelry from Thomas Gifford's store, August 18, 1928, five years.

Wing Fong, Fong Kit and Chang Jung, Ladner Chinese, convicted of distributing and possession of opium, five years each. A $200 fine was also imposed on each, and in default of payment, a three-months' additional term.

Raymond L. Chrane, Agassiz, convicted of a statutory offense, one year.

James Wallace, Indian, Chilliwack, convicted of manslaughter in connection with the death of Lee Kee Tai, 80-year-old Chinese, at Chilliwack, suspended sentence.

"CONFIRMED CRIMINAL."

The judge stated that Bell was a confirmed criminal and had already served a penitentiary term. Chrane, he said, was not a decent citizen, was a menace to the community and had not been supporting his family as he should.

Regarding Wallace, the judge said that if it had not been for liquor, the source of which was Chilliwack's Chinatown, the crime might not have been committed. The jury had recommended mercy, and the attorney-general when consulted had left the disposition of this case to the judge.

Sentenced in court, 1929, Raymond Chrane of Agassiz, BC.

Walter Chrane, our mother's brother, of Yale. As one can see, the Storrings brothers were not the only ones who landed in trouble with the law but straightened out in later life.

Below are newspaper clippings about Walter Chrane we uncovered while searching for family history.

Victoria Daily Times
TUESDAY, DECEMBER 19, 1961

$775 in Fines For Three Men On Betting Counts

Three city men were fined a total of $775 in city police court today on betting offences.

William Paul, 633 Johnson, was fined $400 for recording horse racing bets; Wallace Lindell Mitchell Chrane, 630 Johnson, was fined $200 on a similar charge, and George W. Barber, 709 Johnson Street, was fined $175 for providing information intended for use in connection with bookmaking.

The charges were laid after three police officers, two in plain clothes, visited the three Johnson Street premises and found racing forms and paraphernalia.

All three accused pleaded guilty.

Bookie charged in newspaper article below clipping, 1961.

VICTORIA DAILY TIMES, WED., JAN. 19, 1966

Bookmaking Charge Dropped

Defence counsel Dermod Owen-Flood Tuesday in central court used a legal technicality to have his client acquitted of recording bets.

He was defending Walter L. M. Chrane, 976 Humbolt, charged last August with recording bets.

Mr. Owen-Flood argued the charge was a nullity because it alleged two separate offences in the one information.

The charge read: ". . . did unlawfully use or knowingly allow a place under his control to be used . . ." for recording bets.

There is a difference between using a place for recording bets and allowing someone else to use it, Mr. Owen-Flood said.

Magistrate William Ostler ruled the charge was not a nullity but was a bad charge because of the duplication.

Clippings from Victoria, BC, of bookie charges.

Times Colonist (Victoria, British Columbia, Canada) · 03 Feb 1966.

Betting House Charge

Walter Lindell Chrane was remanded to Feb. 23 for plea in central court today when he was charged with keeping a common betting house Aug. 21, 1965, at 1023 Linden Ave.

Walter Chrane remanded, 1966.

Victoria Daily Times
VICTORIA, B.C., WEDNESDAY, FEBRUARY 6, 1963—PAGE 13

Betting Offence Brings $300 Fine

A man was fined $300 in city police court today after pleading guilty to recording horse-racing bets.

City police arrested Wallace Chrane at 630 Johnson Jan. 30.* He was in possession of a tally sheet and other horse-racing information at the time.

He had a similar conviction in December, 1961, court was told.

More charges on Walter Chrane.

The VANCOUVER SUN:
FRIDAY, FEB. 25, 1966

Bookie Gets $2,000 Fine Or 6 Months

VICTORIA (CP) — A man who pleaded guilty to keeping a betting house was fined $2,000 Thursday.

Walter L. M. Chrane was given two weeks to pay the fine or face a six-month jail term.

Magistrate William Ostler also ordered forfeiture of $517 taken from the man in a raid on his home by police Aug. 21, 1965.

Chrane was acquitted earlier this year on a charge of recording bets because the charge was improperly laid.

Court was told Wednesday city detectives Lyle Somers and Edward Hardy knocked twice on his door the day of the raid.

"This is the police," Det. Hardy called out.

A voice inside told them to "Go away".

Police broke open the door and went inside where they found Chrane burning paper.

Police confiscated several racing forms, a list of telephone numbers and the $517 found in Chrane's wallet.

Court was told Chrane had been convicted in 1961 and 1963 for recording bets.

Chrane fined in court in Victoria, BC.
Our Uncle Walter liked to gamble.

Victoria Daily Times
THURSDAY, FEBRUARY 24, 1966

Fine of $2,000 For Bookmaker

A man who pleaded guilty to keeping a betting house was fined $2,000 in central court today.

Walter L. M. Chrane, 1023 Linden Ave., was given two weeks to pay the fine or face a six-month jail term.

Magistrate William Ostler also ordered forfeiture of $517 taken from the man on a raid on his home by police Aug. 21, 1965.

Chrane was acquitted earlier this year on a charge of recording bets because the charge was improperly laid.

Court was told Wednesday city detectives Lyle Somers and Edward Hardy knocked twice on his door the day of the raid.

"This is the police," Det. Hardy called out.

GO AWAY

A voice inside told them to "go away."

Police broke open the door and went inside where they found Chrane burning paper in a soup tin.

Police also answered the telephone while in the house and three callers were trying to place bets.

Police confiscated several racing forms, a list of telephone numbers and initials and the $517 found in Chrane's wallet.

Court was told Chrane had been convicted in 1961 and 1963 for recording bets.

Bookie fined $2000 dollars in court
(that was a lot of money in the mid-60s).

This Book is Dedicated to all the Children who were placed in Foster care and survived, and, the ones that did not Survive.

MURRAY'S STORY

Murray Kenneth Storrings was born May 18, 1946, and from foster care was committed to the Superintendent of Child Welfare in BC starting July 9, 1948.

Re: STORRINGS, Gladys & John
___Ch: Murray, b. 18.5.46___

5.8.60 (cont'd)

We tried to interpret to Murray why Dennis   and told him
that he could write to him. Mrs. Rausch says Murray was very quiet at first
but had been out picking peas with her husband, and watered the goat for her.
She feels her older son can be of help to Murray. He is an honour student and
going into Senior Matric this year. Murray commented that he had all the things
he liked to eat since he came to Rausch's.

We interpreted C.W.D. policy to Mrs. Rausch regarding medicals and clothing
purchases.

Murray goes into hospital Aug. 16th to have 4 teeth out.

Foster home agreements were left for Mr. Rausch to sign.

9.8.60 B. Barber/cew

17.8.60

Memo from S.C.W. authorizing special rate of $80.00 per month for Murray in
the new foster home. #114.

17.8.60 Summary to date

Murray is in hospital today having 4 teeth extracted. He has been very quiet
and passive at the Rausch home recently. They are not imposing too many restric-
tions at the moment, but are hopeful that he may fit into the family and then they
will expect the same of him as they do of their own children. We are not too
hopeful that Murray will fit in or change very much, but we feel that he will at
least stay in this home for a few months as his pattern has been. He does have
blow-ups now and again, and this is to be expected. It is felt that Murray
should be seen for psychiatric assessment, and Dr. Capling, who knows him quite
well, would refer him if asked to do so by the worker. It is thought that Dr.
Middleton in New Westminster could see him, and possibly therapy would help him.
This should be started as soon as possible. Unfortunately this worker has not
had the opportunity to get him in for this interview, as he could not make an
appointment in the next two weeks, and it is rather useless doing it if it
couldn't be followed through.

Murray, unfortunately, has been involved with
He was involved in a theft, unsolved as yet, recently
at Clappison's. He was also involved with   in other things that we were
not aware of formerly. We are hopeful that now Dennis has gone perhaps Murray
will be away from these things.

Murray will no doubt be asking to see   and we don't know whether he can
visit   but perhaps this could be found out at a later date,

18.8.60 B. Barber/cew

23.8.60

M.S.D.6 received from Dr. Mitdal for Murray's glasses in amount of $13.55. #115.
Letter of authority for Mrs. Rausch to purchase clothing for Murray. #115A.

15.9.60

Mrs. Rausch in with receipts for Murray's text-book and lock rentals and student
assoc. fee totalling $5.75. She also asked if $3.50 per month for rental of
band instrument could be authorized, if it turns out that Murray is interested
in joining the school band.

Memo to S.C.W. enclosing receipts totalling $5.75 for reimbursement to Mrs.
Rausch. #116.

R.A. advised (verbally) that it would be in order to pay $3.50 for instrument
rental per month, but when we phoned Mrs. Rausch to tell her, she said Murray
had decided he wasn't interested in joining the band.

15.9.60 H. Joasalu/cew

Murray Storrings file info.

Me, Murray, as a small child at the beginning of a long road in life, with many moves in foster care.

I noticed I show a small smile in my early pictures while with my loving grandmother Gladys Chrane. It seems that was the only time we were happy—when we were with family, which wasn't often, and it did not take long to get into trouble in our foster homes.

Picture taken on St. Anne St. Haney, 1964, while staying at the Morse home. I was seventeen years old and posing with their cat. This was the first home where I was still a ward of the government and could room and board on my own with Gordon, another foster boy.

Memo from Social Worker Mr. Vander Veen:

Murray is a likeable youngster, however, when angry, which is often in foster care, he is like a caged animal, our files states, but has moved numerous times as a child and as a non-ward and a ward of the government.

This is my story from memory and CFD files from the Information & Privacy Act Division and Department of Social Services in BC. I've had these files for twenty years or more and am reading most of them for the first time, page by page. There are close to three hundred pages, and I cannot write everything that's in these documents. I would like to, but there are many pages that are blanked out (redacted) so I will not know what abuse is in those missing pages unless I get a court order.

I will do my best to tell my part of the story in this book, which is written by me and my brother Dennis, with the help of our brother Glen and many other people. We missed out on a normal childhood, with over a hundred moves between the three of us, but as you will see, us three boys survived and became good citizens. It's a wonder we survived. This story is not written to make anyone look bad; it is to tell as much truth as possible about our life in foster care and prison and our adult lives.

Glen, Murray, Dennis Storrings in Yale, 1948.

Mother Eleanor Storrings and Murray in Yale, 1950, (Murray wishing he had a normal family)

The Ministry said before April 25, 1950, that it would be in our best interest to have adoption plans made for us brothers if possible, as I had had three moves already in less than two years and many more moves as a infant to two years old with my off-and-on parents. Sometimes it was because of illness, and they were leaving me with other people before the Ministry stepped. We were in a temporary foster home together for a few years.

The way it is was then, every female person was Mommy to us, and we don't know what security was (which has been with me for most of my life).

We were not problem children, and all the foster mothers who had us commented on how good we were. I have no memories at that early age, but Glen had more bad memories, as he was four years older than me and two years older than Dennis. He saw more than we did, and he does not like to talk about or remember that part of his life but I know he is hurting inside , I am writing from the information from our CFD files from Victoria on what the workers have written and on our memories.

It was a difficult situation, as my mother cared for us and sent us parcels. She came to see us but yet did nothing about setting up a proper home for us and it seems the only relative that would take at least one of us into their home was our grandmother, Gladys. But she could only handle so much as she was in her sixties.

Welfare stated that they did not think they could sacrifice the children (which they did) while she took her time doing something about the situation. Welfare felt the older we got, the harder it would be to adjust to adoption. This was the mistake the Ministry made with us; they waited too long and we suffered for this in our childhood.

There are hundreds of pages in the file with the workers going back and forth about what to do. Years went by and nothing changed, but we were hurting the most while the adults did nothing but talk about what to do with the three of us. It was normal for them, but not for a child.

I am going to scan file documents to show what we were going though all those years. I moved more than thirty-five times to different homes. There were over a hundred moves or placements for all three of us in the years of commitment and non-commitment. Our father was no help; he never provided for us or helped our mother, who tried but was unsuccessful in her dream of having a normal home with her three sons.

From the files:

Murray is a slender youngster with medium-brown hair, blue eyes and fine features. He is tense and anxious when dealing with adults and tends to speak only when asked a direct question. His reasoning ability can be good and his memory and comprehension ability are above mental age level. Briefly, he is shy, unhappy and scared at times, and is a withdrawn little boy. To all intents and purpose unable to relax. Murray is intensely loyal to his brothers and it is understandable that he would want to do the things they do no matter how detrimental to himself.
Written by Miss Verna Negraiff, social worker.

In another memo they say:

We have not totalled the number of social workers who have had contact with Murray, but the figure would be frightening, and he wonders why this is happening.

This gives the readers some information about me as a child in my very early years. Below is a scan of my files from the government in Victoria. I read an article that says there are very few support groups or information about what happens in the lives of a foster children later in their later lives, but my friend Sandra sent me an article on foster-care relationships written by Jessica Wendroff. She writes about how being taken away from your parents and placed in the foster-care system at a young age can produce lasting, detrimental effects that can carry over into adulthood and effect relationships. The Northwest foster-care study concluded that 54% of people who had been in care had mental health problems, including depression, social problems, anxiety and PTSD. This was so interesting to me, as it answers a lot of questions I had about myself and my brothers. It also says these results were due to foster care's disruptive nature between a child and caregivers. I've often wondered why the Canadian government never addressed the foster children's problems and only addressed and supported other groups. There was never a word about our journey through the foster system and what happens to kids as children and later in life.

MEMORANDUM

~~~MENT OF HEALTH AND WELFARE

CIAL WELFARE BRANCH
   FIELD SERVICE

190, Haney, B.C.
   April 13   19 51

TO   Child Welfare Division,

Court House,

Vancouver, B.C.

Re: STORRINGS, Eleanor & Douglas,
   Present Add.: 935 Denman St.,
           Vancouver, B.C.
   Chn: Dennis, b. 9.2.44
        Murray, b. 18.5 46
        Glen, b. 16.8.42
   c/o Mrs. P. J. Bourelle,
   17th Avenue North, Haney, B.C.

On February 23rd we wrote to you to advise that we had received a parcel from Mrs. Storrings from Vancouver and assuming from this that the woman was still a resident in the city we would, therefore, appreciate arrangements being made for a C.A.S. worker to interview Mrs. Storrings.

We have been reviewing our file and note that it will be three years this July since the children were committed to the Superintendent. During this period we have supervised Glen in the foster home and for the past year have also had Dennis and Murray in the same home. We have made many attempts to have the mother interviewed with a view to planning for the children but regret there has been no progress whatsoever regarding this due to mother's vagueness and indecisiveness with any worker who has seen her. The boys are getting older and we feel it imperative that permanent plans be made for them. The present foster home appears to have met their need but placement was originally made temporarily as it was always hoped the children could and would be placed with parent when her future plans could include their care. However, concrete plans have to date never materialized. Mother is no nearer to offering a plan than she was three years ago. She has not seen the children for many months and the only contact has been through the media of gifts for birthdays and holidays. When approached last summer regarding plans for the children she offered the suggestion of their going to relatives – her mother and sister. Because of the maternal grandmother's health the plan was not feasible and also maternal grandmother was not willing to accept responsibility for Glen.

Foster parents of the children are both elderly and while being fond of and attached to the youngsters, through their own experiences in raising a large family they feel that it is important the boys should have the companionship, understanding and affection of younger parents who would be able to grow along with them. We feel the present foster parents have certainly brought the youngsters along through many little trials but are reaching the age when they will in a year or so be unable to care for the youngsters and we will of necessity have to move the children who by that time will be older and more difficult to place.

Storrings files.

MEMORANDUM

MENT OF HEALTH AND WELFARE

┌───
AL WELFARE BRANCH   TO   Child Welfare Division,
   FIELD SERVICE
                          Court House,
190, Haney, B.C.
     April 18   19 51   Vancouver, B.C.

> Re: STORRINGS, Eleanor & Douglas,
> Present Add.: 935 Denman St.,
>   Vancouver, B.C.
> Chn: Dennis, b. 9.2.44
>   Murray, b. 18.5 46
>   Glen, b. 16.8.42
> c/o Mrs. P. J. Bourelle,
> <u>17th Avenue North, Haney, B.C.</u>

On February 23rd we wrote to you to advise that we had received a parcel from Mrs. Storrings from Vancouver and assuming from this that the woman was still a resident in the city we would, therefore, appreciate arrangements being made for a C.A.S. worker to interview Mrs. Storrings.

We have been reviewing our file and note that it will be three years this July since the children were committed to the Superintendent. During this period we have supervised Glen in the foster home and for the past year have also had Dennis and Murray in the same home. We have made many attempts to have the mother interviewed with a view to planning for the children but regret there has been no progress whatsoever regarding this due to mother's vagueness and indecisiveness with any worker who has seen her. The boys are getting older and we feel it imperative that permanent plans be made for them. The present foster home appears to have met their need but placement was originally made temporarily as it was always hoped the children could and would be placed with parent when her future plans could include their care. However, concrete plans have to date never materialized. Mother is no nearer to offering a plan than she was three years ago. She has not seen the children for many months and the only contact has been through the media of gifts for birthdays and holidays. When approached last summer regarding plans for the children she offered the suggestion of their going to relatives -- her mother and sister. Because of the maternal grandmother's health the plan was not feasible and also maternal grandmother was not willing to accept responsibility for Glen.

Foster parents of the children are both elderly and while being fond of and attached to the youngsters, through their own experiences in raising a large family they feel that it is important the boys should have the companionship, understanding and affection of younger parents who would be able to grow along with them. We feel the present foster parents have certainly brought the youngsters along through many little trials but are reaching the age when they will in a year or so be unable to care for the youngsters and we will of necessity have to move the children who by that time will be older and more difficult to place.

Storrings files.

Re: STORRINGS, Murray, b. 18.5.46

2.   poorly developed physically and somewhat undernourished, although I feel sure   in much better condition now than four months ago. It was noted in the history submitted to us, weighed less in 1953 than   in 1951, which suggests neglect by the previous foster parents.

3.   enuretic and encopretic.

4.   showing seclusive, withdrawn behaviour staying away from the other children.

5. Stealing of food and money is a problem but to a lesser degree.

6.   backward in school, as a result of their emotional disturbance, having passed only conditionally this year.

7. Sibling rivalry is marked.

8. There is obviously considerable repressed hostility   need to be encouraged to express   hostility through play interviews. It was agreed at the staff conference that Miss Stevenson would work

9. The foster mother, Mrs. Fulljames, is a strength in this case. She has a remarkable facility for sizing up the situation and, I think, for coping with it. It will be necessary that both she and her husband spend a great deal of time stimulating   as much as possible.

10. It would seem advisable that the teacher be advised of the problem   and she might also encourage some aggression   The foster mother was asking whether or not she should help   with their school work. I feel that it would be better if she didn't, as one usually finds that children who are being coached by their parents at home become more confused than ever."

15/9/53 - E. Vivian Stevenson/dj

September, 1953

    We visited the foster home twice this month and spoke with Murray alone each time. Our last talk with Murray on September 29th, revealed that he was able to make some remarks on his own. He volunteered some information about the farm animals, mentioned that one of the cows was going to have a calf and that he and Dennis occasionally rode the horse. He was able to tell us the names of all the animals excepting one, and when we suggested that he give the calf a name he suggested "Billy Joe."

    The foster mother reported that Murray did not seem to be making as good adjustment in the home as Dennis.   Murray continued to remain rather quiet and withdrawn. During our interviews with him, he showed some signs of humor.

October, 1953

    We saw Murray several times during October, usually meeting him on the road and giving him a lift home from school. He showed some pleasure over this and not too much concern if the other children missed the ride.

    On October 23rd, we had an evening appointment in order to have the foster home agreements signed by both foster parents. However, just prior to going out to the home, the foster mother contacted us saying that Murray had set fire to their barn and that there was quite a number of firemen also the chief fire inspector at their home. After making certain that there was nothing we could do at this time, we arranged an appointment for the following day. On October 24th, we saw the foster parents, their natural child, Beverly and the six foster children in their home. After a general discussion and admiration of new clothing which had recently been purchased, we spoke with Murray alone in the car. We asked what had started the fire and Murray said he had. That he lit a match and dropped it in the hay and that Dennis had given him the match.

Murray's files.

REQUEST FOR PLACEMENT.

Can child be placed in your

region? **Yes**

Worker **Vivian Vincent**

District **Chilliwack**

Case No. **17545** Type **Prot.**

Date of request **October 9, 1947**

1. Date case opened **August 29, 1944**   2. Referred by **mo. Gladys Storrings**

3. Reason for referral **Deserted by her husband,**

4. Name of child **Murray Storrings**   5. Present address **Restmore, near Hope**

6. Birth date **May 18, 1945**   7. Sex **Male**   8. Religion **Protestant**

9. Status **Non-ward** (Ward, non-ward, etc.)   10. Proposed placement date **Oct. 9/47**   11. Date placed **Oct. 9/47**

12. Residence **Unorganized....Responsibility of Provincial Government.**

13. If municipal residence, has letter underwriting cost been obtained?

14. Will parents be contributing? **Yes**   15. How much? **$15.00 mo.**

16. If non-wards, have parents' consents been obtained? **Yes**

17. Child's health, including serious illnesses, operations, and date of last medical report

   Good...last medical report in May 12, 1947
   Dr. A. Wilson, Chilliwack.

18. School—grade and adjustment   **Pre-school**

19. Ability and interests   **Average**

20. Appearance **Beautiful, well nourished child..large blue eyes, blond curly ha**

21. Behaviour   **Good..placid, easily managed.**

22. Reason for placement **Mother deserted, father unable to take care of children,**
   danger of eviction in present home, long history of marital discord.

23. Type of placement required **good foster home where at least two of the boys**
   can be together.

24. Length of proposed placement   **Three months**

25. Names of persons who should not see or know whereabouts of child

26. Is child in receipt of Family Allowance? **Yes**

27. Has child a ration book? **Yes**

28.   FAMILY

	Name.	Nationality.	Age.	Present whereabouts.
Mother:	Gladys Eleanour	British	23	Unknown, probably Hope
Father:	Douglas Storrings	British	28	Restmore, near Hope
Children:	Glen and Dennis, age 4 yrs. and 2 yrs...also non-wards.			

Murray's files from Victoria.

46

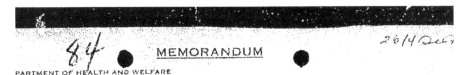

84   MEMORANDUM   *26/4 Sec*

PARTMENT OF HEALTH AND WELFARE

SOCIAL WELFARE BRANCH   TO The Superintendent,
    FIELD SERVICE   Child Welfare Division,
                                               Court House,
                                               Vancouver, B.C.

Chilliwack, B.C., April 25th, 50

RE: STORRINGS, Gladys Eleanor and Douglas
    Woman - Vancouver, B.C.
    Man - Unknown
    Children: Glen, b. 16.8.42
              Dennis, b. 9.2.44) c/o Mrs. Odell,
              Murray, b. 18.5.46) Sardis, B.C.

As these children have been in care since their committal to the Superintendent on July 9th, 1948, we feel that it would be in their best interests to have adoption plans made for them, if possible, as Dennis and Murray have had three moves since November, 1949. In each case these moves have been necessitated through illness of foster mother, and they are still in a temporary foster home. They are not problem children and all the foster mothers who have had them commented on how good they were.

We would like to make a permanent plan for these little boys. The way it is now, every female person is "Mummy" to them, and they do not know what security means.

This is a difficult situation in that the mother is interested in these children. She sends them parcels, comes to see them, but yet she does nothing about setting up a decent home. In the interests of the children we do not feel that we can sacrifice them while she takes her time about doing this. They are very fond of her and ask about their mother practically every time we see them, but if the mother is not going to do anything constructive about working toward setting up a home, we feel that it would be in the best interests of all if the relationship were to cease. We believe that as the children grow older it will be more difficult for them to adjust in an adoption home.

We have heard indirectly that mother is living in a poor district in Vancouver   Of course, this would have to be proven as we are not certain such is the case.

If adoption cannot be worked through with the mother, would the Superintendent consider waiving mother's consent?

GM:KD   *[signature]*
                                          (Miss) G. Millard,
                                             Social Worker

Murray's government files.

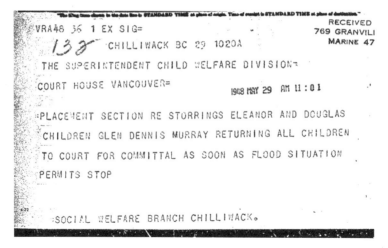

May 29, 1948. Telegram on the Storrings brothers.

In turn, foster care children tend to struggle to attach, or become overly attached to caregivers, which is what my social workers said in my files. Sadly, it says, attachment issues are deep-seated and tend to transfer from caregivers to partners. As a result, foster care survivors tend to push people away, either through distancing or smothering others, which I found to be very true in our case. It says that those who distance themselves have a lack of desire for a relationship because they fear being hurt and abandoned, so they prevent bonds altogether in some cases. Others want to secure a relationship so badly they accidentally push partners away by suffocating them with neediness.

As I read this article, I realized what I was feeling during my years in my relationships. Even today I don't really know the meaning of love; its just a word to me. I could be with someone for years but worry and fear they would leave me and I'd be alone once again. I thank Jessica for her article, which gave me this wonderful insight, and hope it answers some questions for foster children everywhere.

Trying to write this is hard today. It's Christmas Day, 2018, and I am alone again, which is fine as I need to be alone in my thoughts. My daughters and granddaughter go to their mother and grandmother for Christmas, so I don't have an interest in Christmas— it's all about being with family. It's a terrible feeling for my brothers as well. As I see it, we were robbed of our feelings in foster care with all the movements from one place to another, and so has anyone in foster care. This book was not easy for us three, as lots of emotions came back as we were writing, but it helps us understand some of our feelings. I recently had to go back and delete some things I'd written, as it looked like I felt sorry for myself, which was the case, but this is not why were are writing the book. For me it's about trying to express myself and what I was feeling in those dark days as a foster child and to help others that have gone though the same things.

Grandmother Chrane with Murray, taken at Yale, 1950.

A friend asked why I didn't like Christmas, I said I'd rather be with my family and not alone. But I had one friend from the 1950s that cared and gave me some hope and understanding at Christmas time this year when I really needed it.

I collected many pictures of my family over the years with the help of my Uncle Walter. If I'd not looked ahead, I wouldn't have them now. I tried to have a few family members be a little involved with comments or photos of our family, but Wally and Lynette, my cousins, seemed interested. This brought me to think back to when it was only our grandmother who tried to give us a family home, knowing what we had gone though. My wife and I would never let our granddaughter be put in a foster home, as her mother worked, and we would have taken her if anything happened to our daughter or her mother. To this day, Chesley's grandmother Betty watches over her in White Rock where they reside.

I have to write the truth and what I am feeling. It hurts to write this book, but at least my daughters and granddaughter and many other people will maybe understand us much better. One thing that stood out in the files is how many pages were about the foster parents wanting to know where the three or four dollars in payment were for things like going on a small trip. There were requests to the social workers to pay my expenses, and as we grew older the foster parents wanted more money as we were more of a problem to them. It seemed the Ministry did not keep up to date in paying the foster parents.

My mother at times agreed to have me adopted out, which may have been a better idea than the mess that occurred. She mentioned that she was going to divorce my father, but this never happened, just like the adoption never happened.

I often wondered as a child if the parents of other kids who did something wrong would send them away or put them in a reform school if they were quarrelsome. This happened to us; the first time there was a problem, there was a phone call to a social worker saying "We want Murray out of here." It was easy for them to do this, as there was no commitment—we were just loaners to the foster parents or extra money to pay their bills, which still happens today. But not all foster parents are like this. There are and were some caring foster parents.

Below is a file about our parents and a telegraph for us three for committal dated July 12, 1948. I was two at that time.

-2-

The Storrings are being evicted from their home, The only reason they have not been put out before was because when Mrs. Storrings left we asked the Cultus Lake Parks Board to give us a few days to make some plan for the children. This they consented to do. Even if Mrs. Storrings could be established with the children there is no place they could live, as the Parks Board definitely wish them out of Cultus Lake. The rents there will be doubling next month for the summer season in any case.

Mrs. Storrings said she did not wish to separate permanently from her husband if only they could get established and have a regular income. She said she would work and do her part. It is almost too much to hope that he would do his. He states that on May 15th, he will be going to Prince George, where he was raised, to start a sawmill.

However, if we accept the children into non-ward care and give the parents a chance to work out such a plan, with a definite time limit set, it will perhaps mean the home could be re-established on a better foundation that if the Storrings place these children in a sub-marginal home, and merely postponing our taking the responsibility, as will almost inevitably happen. The parents are also capable of deserting their children, which could only result in committal. The only way we can guarantee adequate care for these children, who have already been undermined by the physical and mental poverty in the home, is to accept responsibility for their placement.

We suggested to Mrs. Storrings that she take the baby and go to her mother's, if we placed the older children. She said her mother at the present time cannot offer a home to any of the family.

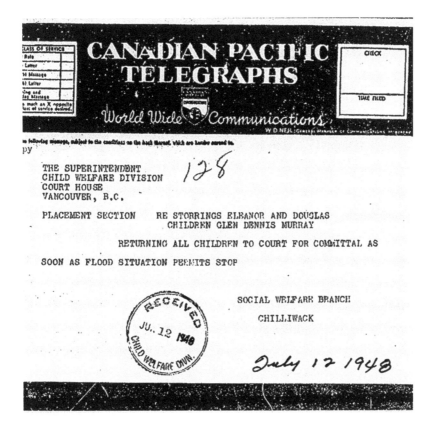

Prior to July 1948, from April 17, 1947, to May of 1947, Murray, who was only one years old, was in a foster home in Abbotsford under non-ward then returned to his own home again. In 1948 he was in another foster home for a period of three months then returned to his mother and then from 1948 to November 1949 was in another foster home in the Chilliwack area. During that period, he was out of the foster home for a short period while his foster mother went on vacation. He was again moved in February 1950 when his foster mom took ill. Then from April 1950 to June 1950 he was in another foster home. We believe that some of the moves were required because of circumstances in the foster home rather then any complaint about Murray's adjustment.

We were always happy when we could go for a holiday to spend time with our lovely grandmother in a happier family setting like other children we knew.

I hope my part of the book will help others know there is hope and that we three survived to try to live a normal life. It was not easy but we made it so we could let other foster children know they're not alone. The people who were put in charge of our lives did make mistakes, and in our case they made plenty of mistakes, as one social worker told me some fifty years later.

Development file:

Murray was exposed to severe neglect and quarrelling in the family during the first two to three years of his life. During that period, he had been placed in foster homes as a non-ward and returned periodically back to his home with his parents and aunts and friends even with police officers friends when the police would apprehend us from our parents and there was not any place to put us .

Physical Development of Murray:

Murray was around the age of one year when while living in his own home he had pneumonia and was reported to be suffering from malnutrition. He seems to have also had a condition of acute bronchitis and had been subjected to chest colds in 1952. It states he had a tonsillectomy and in July 1953, Murray was hospitalised following an acute attack of asthma. Medical reports show that also in 1953 Murray had bronchitis and malnutrition again. Medication was prescribed for these conditions. His weight on June 10, 1947, was 28 lbs at one year old but in 1953, six years later, his weight was only 40 lbs and his hemoglobin was 62%. Three months later, on August 19, 1953, his weight had only gone to 48 lbs. Murray's medical history also shows he had diphtheria toxoid and scarlet fever toxoid ,also chicken pox .

This shows what was happing to me as a child being moved from place to place. I am learning this information for the first time, which is depressing, to say the least.

Family History

Residence List of the Storrings Family from 1942-1946

- Township of Chilliwack, Mar. 1930/1942 to Sept. 1942
- Chilliwack City, Regina Auto Camp, Sept. 1942 to April 5, 1943
- Chilliwack City, Orchard Park Auto Camp, April 5, 1943
- Hatzic, Aug. 30, 1943, to July 16, 1944
- Cultus Lake, July 16 to Jan. 1945
- Laidlaw. Jan. 1945 to March 1945
- Chilliwack City, Preston Auto Camp, Mar. 1945 to Dec. 31, 1945
- Cultus Lake, Jan 1, 1946, to present.
- At this time, our mother was pregnant with Murray, born in May of 1946

Emergency assistance of ten dollars from August 28/46 to December 31. /1946 was in the file that our mother had no food to feed us and she needed help.

Our father, John Douglas Storrings, was born in Saskatoon, Saskatchewan, in 1919, and died in 1971. He came to Prince George as a child and moved to Yale with his family in 1940, living common-law with Eleanor Chrane prior to their marriage in 1943. He deserted his wife and children for months at a time and was a poor supporter. He was employed for short periods of time in logging camps, and later in my life we never heard from him, as he never really cared about his family.

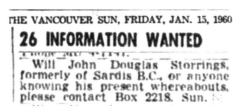

Newspaper article asking the whereabouts of John Douglas Storrings (our dad) for reason we don't know, but I think he had to sign some adoption papers for our two sisters, Charlotte and Valerie, (those were their birth names).

Our father was into drugs in the 1960s, as I uncovered from newspaper files (with the help of Janice).

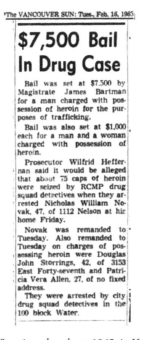

Douglas Storrings drug bust, 1965, in Vancouver.

THE CHILLIWACK PROGRESS, Wed., July 10, 1963

Police Court

Douglas Storring, Vedder, was fine $10 and costs for being intoxicated.

Clipping of police court.

Douglas Storrings.

Mother around age thirteen at home in Yale 1930s. Mother always loved her cats.

Grandmother and daughter Norma (Babe) Dalstrom in Yale in the 1930s.

Our father's information from the files

He is reported to be a tall, slim fellow with dark hair and a sallow complexion. He was frequently disorderly and drunk and threw my mother out of the cabin once where she sat there for three hours in the cold before he let her back in. The children at this time, the file says, were showing strain from the constant bickering of their parents.

On April 8, he left the boys with his sister Joyce Storrings, who was only nineteen at the time. We went to the home and found she was doing a satisfactory (job) given her age at this time so on a temporary arrangement and in no way permanent, Mr. Storrings told us he knows of no home where he could get boarding care for these children other than a family at Cultus Lake whom we already know about. They live in a overcrowded house and would be entirely unsuitable for these boys so we cannot recommend any home where the father could make private arrangements for these boys at this time. And from his past record it is obvious that he could not supply maintenance with any degree of regularity. If we take these children into non-ward care, there is a possibility that we can work something out with their mother as she has been a good mother as far as she is being able. Apart from two occasions when she left overnight, she has given them good care, and when she left the husband had been alarmed by his wife's disappearance and wished her back and we feel he has learned his lesson but that is wishing a lot. Then shortly afterwards he was drinking and was drunk and disorderly and had thrown his wife out of the house for three hours in the cold where she sat till, he let her in three hours later. The next day the children were showing the stain of constant bickering of their parents, and in the morning the father took a bus to Prince George to look for work and said he would send her a cheque. In the meantime she was destitute, and the boys had no food on that September day. She was given a second emergency order for food to feed these poor children. One thing Storrings always told the social workers and police was (that) it was never his fault.

John Douglas Storrings, working for Emile Anderson in Hope, BC.

31 32

Reg. No. (Office use only)

PROVINCE OF BRITISH COLUMBIA
DEPARTMENT OF HEALTH SERVICES AND HOSPITAL INSURANCE
DIVISION OF VITAL STATISTICS
REGISTRATION OF DEATH

Form 6

71-09-005916

1. PLACE OF DEATH

Name of city, village, town, district municipality or place _____ Vernon, B. C. _____
(If outside city or municipal limits add "Rural")

Street or road _____ Vernon Jubilee Hospital _____ House No. _____
(If death occurred in a hospital or institution, give the name instead of street and number)

2. LENGTH OF STAY (in years, months and days) | In Municipality where death occurred | In Province | In Canada (if immigrant)
| 5 years | 46 years | life

3. PRINT FULL NAME OF DECEASED _____ STORRINGS _____ Douglas John _____
(Surname) (All given or Christian names in full)

4. PERMANENT RESIDENCE OF DECEASED:

Name of city, village, town, district municipality or place _____ Vernon, B. C. _____
(If outside city or municipal limits add "Rural")

Street or road _____ 35th Ave. _____ House No. _____ 3308 _____

5. SEX	6. CITIZENSHIP (See marginal note)	7. RACIAL ORIGIN (See marginal note)	8. Single, Married, Widowed or Divorced (Write the word)	9. BIRTHPLACE (City or Place and Province or Country)
Male	Canadian	white	married	Saskatchewan

10. Date of Birth
September (Month by name) | 22 (Date) | 1922 (Year)

11. AGE (Last Birthday) | if under 1 year | if under 1 month | if under 24 hours | if under 1 hour
48 years YEARS | MONTHS | DAYS | HOURS | MIN.

12. (a) Trade, profession or kind of work as logger, fisherman, office clerk, etc. _____ labourer _____
(b) Kind of industry or business, as logging, fishing, bank, etc. _____
(If labourer specify kind of work above) (If Housewife in own home answer "At Home")

13. Date deceased last worked at this occupation _____ January 1970 _____
14. Total years spent in this occupation _____ adult life _____

15. If married, widowed or divorced give name of husband or maiden name of wife of deceased _____ Marion Rutledge _____

16. Name of father _____ Storrings _____ Arthur _____
(Surname) (All given or Christian names)

17. Maiden name of mother _____ nk _____ Minnie _____
(Surname) (All given or Christian names)

18. Birthplace – Father _____ nk _____ Mother _____ nk _____
(City or Place and Province or Country) (City or Place and Province or Country)

19. I certify the foregoing to be true and correct to the best of my knowledge and belief.
Given under my hand at _____ Vernon, B. C. _____ this _____ 23 _____ day of _____ April _____ 19 _71_
Signature of informant _____ M. Storrings _____ Relationship to deceased _____ wife _____
(Married woman not to use Husband's initials or given names)
Address of informant _____ 3308 - 35th Ave. _____ Vernon, B. C. _____
(House No.) (Name of Street) (Name of City, Municipality or Place) (Province)

20. Burial, Cremation or Removal _____ Burial _____ Date _____ April _____ 27 _____ 19 _71_
(State which) (Month by name) (Date) (Year)
Place of Burial or Cremation _____ Vernon, B. C. _____ Name of Cemetery _____ Pleasant Valley Cemetery _____
(Municipality, etc. where Cemetery located)

21. Undertaker:— Name _____ Vernon Funeral Home Ltd _____ Address _____ Vernon, B. C. _____
(Name of City, Municipality or Place) (Province)

MEDICAL CERTIFICATE OF DEATH

22. DATE OF DEATH _____ April _____ 22 _____ 19 _71_
(Month by name) (Date) (Year)

23. I HEREBY CERTIFY that I attended deceased from _____ 1967 _____ 19 _____
to _____ April 22 _____ 1971, and last saw him alive on _____ Apr 22 _____ 1971.

492×

CAUSE OF DEATH	Approximate interval between onset and death
Disease or condition directly leading to death (This does not mean the mode of dying e.g., heart failure, asthenia, etc. It means the disease, injury, or complication which caused death.)	(a) _____ Emphysema _____ due to (or as a consequence of)	2 yrs.
Antecedent causes Morbid conditions, if any, giving rise to the above cause, stating the underlying condition last. II	(b) _____ due to (or as a consequence of)	
	(c) _____	
Other significant conditions contributing to the death, but not related to the disease or condition causing it.	{	

24. If a woman, did the death occur either during pregnancy or within 90 days following pregnancy? _____
Yes or No

25. (a) Was there a recent surgical operation? _____ **(b)** Date of operation _____ 19 _____
(c) State findings of operation _____ **(d)** Was there an autopsy? _____ no _____

26. If a violent death, fill in also: **(a)** Accident ☐; Suicide ☐; Homicide ☐ **(b)** Date of injury _____ 19 _____
(c) How did injury occur? _____
(d) Injuries sustained? _____ (e.g. fracture of skull, left leg, etc., dislocation of -, burn to -, etc.)
(e) Where did injury occur? (home, farm, industrial place, highway, etc.)

27. Signed by _____ James A. Barr _____ Designation _____ M.D. _____ M.D. or Coroner
Address _____ 3005 - 31 Ave Vernon _____ Date _____ April 23 _____ 1971

28. Print name of Doctor or Coroner, whose signature appears above _____ I.A. Barr, M.D. _____

29. Notations

30. I hereby certify that the above return was made to me at _____ VERNON _____
Dated _____ April 23 _____ 19 _71_

District Registration No. _____ 101 _____ (Signature of District Registrar)

(SEE REVERSE SIDE FOR INSTRUCTIONS)

9004–3.14: 11-12-68

87

IMPORTANT: Any change or correction made in the completion of this form must be initialled by the person certifying the information.

CITIZENSHIP (NATIONALITY) is defined in terms of the country to which the person owes allegiance. The term "Canadian" should be used as descriptive of a person who was born in Canada or who has rights of Citizenship in Canada, unless he or she has subsequently become the citizen of another country.

RACIAL ORIGIN — State the racial origin, traced through the father, in terms of the people or race to which the person belongs such as: English, Scottish, German, etc. or in terms of one of the following racial groups: – White, native Indian, Negro, Chinese, Japanese or other.

22
2
920
941

Father's obituary, 1971.

THE CHILLIWACK PROGRESS, Fri., May 19, 1961

9 Months Jail For Theft

Donald Hunt, 29, of Chilliwack will spend nine months in Oakalla for theft of a radio from a city business establishment.

He was found guilty of the offence in city police court last week.

Another man, Douglas John Storring, Vedder Crossing, was also accused of the same offence, but the charge was dismissed.

Theft, Doug Storrings.

Glen, in the meantime, has impurities in his bloodstream that are causing him to break out with large festering sores. This father has said he would have this problem looked after, but he never did fulfill his promise once again, so he came back to the home. But on December 31, 1946, he took off to Vancouver and left his wife and children destitute again with not a care in the world that his family had no food. It is in our opinion this man's habitual pattern to desert, leaving no food or money at home, is hard to understand. We subsidizes the home for the sake of the children, but before we can take any action he returns and things drag on like before. At this time the Community Chest provided and supplied the family with necessities, but now Glen's condition worsens, with sores over his complete body, and it seemed (to make) no difference to her husband to see his son like this and without food for the family. He has made no effort to find employment and support his family.

During January the situation dragged on as before, although the children were always clean, and at our request BC Provincial Police Sergeant. Raybone had a talk with the mother, which is blanked out in our files.

Mrs. Storrings showed signs of a highly nervous condition and finally he left and said he would send her a cheque, as she was almost destitute, and she stated she wished the children to have a father. Storrings wanted her husband to provide for the family and have a normal home life for the children but he was not interested, instead going to Vancouver and doing drugs and drinking in bars while not looking for work unless he was forced to do so.

At this time Murray was suffering from malnutrition, and on September 27 the children had been without food all day and Murray now had pneumonia and was not in good condition.

The father promised to have these conditions seen to but never fulfills these promises. On December 31 the mother was again destitute and her husband had gone off to Vancouver. He also goes to his mother's home in Sardis and she makes him a meal and always takes his side and never takes a interest in her grandchildren. Mr. Storrings beat Murray's mother in the presence of the children and these children were heard screaming and crying by neighbours when this fighting was going on. Older brother Glen tried at his young age to console his two little brothers as best he could.

```
STORRINGS, Gladys and Douglas          October 15th, 1947


          By October 9, 1947 we had been informed that Mrs.
Storrings had been seen in the Hope liquor store the previous
day




          We discussed this case with the C.W.S. and then
phoned the C.W.D. to request non-ward care in view of the fact
that the relatives would not keep the children another night,
the father cannot care for them, the mother could not be located
and the family are facing eviction
          The C.W.D. agreed to non-ward placement. Mr. Stor-
rings came back to the office but had evidently come to no
agreement with his wife and did not know her plans. He said
he had a place rented for September 15th at Vedder Crossing and
had a steady job                          for the winter if hi
wife would return to him. We later ascertained Mr. Storrings
had lost his job

          He signed the non-ward consent forms and agreed
to pay $15.00 per month for each child. We placed the three
children with Mrs. Helen Pryor (F.H.), Vedder Crossing, for the
night. She cannot keep more than two of the children. Before
we got to the sister's home to take the children, the sister
had left them in the office.

          Mr. Storrings got the bus to Hope with the intenti
of finding his wife and bringing her in to the office.

          On October 10, 1947 Mrs. Storrings came in to the
office.


                              when they had returned
to Restmore on Sunday night had whipped her with a belt. The
children were awake in the one-roomed cabin and were crawling
around and crying.


          We asked her about her plans and she said she woul
get a job and try to make a home for the children. We could
not see the immediate purpose in discussing the children's futu
as she was in such a poor physical and mental condition. We
requested her to come in to the office in two days time.



          These children have certainly had a difficult time
in their parents' home and while their mother has given them
good physical care,                     show signs of being upset
and unhappy. The parents have agreed to non-ward care for thre
months, at which time some permanent arrangements with the
possibility of committal may be reached.
```

Parents' files from Victoria.

NAME: STORRINGS, Gladys Eleanor (dd) & John Douglas

Maiden name: Chrane

Address:

Birthdate: 14.4.23   Birthplace: Agassiz, B.C.

(1) SECTION 2

FATHER: STORRINGS, John Douglas   Birthdate: .20   Birthplace:

MARITAL STATUS: MARRIED: John D. STORRINGS 16.4.43 - Chilliwack, B.C.ver.
Husband Deserted on May 27, 1944

CHILDREN:

		Birthdate	Birthplace	Ver.	Legitimate Yes	No
1	STORRINGS, Glen Douglas	b.16.8.42	Mission, B.C.			
2.	" , Dennis Raymond	b.9.2.44	"			
3.	" , Murray Kenneth	b.18.5.46	Chilliwack, B.C.			
4.	, Valerie Linda	b.20.12.58	Vancouver, B.C. x			x
5.	.. , Judy Charlotte	b.9.4.57	"			
6.						
7.						
8.						
9.						
10.						

CATEGORY	Date Opened	Date Closed	Initial Stat.	CROSS-REFERENCES
Child in care	17.4.47	24.5.67		SEE: Bourelle, Agnes & Philip
				SEE: Tolmie, Joyce M. & John F.
Repatriation				
Sundry				
Immigration				
Supreme Court custody				
Legitimation				
C.U.P.A.				
C.U.P.A. sundry				

STATUS OF CHILD				AUTHORITY TO BOOK-KEEPING		Initial	
Name	Status	Date Admitted	Date Discharged			S.W.	B.K.
Murray	w/dSCW	9.7.48	18.5.67				

Files on the Storrings.

In March 1947 our parents were out to a party and refused to go home to their children. We had been left with a young neighbour girl whose mother came and took her home, leaving us alone. Finally our father came home and looked after us and our mother came home at ten the next morning. When Welfare called the next morning, my mother told them she had taken enough and to come and take the kids to a better home life.

John Douglas Storrings died ten years after our mother, in 1971 in Vernon, BC, of emphysema lung disease. We were not notified until I made inquiries in 1972 after the birth of my first child, Marie Eleanor Storrings. Glen had the most contact with our father. Dennis and I had seen him when we were about eight and ten years old at his aunt's in Chilliwack (the Tolmie home). Dennis and I went to our father's mother's place in Sardis a few years later, to Margaret and Alex Storrings's home. The first thing he asked was, "Have you guys got a cigarette?" We saw him again in 1961 at our mother's funeral in Chilliwack, and then in 1963 we saw him in the penitentiary for possession of drugs. He was in there at the same time as Glen, who was there for robbery. He never showed us any affection or acknowledged that we were even his sons.

These files show that this cat and mouse game continued back and forth between our parents and the Child Welfare Division for years at our expense.

Gladys Eleanor Chrane Storrings walking in Vancouver, 1940s.

Eleanor Storrings in the 1950s, Stanley Park, Vancouver.

PROVINCE OF BRITISH COLUMBIA.

SCHOOL YEAR *1924-35*

MONTHLY REPORT

—OF—

Eleanor Chran

Fifth Grade.

Yale School.

Yale City or District.

Jean Cameron Teacher.

100M-433-3058

Report card (front) for our mother, 1934-35.

Eleanor

	Sept.	Oct.	Nov.	Dec.	Jan.	Feb.	Mar.	Apr.	May	June
Reading, Oral	B-	65	B	64	B		B			
Reading, Silent										
Spelling	B-	75	B	90	B	64	B	73		B
Language and Lit.	C+	68	B	75	B		B5			
Grammar							69			16
Composition				B		B	22			32
Writing	B+	68	B+	69	B	75	B	70		70
Mathematics	C	60	C+	68	C	50	C+	38		36
Geography	B			B	53	C				30
History										
Man. A. & Home Ec.										
Nature Study										
Music Lit		B	51	B	14	D		C	57	57
Hygiene										
Drawing	B	65	B		B	64	B	58		
Rank in Grade	1	1		1	2	1	1	1		1
No. of Pupils in Gr.	2	2		2	2	2	2	2		2
Times Late										
Days Absent					1½		3			52
Average		65		62		63		B		52

NOTE.—Rating in subject should be made as follows:—
A indicating superior work, received by top 5% of pupils (approximately).
B indicating good work, received by next 20% of pupils (approximately).
C+ indicating very fair work, received by next 15% of pupils (approximately).
C indicating fair work, received by next 20% of pupils (approximately).
C— indicating fair to poor work, received by next 15% of pupils (approx.).
D denoting poor work, awarded to the next 20% of pupils (approximately).
E representing very poor work (promotion is endangered).
I indicating that the work was incomplete and could not be rated.

	Sept.	Oct.	Nov.	Dec.	Jan.	Feb.	Mar.	Apr.	May	June
General conduct	2	2	2	2	3	3	3	3		3
Attitude to work	2	2	1	3	4	3	3			2

N.B.—In reporting on the pupil's General Conduct and Attitude to Work, use 1 for Excellent; 2, Good; 3, Fair; 4, Poor.

OTHER REMARKS *Eleanor is don fool work & shows improvement Sept. Promoted to 5A. Jan. 31, 1935*

Promoted to Grade 6 B. June 1935

Report card (inside), 1934-35.

Mother was deserted by her husband on several occasions. The official reports in the files are as follows in Murrays words

Mrs. Storrings is a very attractive woman, 5 feet 3 inches, and has a slim build. She has light-brown hair and large blue eyes. She has appealing manners and is outgoing and quite a friendly person. She has had an unhappy life, with a domineering mother and an unstable marriage and has been unable to accept parental responsibility. She is unable to plan for her children but has shown interest in their well being. Her mother is living in Yale and her father separated from her mother and is a chiropractor in Vancouver. Mrs. Storrings they Ministry says in the files inferred with the children and did not let the children forget her either; just as the children were getting along in a foster home she would appear with candy and then disappear for a year. This is a major factor and must be taken into consideration when observing Murray's behaviour today. Mrs. Storrings on Nov 6 1947 was charged with obstruction of a police officer in a item in the Vancouver Sun *and given 24 hours to leave the city, which she did not do, and a sentence of 30 days in Oakalla prison farm for women.*

On Oct 10, 1947, my mother reported that she and her husband were with some friends in Sardis, BC, and our dad abused her in front of the friends. Us boys were awake in this one-room cabin and were crawling around on the floor crying and in need of food. My mother told our dad she was going to leave him once again, but she was in such a poor physical condition and she was asked to report to the Welfare office in Chilliwack.

These children have had a most difficult time in their parents' home, and while the mother has given good physical care at times, the older boys shows signs of being upset and unhappy in their young lives. On April 8 ,1947, when Murray was one year old, the mother deserted her family from cabin 2, Cultus Lake Auto Park in Chilliwack, BC, where they were living. She left the children in the care of her husband and came asking for help at the Chilliwack welfare office. As noted, the contact with this family is long-standing, for reasons in our report. The mother and father were married April 6, 1943, after the birth of Glen, the man has been a poor provider ever since the marriage, and he deserted his wife in Hatzic, BC, on May 27, 1944.

In a memo from 1947 regarding the year 1946, it was noted that on August 18, 1946, the mother left the boys on Saturday night, had not yet returned and did not return until Monday morning. Their father had left too for several days but had promised his wife he would be home that Friday night. The boys were left alone until Sgt. Anderson of the BC police placed them with friends of his until the parents came back, and then he took them home to their parents in a one-room cabin in Cultus Lake. Then in the fall, when Murray was a infant, trouble in the family was brewing. The boys were in poor health but no information on their physical condition was given at this time. We may leave the children with their father at this time until the anticipated return of the mother in the near future.

If the children are not well, in view of the fact that their father is not capable or dependable, we felt the boys will be apprehended and we may work out a plan with the mother to care for these lads apart from Mr. Storrings.

Our mother worked different jobs to help her father Raymond (Robert) Chrane when none of the family wanted anything to do with him as he had left his wife, our grandmother, to raise five kids alone. Mr. Chrane was a chiropractor in Vancouver but was in ill heath. Our mother was always trying to think of others. She sent her brothers in the war parcels and always remember her sons' birthdays and Easter and Christmas with gifts.

My mother worked in restaurants and movie houses to care for herself and to buy a few things for her three sons. She worked in Vancouver at the Bay Theatre as a cleaning lady and at a café in the same area called Mayfair Café on East Hastings. Her hope was to find a home for us but that was not to be, and it was as sad for her as it was for her three boys. She did say in a memo that Glen had a difficult, stubborn nature like his father.

My sister Judy Charlotte Storrings was born at Grace Hospital in Vancouver, BC, 09-04-1957. Judy was placed with her adopted parents as a young infant on a private basis as she was not free for adoption until 1960. Her name changed to Kim. It seems that when Judy was born our mother wished to have her adopted out as she felt she must take responsibly of her three sons first. On July 18, 1957, she stated that she was the only one in a position to help her sons. But because of our age we would not be adopted and would stay in foster care. Maybe she could have helped us in some other ways, but because of Judy's age, the baby would more readily adjust to a new home. Our mother indicated a strong feelings of failure, which she attributed to her husband who has not helped her in any way in bringing up us boys.

Judy's bio in the files says:
Judy is a most appealing little girl with very blonde hair and big blue eyes. She is quite chubby and healthy in appearance and lives in a home with her birth mother and another child, Vivian, born in 1954, who is Chinese in appearance, with oriental features.(Most of the info on Judy is whited out as she was adopted out and maybe that was private information)

Judy, who is now called Kim, was adopted to a nice family on the Island and now resides in Maple Ridge with her husband. They have no children.

Sister Charlotte's info

#205, 11965 Fraser Street
Maple Ridge, B.C.
V2X 8H7

October 5, 1979

Mr. Murray Storrings
11682 Morris Street
Maple Ridge, B.C.

Dear Mr. Storrings:

The following is taken from the microfilmed copies of your sisters'
files.

Re: Judy Charlotte - bn: April 9, 1957

Charlotte appears to have been placed as a young infant with her
adopting parents on a private basis. She was not free for adoption
however, until 1960.

I can tell you a little bit about her adopting family. The adopting
father was born in Latvia in 1932. He finished Grade XII and took
additional courses in electronics. He later became a radio and television technician.

The adopting mother was born in 1932 in England, where she and her
husband met and married. She also completed Grade XII.

They were both in good health and live in an average working-class
area in a nicely kept house.

They enjoy community type gatherings with a group that includes the
children. They believe in doing things together and throughly enjoy
camping and picnicing outdoors.

They had no children of their own when Charlotte came into their
home, but later had a little girl in 1960. Charlotte was described
in 1960 as "a lovely looking child with blonde hair and blue eyes".
She gave every indication of receiving excellent care. The younger
child born to the adopting parents, was said to resemble Charlotte
remarkably. At first, Charlotte was jealous of the baby sister, but
this disappeared rapidly and there appeared to be a good atmosphere
in the home between the girls and parents.

..... 2

Murray trying to locate sisters (took me thirteen years of newspaper ads).

Micro-film Section
2nd Floor 614 Humboldt Street, Victoria

Attention: E.M. Bowker

AUG 13 1975

RE: STORRINGS, Valerie *Linda* bn. 1956 (?) b. 20 12·58 Vanc.
_____ *Judy* Charlotte bn. 1958 (?) 9·4·57· Vanc.

A Mr. Murray Storrings, for many years a child in care and now a
man in his thirties, who owns his own business, is anxious to
find out something about two younger sisters of his, whom he
never lived with.

His mother, Gladys <u>Eleanor</u> Storrings, gave birth to Valerie
andCharlotte while living in Whiterock. Mr. Storrings thinks that
the girls lived with their mother until her death in 1961.
He does not have any idea what happened to them after that time
but he thinks they became wards.

Would you be able to find any more information through your
records? Were either of the girls (or both), placed for
adoption?

Murray would really appreciate knowing something about these
two women.

(Mrs.) June Haner
Social Worker

JH/mec

MINISTRY OF HUMAN RESOURCES
205 - 11965 FRASER STREET
MAPLE RIDGE, B.C. V2X 8H7

Mrs. Storrings then said she was expecting another baby in December and the father is (this
was whited out, but we believe it is our father*). But she says this pregnancy gives her a
certain urgency in her planning for Judy and gives her a rather deep-seated guilt concerning
this pregnancy. Perhaps she feels she cannot realistically cope with a fifth child* (then it is
whited out for about ten lines). *She does recognize that it is not good for Judy to be moved
from home to home as exemplified very forcefully as her own sons were. Therefore she believes
adoption is best for Judy...* (more lines whited out here; they did redact many pages of
information in our three files)

65

I looked back in the late 1970s when finding adoptees was harder, and I spent thirteen years looking and found the two sisters in early 1990s. I put ads in the *Province* or *Sun* papers for all those years until fate stepped in and I made contact with Judy (Kim) first, and then eighteen months later Valerie was found though Parent Finders.

Valerie's file:

Born December 20, 1958, in Vancouver, BC.

Mr. Murray Storrings   - 2 -   October 5, 1979

Re: Valerie - bn: December 20, 1958

Valerie was born in December 20, 1958. She was committed to the custody of the Superintendent of Child Welfare in February 1960 at age one. She was placed with her adopting parents in March 1960.

The adopting father had a good job as a Sales Manager and provided a comfortable standard-of-living for his family. The adopting mother is described as being "friendly and relaxed with a quiet and gentle manner. She shows great patience and understanding of children." The couple had adopted one other child - a boy, born in 1951. He was placed for adoption with them at age 6. Coming to them as a frightened and upset child, he subsequently became very well adjusted.

Valerie was described at the time of her adoption as "a most attractive, pretty child with dark blonde hair, large blue eyes and fair skin. She is a vivacious, friendly little girl whose intelligence is obviously above normal. She is a very feminine little girl who is completely accepted as a member of this family group and who is obviously secure and happy with these parents."

I trust the above information is to your satisfaction.

Yours truly,

(Mrs.) June Haner
Social Worker.

JH:jhk

blind copy: Miss M. Evans
                 Co-ordinator - Adoption Archives
                 Family & Children's Services - MHR
                 Victoria, B.C.

Valerie Lynn Storrings born to Gladys Eleanor Storrings and we think John Douglas Storrings in Grace Hospital. Her name was changed to Penny Joy Doiron after she was adopted in 1960. She was committed to the superintendent of Child Welfare at age one in February and then placed with her adopted parents in March of that year. Since then her adopted parents have passed away. Their home was in North Vancouver, BC. I found Penny in 1992 and met her soon after. At that time she was married to Mark Hartle, who has since passed away, and they had a boy and a girl named Shane William Hartle (Shane Williams), born 1994, and Erin Mariah Doiron Hartle, born in 1990. Erin is in Montreal and her mother had a business at one time, Mariah Casting, in Vancouver. Shane is a musician in Vancouver (Shane Williams and the Vibrations).

Our sisters Penny and Kim with me in 1992 in Maple Ridge at my home.

Erin Hartle, our niece.

Mother was always worried that us boys would grow up to resent her and blame her for not being there for us, but to this day we still miss our mother and don't blame her for what happened in our lives. There were no lifelines or groups for addicts she could go to for help back then like there are nowadays.

Mrs. Gladys Eleanor Storrings was killed in a taxi accident on May 10, 1961, on her way to her mother's home in Yale on Mother's Day.

The VANCOUVER SUN, Wed., Mar. 22, 1961

36 INFORMATION WANTED

Will anyone knowing the whereabouts of Gladys Eleanor Storrings, last known address 2676 E. 1st Ave., please contact Box 1336, Sun.

Whereabouts of our mother in March of 1961, two months before her death.

THE VANCOUVER SUN
NOVEMBER 6, 1956

INFORMATION WANTED

Anyone knowing the whereabouts of Eleanor Storrings, please write Box 93, Sun.

Where is Mother? 1956.

Trip Home for Mother's Day Kills Woman in Taxi Crash

CLOVERDALE (Staff) — A woman going home by taxi to be with her elderly mother on Mother's Day was killed here Wednesday when the vehicle crashed into a ditch.

The Sun

VANCOUVER, BRITISH COLUMBIA, THURSDAY, MAY 11, 1961

WOMAN PASSENGER WAS KILLED when this taxi went out of control and crashed in ditch a half-mile west of Fry's Corner on Trans-Canada Highway. Dead is Mrs. Gladys Storrings of Vancouver.

Mrs. Gladys Eleanor Storrings, 38, of Vancouver, was pronounced dead on arrival at Royal Columbian Hospital in New Westminster.

Driver of the Yellow Cab, Guy Vernon Myrick, 40, of 1245 West Twenty-seventh, Vancouver, is unconscious and in fair condition in the same hospital with head and back injuries.

Police said the driver apparently lost control of his vehicle and crashed into a wooden culvert on Hartnell Hill, a half mile west of Fry's Corner on the Trans-Canada Highway in Cloverdale.

Mrs. Storrings' son, Glen, 18, of Yale, said his mother telephoned him Wednesday at 5 p.m. and said she was taking the 6 p.m. bus home.

Mrs. Storrings missed the bus and, instead, hired a taxi for the 114-mile trip to Yale. Yellow Cab officials said today the fare would have been about $47. A return bus ticket to Yale is $6.15.

Young Storrings said his mother had not seen her mother or him in six months.

"I guess every person wants to see their mother Mother's Day," said Glen.

Mother's Day is Sunday.

Glen, an unemployed logger, lives with his aunt and uncle, Mr. and Mrs. Mike Doern.

He said his mother had been working in Vancouver for eight years as a waitress and housekeeper.

THE PROVINCE,
Saturday, May 27, 1961

Inquest told woman had two seizures

Taxi driver Guy V. Myrick said Friday a woman passenger had two seizures while he was driving her from Vancouver to Yale.

He was testifying at an inquest into the death of the passenger, Mrs. Gladys Eleanor Storrings, 36, who was killed when the cab left the Trans-Canada Highway near Fry's Corner in North Surrey and crashed into a culvert.

Mr. Myrick said that he was pulling off the road during Mrs. Storring's second seizure when the woman lashed out with her foot and kicked him across the instep, causing him to lose control of the vehicle.

The jury returned a verdict of accidental death with no blame attached to anyone.

Mr. Myrick said Mrs. Storrings had the first seizure while they were travelling through Burnaby. He said he pulled off the road and asked if she was all right and she said she was.

Dr. C. J. Coady, Royal Columbian Hospital pathologist, said Mrs. Storrings had .36 per cent of alcohol in her blood.

He said that .15 is considered the average impaired level and any level over .4 per cent is lethal.

Newspaper article on our mother's accident in Surrey, BC, 1961.   *Accident, Eleanor Storrings.*

WOMAN PASSENGER WAS KILLED when this taxi went out of control and crashed in ditch a half-mile west of Fry's Corner on Trans-Canada Highway. Dead is Mrs. Gladys Storings of Vancouver.

—Don LeBlanc Photo

Clipping in The Province newspaper, May 27, 1961
(sent to me by Janice Wilkin, who helps people find information on birth families etc.).

Form 6

44-065
Reg. No. (Office use only)

61-09-006205

PROVINCE OF BRITISH COLUMBIA
DEPARTMENT OF HEALTH SERVICES AND HOSPITAL INSURANCE
DIVISION OF VITAL STATISTICS
REGISTRATION OF DEATH

1. PLACE OF DEATH

Name of city or place _Frys Corner_ (If outside city or municipal limits add "Rural") Name of Municipality (if any) _Surrey_

Street or road _Trans Canada Highway_ (If death occurred in a hospital or institution, give the name instead of street and number) House No.

2. LENGTH OF STAY (in years, months and days) | In Municipality where death occurred _passing through_ | In Province _38 yrs._ | In Canada (if immigrant)

3. PRINT FULL NAME OF DECEASED _STORRINGS_ (Surname or family name) _Eleanor Gladys_ (All given or Christian names in full)

4. PERMANENT RESIDENCE OF DECEASED:

Name of city or place _Haney, B.C._ (If outside city or municipal limits add "Rural") Name of Municipality (if any) _Haney_

Street or road _Dewdney Trunk Rd_ House No.

5. SEX	6. CITIZENSHIP (See marginal note)	7. RACIAL GROUP (See marginal note)	8. Single, Married, Widowed or Divorced (Write the word)	9. BIRTHPLACE (City or Place and Province or Country)
female	Canadian	White	married	Agassiz, B.C.

10. Date of Birth _April 27 1923_ (Month by name) (Date) (Year)

11. AGE (Last Birthday) _38_ YEARS | If under 1 year MONTHS | If under 1 month DAYS | If under 24 hours HOURS | If under 1 hour MIN.

12. (a) Trade, profession or kind of work as logger, fisherman, office clerk, etc. _housewife_

(b) Kind of industry or business, as logging, fishing, bank, etc. _at home_ (If labourer specify kind of work above) (If Housewife in own home answer "At Home")

13. Date deceased last worked at this occupation _May 10, 1961_

14. Total years spent in this occupation _life_

15. If married, widowed or divorced give name of husband or maiden name of wife of deceased _Douglas John Storrings_

16. Name of father _Chrane_ (Surname or family name) _Raymond_ (All given or Christian names)

17. Maiden name of mother _Teague_ (Surname or family name) _Gladys_ (All given or Christian names)

18. Birthplace — Father _Florida, U.S.A._ (City or Place and Province or Country) Mother _Yale, B.C._ (City or Place and Province or Country)

19. I certify the foregoing to be true and correct to the best of my knowledge and belief.

Given under my hand at _Chilliwack_, this _12_ day of _May_ 19_61_

Signature of informant _Walter L. Chrane_ (Married woman not to use Husband's initials or given names) Relationship to deceased _brother_

Address of informant _Yale, B.C._ (House No.) (Name of Street) (Name of City, Municipality or Place) (Province or State)

20. Burial, Cremation or Removal _burial_ (State which) Date _May 16_ 19_61_ (Month by name) (Date) (Year)

Place of Burial or Cremation _Chilliwack_ (Municipality, etc., where Cemetery located) Name of Cemetery _Anglican Cemetery_

21. Undertaker: Name _Henderson's Funeral Homes Ltd._ Address _Chilliwack, B.C._ (Name of City, Municipality or Place) (Province or State)

MEDICAL CERTIFICATE OF DEATH

22. DATE OF DEATH _May 10th 1961_ (Month by name) (Date) (Year)

23. I HEREBY CERTIFY that I attended deceased from _held an inquest May 12_ 19_61_ to 19___, and last saw h___ alive on 19___.

	CAUSE OF DEATH	Approximate interval between onset and death
Disease or condition directly leading to death. (This does not mean the mode of dying, e.g., heart failure, asthenia, etc. It means the disease, injury, or complication which caused death.)	(a) _traumatic rupture of heart_	
Antecedent causes Morbid conditions, if any, giving rise to the above cause, stating the underlying condition last.	(b) _with ruptured pericardium_ due to	
	(c) _multiple rib fracture_	
Other significant conditions contributing to the death, but not related to the disease or condition causing it.	_fractures R. at elbow, both femurs, left Patella, left ulna & fibula_	

24. If a woman, did the death occur either during pregnancy or within 90 days following pregnancy? _no_ Yes or No

25. (a) Was there a recent surgical operation? _no_ (b) Date of operation 19___

(c) State findings of operation

(d) Was there an autopsy? _yes_

26. If a violent death, fill in also: (a) Accident [X]; Suicide [ ]; Homicide [ ] (b) Date of injury _10 May 1961_

(c) How did injury occur? _subject was passenger in truck which ran off roadway, striking a cement culvert + subject thrown against guardrail._

(d) Injuries sustained? _as above with multiple lacerations_ (e.g., fracture of skull, left leg, etc., dislocation of, burn to-, etc.)

(e) Where did injury occur? (home, farm, industrial place, highway, etc.) _highway_

27. Signed by _[signature]_ Designation _Coroner_ M.D., Coroner, etc.

Address _Coroners Office New Westminster._ Date _15 May 1961_

28. Print name of M.D., Coroner, etc., whose signature appears above _Coroner Pat Oaks J.P.Warwood_

29. Notations

30. I hereby certify that the above return was made to me at _New Westminster_

Dated _[illegible]_ 19_61_

District Registration No. _890_ _[signature]_ (Signature of District Registrar) Deputy

DO NOT WRITE BELOW THIS LINE OFFICE USE ONLY

9004—3,14: 31-7-59

(SEE REVERSE SIDE FOR INSTRUCTIONS)

Mother's accident death certificate, 1961.

The Sun

VANCOUVER, BRITISH COLUMBIA, MONDAY, MAY 15, 1961

Taxi Crash Victim Drunk, Jury Told

NEW WESTMINSTER (Staff) — A coroner's jury here was told a 36-year-old Yale woman killed in a highway accident Wednesday was in an advanced state of intoxication.

The woman, Gladys Eleanor Storings, was returning to Yale when the taxi in which she was travelling went off Trans-Canada highway west of Frys Corner and crashed into a culvert.

Dr. C. J. Coady, Royal Columbian Hospital pathologist, told the jury that alcoholic content of Mrs. Storings blood was .36 per cent, indicating an advanced state of intoxication.

The inquest was adjourned to May 25, pending recovery of the driver, Guy V. Myrick, Vancouver.

Newspaper clipping on Mother's accident, 1961.

The taxi crash happened near Fry's Corner in Surrey. The driver was hurt in the crash but Mrs. Storrings, without a seat belt and in the front seat of the taxi, went though the windshield and was killed on impact. She was DOA (Dead on Arrival) at the hospital. I had seen her for the last time in a taxi in Haney, BC, when she was staying at an Auto Court to visit us. I said goodbye to her as two men picked her up in a Taxi from Vancouver. She was looking terrified from the back seat, screaming to me that she did not want to leave. I was thirteen at the time and to this day I still see that terrible day and the look on my mother's face; it was as if she knew it would be the last time she would see me. Three weeks later she was killed in the taxi and then buried in Chilliwack in May of 1961. Only her sons were at the funeral, and Dennis had to be escorted in handcuffs to the cemetery from Haney Correction Institute Prison in Haney. He had heard the news of our mother's death on the news in prison.

At the time, Dennis was waiting for her to visit him in HCI, but she was blocked from her visit as the social worker thought she had been drinking. He never forgot that he didn't have the chance to see his mother; it would have been the last time, and this still haunts him to this day.

Footnote RE: Mrs. Storrings's Accident

Miss Joasalu, who oversaw the Welfare branch in Haney and knew the mother and her sons very well over the years telephoned regarding claiming against the taxi company. The driver stopped at a liquor store prior to the accident that killed the mother. Mrs. Joasalu has been closely involved, having to identify the body of the mother and attend the inquest. At this time we don't know the outcome of this claim, as the children are pressing her to take some action (In 2018 Glen Storrings did ask and got the inquest report).

It was suggested to Miss Joasalu that she send the report and accident report to our attorney general department (The findings on this case told to the boys from their Uncle Walter Chrane in Yale, brother of their mother, was she was working and not looking after her children and there would not be any money left to these three children. Again, these brothers were left without a mother and money to try and make a better life in their early years of adult life. One brother made a comment that it seems their mother's life was not worth anything, and also none of the family attended the inquest and the sons were not told about it. To this day the brothers don't believe the whole truth was told at the inquest in 1961.

SIMONE PONNE/News st

Roadside memorial marks spot where Hilda Joasalu was killed. Her sister died in the same place in 1987.

Woman, 91, killed on Old Dewdney

BY MICHAEL HALL
STAFF REPORTER

A 91-year-old woman was hit by a Ford Explorer and killed Friday evening while crossing Old Dewdney Trunk Road in Pitt Meadows.

Her younger sister was killed by a vehicle while crossing the same stretch of road during an afternoon in 1987.

"Her sister was hit and killed by a vehicle in the same location," RCMP Cst. Dwayne Beckerleg said.

Hilda Joasalu lived alone in a house at 19025 Old Dewdney since her sister died. She never married, a neighbour said.

She was quiet, sweet and spry, sa one neighbour who was surprised learn Joasalu was 91.

Joasalu was apparently a retired soc services worker who belonged to Estonian community association. Poli said most of her relatives live overseas.

PLEASE SEE TRAFFIC, PAGE

I was going to see Miss Joasalu few times before she was killed, and she told me they made mistakes with us boys. I wanted to know more but she was killed before I could talk to her again. Newspaper article of her death (Our Social worker in the 1950s)

The maternal grandmother said she would look after Glen if the parents would leave her alone, and she agreed to take Glen at this time. Glen expresses dislike for his father for his mean treatment of the boys' mother and the father show little affection for his son. On September 26, 1947, the file says he was trying to make things difficult for his wife so he could charge her for desertion of the children so Mr. Storrings left the children with a neighbour in Laidlaw until their mother came back to care for them. Once she came back, she reported to the social worker there was no fuel for heat and no food for the children. On October 6, 1947, the mother abandoned the children once again and left them at a neighbours. She went to the welfare office but no one was there to talk to her, and she left the office and called the police to try and locate her. On the morning of October 8, 1947, Mr. Storrings arrived by bus from Restmore near Hope, BC, with the three children and took them to his sister, Mrs. Doris Pasacreta.

On April 15, 1947, Mr. Storrings went to Yale to his wife's mothers to see if his wife was there and to tell her Glen was very ill and she should come back home. His sister, Mrs. Tolmie, was looking after Glen and had called the doctor. Glen was admitted to Chilliwack Hospital and he was diagnosed with bronchial asthma.

The shack above where our mother had to live in a one-room shack.

My mother went to the Chilliwack welfare office to get assistance with food, and apparently she screamed to the worker, "I can't go on any longer living half starved in this miserable shack," but before she could leave the shack, my parents quarrelled. He kicked her out and she then hitchhiked to Yale to see her mother but came back, as she was concerned about Glen's health. She said she did not want to separate from my dad but wished they could get established and have a regular income, and she said she would do her part.

But it was almost too much to hope that he would do his part, and it was only a matter of time before Welfare would step in to care for us three brothers who had gone though hell in our short lives. The social workers suggested to my mother that she take the baby

(Murray) to her mother's if they placed the older brothers. The grandmother had said she would take Glen later if asked to do so, but at the present time could not offer a home for the family.

Later, Murray would find out the story that Grandmother had a boyfriend (Dan), a friend of her son Walter Chrane's who was many years younger than her. Our mother did not like him because, as we figure, it was making it harder for her to leave the boys with her mother. On September 9, 1944, our mother wanted to go to work to provide for her two remaining sons but this memo from the Children's Aid Society and Department states:

It is not the policy of our department to accept children for placement because a mother wishes to go to work to provide for her children, but we have asked the superintendent of Welfare to grant a social allowance for one month only in order to give this mother adequate food and shelter for her and her children while she works out a suitable plan of living. We feel that the two requests, namely "food and shelter" and "placement of the baby" are two phases of the one problem and should be handled by another department. Mrs. Storrings had tried hard to look after her two sons at this time in 1944 with proper food and care but has found it hard without support from the father.

Then, by August of 1947, while living with the children in Cultus Lake the situation was repeating itself and despite the social workers' efforts to encourage our parents in a more rational and normal way of living, Mother reported that on August 2, 1947, her husband was refusing to work and had been beating her regularly and spent every weekend drinking. In this file there is more information blanked out. It says our mother entered the hospital in August in a run-down and nervous condition while the husband stayed at home looking after the three boys. The homes our parents were in were always in danger of eviction.

Glen's behaviour says he has a serious protective attitude towards the younger brothers. Glen is their big brother and tries to protect his mother from his abusive father.

Later in life, as the boys were a bit older, Glen still protected his brothers and when he went to Yale to see his grandmother for a holiday, he took on a tough Native boy, Gerald Bobb, who was picking on his cousin Wally Doern, as well as whoever else was causing trouble for his cousin.

We the social workers then tried to locate Mrs. Storrings and had Constable Dodd of Yale to go to their grandmother's home in Yale to see if she was there. We asked the father's sister to keep the children for the night and she agreed. A mattress was procured. Murray was eighteen months' old at this time and all three boys slept on the floor. At times when a social worker or a police officer went to the boys' home the boys were huddled in fear on the floor crying in a bedroom.

On January 13, 1948, at 4:00 p.m. there was no section on the authority to apprehend. We had used "K"—no proper guardianship—on the information of the complaint, and the Vancouver Police were trying to get a line on the parents for a court date. We also believe that Douglas Storrings has been doing a little business with his wife and sister in Vancouver beer parlors, and if this is confirmed we will alert the police dated this day, January 13, 1948.

On August 18, 1948, the mother left the children alone over a weekend. Murray was two, Dennis four, and Glen had just turned six and was left to look after his two brothers. The children were placed temporarily by the local police, but later the police saw the mother and father together and returned the children to their parents to let it happen all over once again.

In 1942, Glen was born on August 16. Dennis was born Feb 9, 1944, and Murray, the youngest, on May 18, 1946. They were apprehended in 1948 and made wards because of neglect and desertion by both parents. The maternal grandmother and mother were visiting the children without arrangement and supervision and the mother could not accept the reasons for supervisions. Besides the three boys, Mrs. Storrings had two girls, Judy Charlotte Storrings, born April 9, 1957, and Valerie Linda Storrings, born December 20, 1958. While he was in foster care with his brother Dennis, Murray had a dominant personality and Dennis permitted him to do the leading. Through our observations, Murray may imitate Dennis and recognizes him as the leader, but both brothers are very close, as they mostly had each to depend on and were each other's only family at times.

It seems we had a well-documented early life as wards of the Welfare. Children that were wards of the Ministry can write to access their CFD files in the area they were living at the time of commitment.

First symptoms of real disturbance occurred in Feb 1950 when Murray was four and Dennis six and they moved from the Kendall foster home, where they had been for only four months, to Mrs. Dartnell in Chilliwack, where they stayed for a month only. They then moved once again to the foster home of the O'Dell family. Their behaviour regressed there, and their included setting the back yard on fire , became destructive and trampling on the neighbour's gardens. When confronted about these acts, they said it was a stranger that did this, not them. One worker commented that they said these comments with a straight face, always looking sad.

It seems even at that early age I could tell a story. Adoption was considered but not followed through on because consent was not available, and the Ministry dragged their feet on this issue for years. By then it was too late, as we were getting to old to adjust to being separated.

The Bourelles Foster Home:

At the Bourelles foster home in Haney (Maple Ridge), 1951, with Sharon (Singbeil) McGillivray,
a foster child living in the same home with her younger brother.

Tanaka home and Bourelle home.

Foster home we lived at in the 1950 as it looks today.

Murray

My first memory of a foster home was Mrs. and Mr. P.J. Bourelle on 17 Avenue, now 240 Avenue, in Haney (the Tanaka Homestead of 1920), which is still there and on both pictures on our book cover. I was placed in this home in June 6, 1950, along with my brothers Glen, eleven, and Dennis, nine. The Bourelles were in their late sixties and were worries about the connection between the natural children and grandchildren, although there seemed to be a good relationship between the foster parents and foster children. But the social workers felt that there was inadequate supervision as the older grandson used rough treatment on us boys, who were a lot younger. Both foster parents became ill and they had to remove us on very short notice. His files say I seemed apprehensive over the move but did not appear to miss these foster parents to any great degree.

When we removed these children from the Bourelle home, we received the impression that each younger child was teased and "bullied by the next older child. Murray and Dennis called Mrs. Bourelle "Gram."

I attended Alexander Robinson School from 1952 until May 1953 while living with the Bourelle family and then went back at this school in 1956 for a few more years while I was at the Hovis foster home.

Caldwell's' Foster Home in Haney

We had a short stay at the Caldwell's in Haney. We went there for a holiday visit but once we were there for a while it was not good. It seemed they were okay with kids they fostered that were in their teens but with us three they were not so nice, as we were young children. I was four or five and saw Mr. Caldwell put Glen in the scary basement with spiderwebs everywhere and lock him in. Glen would be at the window screaming while I watched outside and then Dennis was locked in there also, but not me. Maybe I was too young or never did anything wrong, but to this day I still see my brother Glen's face and Dennis's face in that window screaming and the looks of terror. Then one day at the small bus stop on the road, Mrs. Caldwell told the lady waiting for the bus that these "welfare kids" were bad kids. Glad I never lived there for any length of time.

Bourelle Foster Home in Haney, 1950-1953

Our foster home with the Bourelles was first owned by the Tanakas, a Japanese family that was given forty-eight hours to get out of their home during the Second World War. It was bought by another family in the area at auction, and the home is now a beautiful place owned by a lovely couple, Bill and Rosemary Calvin, who let us in to look around and take the cover photo for this book in 2018.

My memory of the Bourelle family was that it always seemed to be the best family I lived with as a young child. I learned to tie my shoes from Mr. Bourelle, and I remember me and him tuning in the boxing fights on his old stand-up radio in the hallway. I remember was a Joe Louis fight with Rock Marciano. There were two other foster children there as well as me and my two brothers: Sharon Singbeil and her brother Darryl. I contacted Sharon a few years ago in Alberta where she resides and there is a picture in this book of us on my first day at Alexander Robinson school in Haney, as it was called back then.

We had our room upstairs in the home, and one room we never went into had only a bed in it. It was cold and scary, and we called it the ghost room. Years later, when the Collins family bought the home and then sold it to the Calvin family, my granddaughter went there to see it with me, and I asked Mrs. Collins about the room upstairs. She said, "It's a strange room; we don't use it." They allowed me to go inside, which was strange to do some sixty-five years later ….

The home has been renovated by the new owners, who bought it few years ago. My brothers and I had our picture taken in the same spot in 1951 over sixty years ago.

I remember having my first asthma attack there upstairs and being taken by ambulance to Royal Columbia Hospital, as there was no hospital in Haney at that time. I also remember their son hanging the bear, which was shot, on the front yard pole. Overall the place was relaxing, to some degree, but we all missed having a normal home with our Mother.

Sharon wrote to me a few days ago and sent me some of her memories of us three foster kids at the Bourelles home in 1953. Her memory of us on the Bourelle's farm was one day all of us children were called to line up in the driveway. We were told someone had poured lye, and Glen had thought it was on the shelf and wanted to know who had done it. No one said anything, and Glen had no idea what they were talking about. Mr. and Mrs. Bourelle asked again and said if the person who did this did not confess, we all would get a spanking. Glen looked at me, his little brother, who was only three or four years old, and he thought they were going to spank me, and I did not do anything, as we were playing together. He knew I wasn't at fault, as he was so little. So, Glen said he did it and got spanked for it. Dennis said he had seen Glen do it. Well, later it was found out Dennis had done it and he got a good whooping for what he had done, not only for what he did but for lying and for Glen getting a licking'. To make matters worse, Arthur was sitting in the window and laughing at him.

Another time we were all having supper, and I believe it was Glen who asked for seconds, which was fine, but when he asked for thirds Mr. Bourelle was getting upset. Then he asked for another helping and Mr. Bourelle lost it and got him down on the floor and sat on him and whooped him. Shortly after Sharon said to Murray that all three of us boys were gone. Dennis and I were sent down the road to the Fulljames foster home, where there were at least four or five kids once they got there, and Glen was not to be with his brothers.

Fulljames Foster Home (Haney)

In 1953 Dennis and I moved to the Fulljames foster home of 1953 in Webster Corners. There were four other foster children in the home, and it was a ranch with five bedrooms and electricity but not modern plumbing; they had to go outside to the outhouse. Two of the foster children were Native, Francis Point and her brother Jimmy, plus there were two kids of the parent's own: their daughter Beverly and a brother who later married one of the Asian foster kids, Peggy. She had a sister named Joan.

Dennis pointing to the former foster home of the Fulljames in Webster Corners in Haney BC.

Beverley Fulljames's daughter told me that at one time in the summer her mother had eighteen children there. We all had chores to do and never seemed to mind, and we got along fine. We often swam in the creek in the front of the property. There were four boys including me and Dennis, but there were more girls: Peggy, Joan, June, April, Marilyn, Cheryl and Francis always seemed to be the bossy one. The babies needed somewhere to stay short term while they were waiting for adoption, but things changed after the barn was burnt down by me and Dennis. We didn't stay there much longer after the fire. The foster parents sold the farm and moved to Surrey then to Langley. At the farm there had been farm animals and three dogs, goats, chickens and cows. They were provided with one hot meal a day and at times had ice cream. I attended Webster Corners School and was promoted to grade 2 on trial in June of 1953. A teacher remarked that my work was improving steadily but that I would need extra help. I was rated as satisfactory and normal in all subjects but had missed school with asthma attacks and spent lots of time in RCH in New Westminster hospital in an oxygen tent.

Murray's Evaluation

The plan for Murray is as follows: Murray has been in many foster homes and also experienced a great deal of insecurity in his own home. During his three years at the Bourelle foster home he was describe as a quiet and well-behaved child. It was not until placement in the Fulljames in 1952-3 home that we received any indication that those children were not developing satisfactorily. Murray is anxious and apprehensive. When he is called into the house he comes quietly, but Dennis trembles with fear. Murray lacks initiative and seems disinterested. The other children encourage Murray to take part in the games they are playing. Murray does obey quietly but at the first opportunity drops out of the game and disappears outside or in his room. It's noted that Murray follows Dennis around and maybe imitates Dennis's behaviour. Murray and Dennis sit quietly for hours pulling a leaf or a blade of grass into little pieces and has been observed eating heads of clover also. He seems to lack the ability to verbalize either his fears or his pleasure over anything; it seems his feelings are numb and has no attachment to anyone except his brothers .

Murray, as young as he is, seems to be thinking "why are we here and not with our own family?" and it shows in his behaviour, as he does not want to join in on any of the things happing in this family. Dennis seems to want to be liked by the foster mother and will do anything to please her.

Reports from the foster mother say she is trying to separate the two brothers, but that Murray and Dennis are obedient. Murray does nothing on his own. He never rushes to the table for his meals but waits patiently until he is told to wash his hands and face and sit at the table.

The foster mother would be willing to continue with care of Murray and his brother if she felt she could assist them to a better adjustment. On the other hand, she reports she feels that this child Murray should be in a special school or institution for treatment. She feels if Murray continues in his present behaviour that he might become mentally ill. In view of

*Murray's present unhappiness and behaviour we wish to have a recommendation from the clinic regarding plans and treatment for this child. (*Parts of this report are blanked out*)
~Miss Vivian Stevenson, Social Worker.*

Murray

When I read that report I was shocked— we were just unhappy being moved so many times by the system, and as there were only good reports from the Bourelles, it shows I was unhappy at this foster place and with good reason and not mentally ill, Dennis and I would hide in the bush in front of the ranch and count the loafs of bread that were delivered to the house and then in the middle of the night we would get out of bed and sneak downstairs at around 3:30 am and would go into the kitchen and take a loaf of bread or pastry and eat it or hide the food in there bedroom. I remember one-time Mrs. Fulljames came into the room where Dennis and I were sleeping. Dennis was in one bunk and I was in another lower berth, and she yelled at me, saying, "We know what you have been doing—hiding food."

She grabbed me out of the bed while Dennis watched and she rammed my head into the bar on the top bunk, splitting my head open, which required five or so stitches at the doctor's office in Haney.

A few weeks later two social workers from Victoria came to question Dennis and me because of the doctors report Mrs. Fulljames told us if we said anything about this we would not receive ice cream, so when the workers asked us if everything was okay we said it was. We were scared to say anything more. I had wondered what they said happened to my head because there was a medical report, but I have never seen it in my files. Pages and pages of data have been redacted, so we don't know what more happed to us over the years as children. Deep down, I was never really happy at any these foster homes.

A referral to the guidance clinic was never done for me, as far as I knew. Later, at the Hovis foster home between 1957 and 1958, Mrs. Hovis tried to understand my behaviour and feelings as this was new to her. She asked me to call her Mom, but I refused to do so.

Dennis brought home matches from school while living at the Fulljames home and he said he would show me how they worked in the barn's hayloft. We climbed a twelve-foot ladder up to the loft and Dennis let me light a match. It dropped between the hay bales and caught fire quickly, and we went back down but I fell down the ladder to the hay on the floor. Dennis was quickly gone towards the house with the Billy goat when our foster mom came screaming out of the house asking Dennis what happened. He said he didn't know and but that he saw me coming out of the barn, and then I was blamed for the fire and shunned from the family until they moved me to another foster home. I was glad to leave the Fulljames place for sure. In my files it says that when I was placed there I was suffering from malnutrition in 1953.

The Cameron's Foster Home on River Road, Haney, 1953-4

I went to this foster home after the Fulljames barn fire and liked it right away because the Lougheed Drive-In in Haney was on the north side of their house. I could see it from my bedroom window, but I couldn't hear the sound. There was another foster boy there named Allan Haus and I remember he was older and seem to boss me around. The files say Mrs. Cameron asked me about the fire that was in the local paper and I told her I was playing with matches with my brother Dennis and lit the match and it fell in the bales of hay. Mrs. Cameron took us to the movies at the Haney theatre, and I had never seen one before.

The foster mom said in the report:

Murray reads well and seems fairly clever and asks many questions about the show.

Murray also tells time and is quite smart, but recently Murray expressed an interest with dolls. She found a doll and Murray took it to bed with him and she thought being separated from his brother has something to do with his thinking. At Christmas he sat on Santa Claus's knee and when Santa asked him what he wanted for Christmas he said a doll. Santa asked again and Murray said a doll and Santa again asked, saying, "Murray, you mean a dog?"

"No," said Murray, "a doll." Santa went to the next child without saying a word. But once Murray got his doll at Christmas he put it away and never asked for it again. The main complaint was that Murray and Allan were destructive around the home; they were always tearing sheets and pillowcases. The Cameron's were planning on selling the home so it would be better to move the boys. She thought she would like to keep Murray, but her husband said if they kept one they had to keep both. Murray remarked that he liked the place and that there was always lots to eat in this home and he could express himself quite freely.

So in 1954 the Cameron's decided to keep both boys. But then Mrs. Cameron went into the hospital and Murray was sent to a neighbour's home, Mrs. Moody. The boys both got along well at this home and Mrs. Moody indicated they became quite fond of Murray and were thinking of a permanent place in their home for Murray, but that never happened. Then he went back to the Cameron's' home where Mr. Cameron was away working most of the time. He asked his wife to move the boys and stated that she paid no attention to him. Mrs. Cameron enjoyed the company of the boys even though Murray threw a rock through the back window and had to wait a week till Mr. Cameron came home to spank Murray in the woodshed.

My memory of that was that if I cried, he would stop spanking me. Thinking back on all these places, I remember that if you did something wrong, they either sent you to another foster home or to the reform school, which they did later in 1962. I left the Cameron foster home in late 1954 and went for holidays at my grandmothers' home in Yale, then to several other places until I landed with the Hovis family in Haney once again.

The Hovis foster family were a religious family (Pentecostal). I was nine at this time and feeling fed up with this constant moving, as one can imagine. I'd moved maybe twenty times already from one home to another, and other smaller moves, so being a little older I was running out of patience.

Murray at Hovis foster home in Haney, BC, 1957, on our bikes. David Hovis on left, Murray on right on bike his mother bought for him.

Murray, David Hovis, Randy Gray
and Mr. Hovis 1958 in Haney.

Now, this home was very different as we went to church at least four to five times a week. Sundays was at least twice and then on Fridays, Mr. and Mrs. Hovis and their son David and me would stand in front of Fuller Watsons store and Mr. Hovis would preach to anyone who would listen. At times my older brother Glen and his friends would pass by on their way to the Haney café and razz me a little in a good way. Then Saturdays we always knelt and prayed and in summertime the kids went to church camps. One was in Abbottsford, and I remember I liked it.

In January 1956 the files state:

Murray is quite nervous and is constantly chewing pencils, toothpicks, matches and anything he has in his hands. Murray is in grade four at Alexander School and is not doing well this year. He appears to be absentminded and unable to concentrate. Mrs. Hovis states that there always seems to be something else on his mind and he does not care if he has friends at any time. Murray also suffers from asthma attacks and spends time at Royal Columbia Hospital in oxygen tents. Dr. Capling says Murray is high strung and suggest that he attend the guidance clinic or a pediatric psychiatrist, as he believes the asthma may be psychological.

For the most part, David and myself got along, but we had our issues at times, being young kids. Then came two more foster children, and they were adopted by the Hovis family. They were named Randy and Susan, and I talked to them a few years ago and still do once in awhile on Messenger. I've kept in touch with David from time to time, and they sent me three pictures, which was important as we had not many pictures from certain ages.

The Hovis family noticed Murray was shy with strangers and once went to brother Glen's foster home without permission. Murray shows more interest in his brothers then his foster parents.

My mother bought me a three-speed bike for my birthday 1956, and I learned to ride it on the front yard grass. The Welfare didn't like that my mother bought us gifts, but she always did and always wanted to know how we were doing even though she could not make a home for us. I was showing more inward hostilities as I got closer to my teens, according to reports by Mrs. Hovis. The social workers wanted her to discuss certain things with me but she seemed to need help to understand me. Welfare wanted her and I to go into Vancouver General to the out-patient department to see a psychiatrist and a social worker psychiatric. They wanted to discuss these things with Mrs. Hovis to help her and instruct her on touchy problems such as religion, discipline and sex, but she never discussed these with me.

They sent me to a probation officer to try to explain the birds and bees and Mr. Mclean tried to tell me, but I never knew what he was talking about. In my early teens I thought a baby came from the belly button, so I had to learn most everything on my own in life.

I had difficulty relating and showing any affection to Mrs. Hovis. I remember shouting at Mrs. Hovis, who wanted me to call her Mom. I never felt I could and never did with any of the foster moms except maybe I was two or three. When I called Mrs. Hovis, I'd say "HEY."

Moving to the Hovis foster home, I had to go to new school and thought I would pass but I failed again. I got kicked around a great deal in Vancouver General. I needed a great deal of understanding and support, and the social worker thought at this time that someone skillful like a worker should go in with me rather than my foster mother, as she tended to be too cold. They suggested we both talk to the psychiatrist and that they needed a social history on me.

My thought today is that they tried to help as much as the family and workers could at that time, but the damage was done in the early years. In this foster home the family and workers did try and boost my ego, as it was very low at the present time. But as time went on, my thoughts were about my family, and Mrs. Hovis said to my worker that I wanted to stay with Glen and at times pined away for hours and hours for my brothers. Sometimes I would cry but try to hide it, and I would not go play with other boys. I said I did not like them.

My foster mother said my older brother Glen was a bad influence. Then when a holiday came, I went to Yale to see my grandmother, Mrs. Chrane, and one day I was riding on the handlebars of my cousin Wally's bike. Some boy threw a sack in front of the bike and my foot caught in the wheel and threw me headfirst onto the pavement, breaking both front teeth in half and breaking my nose. I also got a concussion. The day before this happened, my grandmother said, "What beautiful teeth. They are like pearls." I was not able to go back to school for some time until everything was healed.

A few times early on that the Hovis house I'd run away, but not too far. Once I hid under the house, then in the garage and once I went uptown in Haney. Dennis also ran away and hid in a garage, and I brought him food to eat. Around the end of the stay, Mr. and Mrs. Hovis reported to Welfare that they were unable to help me as I was obviously unhappy himself. They said it was better that they move me once again, as my anger and frustration would erupt violently, and I would pull down drapes etc.

They said, "Murray can't seem to express himself well but likes going to the Welfare office, would also keep his appointments and answer our questions in monosyllables and stated he wanted to live with his grandmother in Yale." In January, Welfare contacted my mother and asked her to come to the office to help me come to grips with her rejection.

With Murray in the office with her we pinned his mother down to making a decision on her three sons …(Part of this memo is blanked out). She gave Murray a wristwatch and said she would be back next week with plans about if Murray could visit her or live with her. His mother contacted us later that week to say that she couldn't make it and she would not be able to care for Murray. The office brought Murray in and told him the situation and Murray merely shrugged and accepted our interpretation.

A memory that has stayed with me from this foster home was that one summer I went to Grandmother's in Yale to spend a few weeks there as I often did on holidays. This time my mother happened to be at Yale with her mother, and she said she would ride the train back to Haney with me, as she was going back home to Vancouver. I was excited to finally be with my mother for awhile. We got on the train and after a few minutes she wanted to go up top to the dome. She walked up the stairs and disappeared. I waited for her to come back to her seat with me but as time went by the conductor came by, and as I was only ten years old, he was wondering where my mother had gone for so long. I pointed to the stairs and he walked away. He came back every so often to check on my well being. Wondering what she was doing there, I crept up the stairs and there she was, sitting at a table with a beer in her hand. She didn't see me, and I went back to my seat. I don't remember if I saw her after I got off the train at Haney, and that memory has not left me since. I don't think I've forgiven her for this memory. Memories like that stay with children for a lifetime. I did settle down, but I was moved again when I was twelve.

Murray on his bike at the Hovis foster home, 1957, in Haney.

Murray and his grandmother's lovely dog Rusty, our favorite dog when we went to see Grandmother.

Cousin Wally Doern and Murray in Yale.

Quesnel, BC, from left Murray, Auntie June, Glen, cousin Wally Doern, cousin Gary Doern and Wally's son Ryan at Wally's wedding.

Alexander Robinson class picture, 1957, Murray fourth from left top row.

The Stephani Foster Home

The Stephani's were a German family living on 17th Ave. South in 1958. I moved there after leaving the Hovis family. There was another boy named Ronnie McCrea who not long after I was moved again died of his illness in this foster home. He was in a wheelchair and had MS. He was an artist, and I think he was about seventeen. We got alone right from the start. He said they were mean to him and he did not like it there. As time went on I found out I knew Ronnie's birth family Carl, Shirley, Allan, Denis and Jeanine. The Foster family spoke German in front of us most of the time, so we never really knew what they were saying. I did not have a bedroom; I slept on the couch in the living room according to what the worker wrote in my file. I remember going up into this nice shed outside and opening a large trunk full of old comics and spending hours by myself reading them. I wish I had them today. They had cows and farm animals and lots of land to walk around on, but I was not happy there either.

I went to Alexander Robinson School and went to Cubs, but only a few times as I thought it was not for me. I also played baseball (hard ball) on a team in Haney and loved to play marbles at school. During the summer holiday I went to Yale to Grandmother's, and when I came back to the foster home, I was depressed. It was like another move every time I came back from my grandmother's home. The foster dad made fun of me because I wanted to live with Grandmother and was crying. I did not want to stay at this home, so a worker took me to her home for the night. They say I kicked up such a fuss and gave my foster mom a bad headache. It seemed at the first sign of trouble I'd be told to leave again, but this time I wanted to leave and refused to go back to the foster home.

Welfare called my grandmother and told her I wanted to live with her permanently, and I wrote a letter begging her to take me to Yale. They heard nothing from her and could not find another home for me, so I had to stay at the Stephani foster home.

I saw more of Dennis, as he lived not far away, and I was happy but I became initiated into small delinquencies. After Grandmother came home from her son's in Toronto she read my letter and set up an appointment in Haney to take me and sign the papers, but I said I would only go if she took Dennis too. Grandmother could only handle one of us, so they told me to make up my mind. They knew I would not know how to decide what was best for me, so they decided for me.

By now the school zones had changed, and I was transferred to Haney Central. One day in class someone knocked on the door and wanted me to come to the office. There was Miss Joasalu, who informed me that I was moving to Yale and my stuff was in the car and we needed to leave. I was happy to live with Grandmother but was not happy to leave friends and couldn't say goodbye to Ronnie, so I never said a word to the worker all the way to Yale. It was a very long and tense ride.

Mrs. Gladys Chrane Foster Home in Yale, 1959

Once a few days had gone by at Yale and I was in another school I was happy. I could hear the trains go by at night from my bedroom window, as the tracks were only about fifty feet away from my room. I enjoyed my stay there and was now a teenager enrolled in elementary school. It was nice, and I met lots of great friends, like Raymond Sakowsky, Ricki Wolf and the Hahn kids. I played ball with Wayne C., Dickie G., Jimmy P. and his brother Eddie and many more kids my age. We had a ball team, and there was always lots of fun for kids in Yale at that time. There were two sisters, Beverly and Sylvia Sandwith, who would stop at Grandmother's on Saturdays to walk in town with me. I was always still asleep, but I did walk into town and enjoyed the day in small-town Yale with all the friends. As time went by, I passed grade seven and went into high school in Hope. We took the bus for the fifteen-mile ride, which was a nice break. My cousin Wally Doern was there, as well as Gary and Auntie June and Mike Doern.

My Aunt June had the telephone operation in her home and she was the operator. I took turns looking after it too. My friend Karla (Conrad) was above the highway, and her mother Queenie was great friends with Grandmother. She called her every night. My friend Skip Cornwell and I always hung out together in Hope and did what teenagers did on a weekend. Then came the heartbreaking news that my grandmother had to stay with her daughter in Williams Lake and I had to leave once again. It was like us boys were on loan to anyone that needed a child at times in their lives—back and forth, again and again.

So, I went back to Haney and a new foster home. It seemed that at the first sign of trouble or if the foster mom got sick, which meant another car ride to a new foster family .When I read my social workers' comments about all our moves, I wondered how we all survived this. There was a lot of information in the files, but so much was blanked out. In 1960 there are almost ten pages redacted. In November 1960 a worker states that they got a file that said "Murray is damaged too much to be helped and will talk to a doctor for a checkup and a possible psychiatric referral to Dr. Middleton." I moved so many times, it's a wonder I knew my own name. It seems from these reports that they wanted us three to see each other as brothers but then they said we shouldn't see each other. We never knew what was to happen next.

Rausch Family Foster Home, 1960

This home was in Webster Corners down 25th Avenue, which is now called 256th Street. The parents had three of four of their own children, but one was on his own. The family moved down the street to a small house with two bedrooms, with the children in one room (two boys, a daughter and me). I went to Garibaldi High School for grade 7 or 8, and the home had a big yard. I kept busy outside, and there were kids my age in the area so it was okay. It was only a few houses from the Fulljames home where I lived with Dennis in 1953.

There were kids I knew in the area, like Ken Nagatti a few houses away, Gerow, David-Sabiston and Billy Barker, and Vern Anderson who lived across from Billy Barkers home ,Vern married a friend from school later Trina Harty . We would hitchhike to Haney back then, and at times I'd sneak up to the HCI prison fence to see if Dennis was playing ball in the field. I was getting to be a rebel as time went by, and during my stay at the Rausch home. And then one night, on May 10, 1961, the phone rang. I was awake in bed and could hear the conversation. My mother was killed in a taxi accident. She was thirty-eight years old, and I'd just seen her a few weeks before in the motel she stayed at in Haney waiting to go see her son Dennis in HCI (Prison) I was the last relative to see her alive which was in a taxi two weeks later she was killed in a taxi . The foster mother told her husband they should tell me in the morning, but I already knew, and it took me many hours to go to sleep that night but it seemed like the car ride to the graveyard was more important to me then the feeling that my mother was gone, maybe I had to hide and keep my feelings inside or id never have made it in life.

My uncle Walter and family picked me up for the funeral in Chilliwack where she was buried.

Age 15- Murray Storrings.

Wasyluk foster home in the 1960s.

The Wasyluk Foster Home

I was living in Haney as a young teenager, and it was a nice home and I was treated fairly, but I was hostile at this age. I was not doing well in school, and my brother Glen had punched out the gym teacher(Dan Buss) at a dance in the gym at MRHS in Haney with brass knuckles, so going to school there was not the best time. I lived across the street from Allan Okeson and his family, who we played with at times. Jerry their son would often take me to the bowling alley where he set pins and to the pool hall. I also remember going to the drive-in with Willie, the foster family's son, who was going with the Okeson girl across the street. For some reason they always took me with them to the drive in but Willie's mother objected to it. I still went, and it was fine with me.

It seemed I did not get into too much trouble at this home except at school. Mrs. Wasyluk had to tell me that there were rules in the home about using the phone, she told the workers I got mad and clenched my fists. She asked why I was doing that, and I said, "I am protecting myself." She said she would never hit me or her own kids, but I said I was hit before and had to protect myself.

The file said:

Murray seemed to have a girlfriend across the street, Maya Okeson. She would call him late at night but wouldn't say anything on the line unless Murray answered. Mrs. Wasyluk would not let Murray talk to her. She was a few years older than Murray and he once again took offence to this order, so she got the okay from Welfare office to punish Murray by keeping him and not taking calls from the girlfriend. He had to come to the office, as we wanted to talk to him about this problem. (Not long after this, my girlfriend started dating Mrs. Wasyluk's son Willie, and in time married him) *It seems Murray never had a girlfriend before this and did not know how to handle the situation. Murray become quite belligerent and hostile to the home and to everyone in general but has settled down and is very co-operative around the house. He has no problem coming home on time or with his personal cleanliness; he is always neat and clean and well behaved in that regard. It is hard to stay mad at Murray, as he seems to charm people but can change in a instant. Murray liked the home, and then Mrs. Wasyluk called the office and said she would not keep Murray any longer. It seemed his face was swollen, and he had a bad toothache. It was a hot summer day and Mrs. Wasyluk told him to stay home but he took off swimming and did not come home until after 10:00 p.m., and he lost his glasses in the river again (the third time in eight months). We advised the foster mother to tell Murray to pack his clothes and bring them to the office. We said he could go out and find himself a home, which we could improve, and until then he is on his own. Maybe when he is without a meal or two and a bed, he may settle down a little. Murray is fourteen years old as of this memo of 19/07/1960.*

Social worker's Comments:

27/07/1960. Summary to date, memo from social worker Miss B. Barber one week later says Murray at 14 years old is a belligerent, hostile child who relates poorly to anyone and does not do well in school in grade seven. He has more likely only about a grade-five education as has missed so much school with moving from foster home and early on had severe Asthma. He finally returns to his foster home after begging for meals and a place to sleep (Which was not the case; I could not have cared less, as I went though more drama then that). *Murray idolizes his brother Glen* (whited out*) and Dennis* (whited out) *… these boys are quite attached to each other, and one finds what happens to one effect the other. The Wasyluk home has become very intolerable once again and he has become very belligerent again and is fighting and extremely "nasty." We could not find a home where a man was home and would be willing to try and keep Murray for a special rate of $80.00 per month*

During this time hopefully we can have a psychiatric assessment made and perhaps have him admitted to a treatment centre. He has been told this is the last foster home and if he loses this last one, he will go to the reform school. However, he was shortly moved on to another home.

Murray will probably require a male worker; however, we have to see.

It seemed to me that they gave up on me, but one could expect this type of behaviour with what I went though in my early life. A social worker took me to HCI prison in Haney to see my brother Dennis, and I was happy to see my brother once again.

Re: the RAUSCH-FOSTER HOME in Haney: Murray has been very quiet and passive at the Rausch home recently. We feel that Murray will not fit in this foster home or change much either. He will stay for a few months, as has been the pattern, and we hope we can get him in to see Dr. Middleton in New Westminster for therapy. For this to happen we must follow up for an interview. It's rather useless if we never follow though with the help this boy's needs, (which never happened). *Murray does feel closer to his brother, as just up a small road is the prison where his brother Dennis is serving a sentence, and he does sneak up though the brush to the fence of the prison and ball diamond hoping to see his brother.*

Feb. 13, 1961:

At fifteen, I landed in court for the first time for breaking and entering into a Haney store the worker appeared at court and recommended that I be placed on probation rather then being sent to a institution. The foster family said they would continue to care for me, but the accommodation for all us children in the Rausch foster home was very poor.

The file states: *Home is very small and during the summer rain or shine the boys have to sleep outside in tents for lack of space.*

Their daughter Helen went to high school with me, and the younger ones were only in grade school. Helen passed away a few years ago. Allan was the older son who married Dorothy Herman later in life. Mr. Rausch was an electrician who worked out of town often to support his family.

I showed improvement in Garibaldi High School, but a few months later Mrs. Rausch wanted me placed in another home. If I was their birth son would the foster families send me away so easily? I think not. One has to remember we did not control our lives as small children. As we got older, we made choices that were at time not good for our well being, but the damage was done early in childhood. As small children we must be cared for better, as that is the most important time in a child's life.

On the Move Once Again. Prasse Family Foster Home in Haney, 1961

Welfare put an ad in the local *Gazette* paper in Haney and placed me once again with a family of German immigrants who had a nice home across from the Welfare office. Mr.

THE STORRINGS BROTHERS (IN FOSTER CARE AND PRISON)

Prasse was away up north painting. I started school, but I was sent home for being imperti-nent to teachers. There were other children in the home, twin sisters and another sister and brother, and for the most part I did enjoy the home. I was getting into trouble at school, in the home and on the street in Haney. One day a worker called me to the office as I wasn't getting along with the foster mother. My temper was getting the best of me, it seemed, and they sent me to the courthouse next door. Before I knew what was going on, I was before a judge charged with incorrigibility.

Brannon Lake School for Boys, Jingle Pott Road in Nanaimo

I was told in the Haney Welfare office that I had only two alternatives left open: the first was a willingness to live a normal life. Reading this in the file, I thought *just like that they want me to live a normal life*? As if my life had been normal for the past fifteen years). The other part was that I was to stay away from police, jails, etc. This would include school achievement. The second choice was a charge of incorrigibility, as it has reached the point where control in the normal sense would not work. I had to choose, and as was expected, my loyalty to my brothers won out.

I was to be back in the office for my decision but failed to show up and was apprehended on the streets of Haney and sentenced to the reform school for boys for an indefinite term. I worked on the tree- planting job there but still suffered from asthma. I did learn how to follow orders somewhat during my close to nine months there. While there, I was asked if I was released back to the Prasse foster home, would I go to school and maybe take a course. I said I would like to take a cooking course (which is now funny to me as I still don't know how to cook). Maybe being hungry most of the time as a child had something to do with that comment.

A letter from the Mental Heath

R. Smith of the youth centre suggested psychological testing and a psychiatric interview again after two years, saying then they could consider placing me at the CCM Ranch or in a Smithers group home.

A report from Dr. G. M. Kirkpatrick from the mental health centre stated that they could not get me in for a complete psychological assessment but that he believed I was a suitable candidate for a group placement, which never happened:

Murray seems not to be able to form relationships, but I think that a foster home setting will not benefit him. I think a group setting will be better. Mental Health, Aug 1, 1962

Mr. Humphries letter about the CCM Ranch included a copy of the assessment from Dr. Kirkpatrick and a completed application for my placement on the ranch. The assessment was whited out.

Just before Murray's release from Brannon Lake, Mr. Smith advised us they cannot accept Murray at the CCM Ranch because of his brother Dennis's influence. Then the Children's Mental Heath Services asked the CCM Ranch to reconsider for this boy and asked the group home for admission once again. They were refused, so Murray will stay in the reform school until we find a placement. (This ended being placed back to the Prasse home in Haney)

We hope Murray will submit to psychiatric counselling and therapy. It is our thinking that he will benefit from this. (This never happened that I can remember. I never really heard about it until I just read it in my file) *Murray has a charm and is a likeable youngster; however, when angry ,which is often, he can be like a caged animal.*

When I got back to the Prasse foster home, there was another boy there, Gordon. It did not take long to get into trouble. Welfare kept saying they needed to get me some sort of treatment but they never did, except to send me to a reform school. Maybe they waited too long to act.

When the Prasse family went to a wrestling match in Vancouver, Gordon and I took the .22 rife and shot bullets out my window upstairs into a building across the street close to the police station. On Monday after school, I came in the front door and a policeman was sitting on the couch holding the rifle. He said, "Do you know anything about shooting bullets into the building across the street?"

I said, with a straight, calm face, "No, I don't," and he said they lined the angle and it came from my bedroom. I said I never shot a rifle, and just then Gordon came in and was asked the same question. His face turned red and he said "no" in an angry voice. The policeman left, and I told Gordon to say it was only him, as he would just get probation but I would go back to jail. He did, and he got probation. I am not sure who shot the .22 rifle, but we were both involved.

In 1963, school was a problem at times because Glen had punched out that teacher at the dance when he found out the teacher had roughed up Dennis. School was coming to end for me, and the files show I was bored stiff with occupational-type training. It states that I seemed to think my intelligence was superior to my classmates'. I also had the police record.

Murray has been removed a second time from the Prasse foster home, as they are fed up with him and blame his brothers for his trouble. Murray stays loyal to his brothers. Murray now moved to a temporary home with the Vanderveen's. Mr. Vanderveen is a social worker and also has Dennis in his home as a foster boy. Murray then says he will find a job soon but wants to go to Penticton in the meantime to pick fruit with a few friends which included ,brothers Stan and Steve K ,Sammie .D ,Jerry (driver of the car) and others (I live in Osoyoos now, and Stan lives five minutes from me. I go over for coffee with him and his wife Heather and their daughter Harley).

Murray was in trouble with the RCMP there stealing campsite food, chicken and beer, and he managed to talk the boys into saying he was not involved. As Murray put it, he was the only one with a record and would be sent back to the reform school. Murray was not charged and was told to get out of town and was given a floater to leave the city of Penticton. Before Murray could leave, he was with some friends in a car sleeping on a stormy night with lighting all around on Lakeshore Drive, and he had his first epileptic seizure. (This was one of five I have had in my lifetime) He was placed in the hospital and his brother Glen came to pick him up and take him back to Haney. Murray felt bad but quit school at MRSS (Maple Ridge Senior High School) before he got expelled, and a boarding home was arranged for Murray and Gordon, who were in the Prasse foster home together a year earlier. Both boys were sixteen years old at this time of this last placement.

Iris Morse Boarding Home on St. Anne Street in Haney, 1963

I was moved to a boarding home with Gordon at a rate of $80 each. As time went by, I formed a relationship with the Morse family's daughter Sandy. She was a beautiful blonde girl. I did like her a lot but found it hard to form any type of relationship or get too close to a person for fear I may lose them as I had in the past. I was also going though a lot of struggles in my teenage life. We had an upstairs suite where we watched an old black-and-white TV, which I rented for four dollars a month. It was nice, so things went okay for awhile. Sandy would come upstairs and watch TV with us.

But then trouble came once again. Gordon and I were getting short on food so we went into the IGA roof and down into the store and carted out lots of food and chocolates. The store was not open yet. Then one day the police came upstairs and saw all the stuff that was taken and we were taken away to court and sent to HCI(Prison in Haney BC) in Haney for one year definite and nine months in-definite which meant we had to do at least one year then had a chance at Parole

I took a painting course with Mr. Bale and also a correspondence course. After a year, in 1965, I was paroled to live at the Morse home again. Dennis, a friend Ben and I drove my car, a black, 1950 Ford, up the canyon, as I remember, past Yale. Late at night, we came across a building that may have been a café so we thought we would break in to see what might be in there. As we were trying to get into the place, we heard a yell and we ran. The car was down the road and Dennis and Ben ran that way and I ran towards the tunnel while I heard shots being fired in my direction. I could hear the bullets hitting the walls of the tunnel, and once though the tunnel I went over a bank and stay there for what seemed like a long time. Then I walked down the dark, lonely road to find the car and there were Dennis and Ben waiting for me—another close call.

I then worked in the winter works programme for awhile and bought another car, a 1949 Ford, for $40 from a person on River Road in Haney. I did not have a licence (which I never got till I was twenty-six and married) and was charge for driving without one and fined $13.50. Gordon and I were fired from the works programme but it was not my fault; it was the other guys. My worker said, "Sorry, there's no help here for you. You're on your own, and if don't think it's fair, write to Victoria."

I took it well and left thinking, *well, after all this I am alone again.* Now my decisions in life were my own to make as an adult, and they were not always the correct ones. For the next five years I was in and out of prison. In December 1965 I was charged with credit card fraud, which I never took but was charged anyhow. I got a legal aid lawyer but got five months in Oakalla anyways, and up till the court case I was wandering around aimlessly. My motivation was non-existent. I was twenty-one and was discharged from care as of 18/5/67. Now I was really on my own, as Welfare had been my parents since childhood, and they were saying, "Murray, make a life for yourself."

So now began the path to be a good citizen, but it had some bumps in the road first. I was in Vancouver with Dennis and we did a B&E, and I get convicted in Vancouver and got eighteen months definite and eighteen months indefinite, which I did in almost two years in HCI Haney Correctional Institute.

HCI prison in Haney.

HCI gatehouse (Haney Correctional Gatehouse).

I was sent to the Hole twice when I was there. Fifteen days of bread and water is what you got most of the time, which meant three days bread and water twice a day and then two meals a day for three days if correct At the time, being in prison didn't seem to bother me; it was just another foster move, in my mind. I missed certain things on the outside. A good friend Danny Brewer and his wife Lindy lived in Vancouver in the 1960s and they would pick me up in Haney and take me to there home and I always remember them playing records of Bob Dylan.

I was released on parole in 1967 then met up with Dennis, who was staying at the Smith home in Hammond with a friend and his wife. I bought his 1955 Chevy car for fifty dollars. It burned lots of bulk oil a week and smoked a lot. One night we were with a friend, a Native boy named Lloyd Cunningham from Haney, and we were drinking. He had to go to see someone on the Katzie Reserve, so as he went to the house, Dennis and I stayed in the car. Then Lloyd kicked the front door in and we saw him running to the car as the person in the house was shooting as us. We got away as fast as we could, and a little way down the road our tire was flat from a bullet. That was another close call in my life as a teenager in Haney.

One night long after that Dennis and I were pulled over by an RCMP officer in Hammond, Don Waite. He was shining his flashlight and looking for anything that seemed to not to belong to us, and he called for backup and found about thirty packages of cigarettes under the front seat. We said they were not ours and we had borrowed the car from our landlord, as we had a landlord then. We did not get charged, and to this day Don Waite has been a friend to us three and helped us so much writing this book.

Then Dennis and I was charged in Chilliwack for five counts of breaking and entering. We elected trial by judge and jury, and as we were arraigned in court a school class came into watch the process, which made us nervous as we did not have a lawyer and we took on the case ourselves. We was remanded in Oakalla till the trial, and we were transferred to South Wing, (four left) overlooking death row. At the time, prisoners were still be sent there after they changed the law.

I kept us in tobacco by playing poker, and we had a small yard for all the prisoners to get exercise. There were some of the most notorious criminals waiting to go to the BC Pen in New Westminster. We got along okay there as our older brother Glen knew many of the convicts who were there for bank robbery, murder and many other crimes. I played cards with the CKNW broadcaster who was charged with poisoning his wife, bank robbers Danny and Mike and well-known Andy B, who later was charged with Dennis and I in a takedown in a Burnaby cellblock while waiting to go to court. He helped Dennis and me fight off police officers when they stormed the cellblock to take me and Dennis out for acting up. We was each charged with five counts of assault and other crimes and we awaited trial for almost a year in remand without bail in South Wing. We had a politician that had written the Victoria attorney general about our case, so when the trial was to begin, we smuggled a hacksaw blade from Oakalla in our transcripts to Chilliwack holding cells. If convicted and sentenced to a long prison term we were going to cut the bars in the cell leading outside to the street and escape. Just before entering the courtroom, Victoria called the court and told them that if we pled guilty on three charges and they dropped two we would get one day each on the three charges, which we did, and I was released that day. Dennis had thirty or so days left on a theft charge, so he had to go back to the prison.

When Dennis got out, we hooked up in Haney once again. I was staying at his rented duplex for a few days while he was away with this lady, and in the early morning the duplex was surround by police officers. I opened the door and they came in with a search warrant looking for drugs, which they found. There were a few pot seeds in a baggie, so they took me away and completed their search, drilling into the side of the outside concrete looking for what the informant had told them was there. They could have gone into the furnace room, opened the trap door and found about five pounds of pot bagged up, which belonged to Dennis.

I spent another three months in Oakalla until my charges were dropped. That was 1970, my turning point in my life. I must say, as teenagers and young adults we got into trouble, and this was our own decision at this time in life. We can blame it on our past in care, and it had something to do with it, but we did not make the decisions as a child; as it was the adults that were in charge of that, but we knew what was right and wrong as we grew older. All three of us brothers had a strong will to survive as we wondered why this was happing to us with all the moves. We felt different, and even kids in school asked me why our mom's name on our report cards was different and I would they were just looking after me and I didn't have a mother.

In Romania, 2003.   *Murray in Graceland at Elvis's Home.*

My turnaround in life begins with a marriage to Betty Ann Nicholson in 1971. Marie Eleanor Storrings was born in August 16, 1972. On that day I celebrated a bit too much, got into a fight and received a black eye, and my blue-lens glasses got broken. My wife wasn't too happy when she saw me at the hospital the next day. Then in 1975 on July 11, Shelly Lynn Storrings was born in Maple Ridge.

I started doing family genealogy in late 1990s and found most of my distant and not-so-distant family members in England, the US and other parts of the world. I had my DNA done and found I am 56% Irish and Scottish and 44% from England, Wales, and northwestern Europe. I am related though my great grandmother Francis A. Rugg and John Rugg to Hannah Prescott, family to the two presidents George Bush and George Senior, among other famous presidents. It says George Washington is a first cousin six times removed. There are more people in the US, including Jesse James's cousin, Clementine Ford, and my great-grandfather was friends with Mr. Pinkerton from the detective agency, along with my great-grandfather A.G. Chrane who rode in the Buffalo Bill Cody wild west show. Only my immediate family know I found almost all my extended family and their history. I was the only family member to search for relatives, and I found lots of information in the past twenty years.

Another turning point was working for a living to make sure I provided for my family, not like my father had not done for us, and I started out painting with my former foster dad Mr. Prasse. I worked for some time with him painting houses.

One day I needed dental work done and I found out that Welfare would not cover it, so I called Miss Joasalu and complain to her, asking why it was not covered. She told me in a firm voice, "Murray, you're married and working—pay for your own dental." I was not to happy to hear this, but I told myself never to ask them for help again and I provided for my family from then on.

Then in 1975, with the help of Mr. Prasse, I opened a stained glass store in Haney next door to Prices Store on the corner of 8th and Dewdney Trunk Rd. I stayed there a couple years before moving into the Morris Electric store. I bought a lot of his inventory and moved my glasswork, along with his lighting and electric business he had for years. After a few years I bought the building from the doctor that owned it and we had a great little business for several years teaching classes in our shop as well as teaching up at HCI, which now was PVI and not a prison. In 1978 the store and two other stores were burned down by arson. We lost a great deal in this fire and we had to sell the bare land for what we paid for the store and land, but we opened up a few months later down the street and continued our business teaching glasswork and retail until 1989 when we sold the business. We still did windows and other items while I got a job with the school board, which lasted fourteen years, for the CUPE Union. I then started working at the senior's centre and took a extra job at the leisure centre for the City in Maple Ridge. I worked long hours doing two jobs, most times working from 3:30 p.m. until 6:00 a.m. double shifts most weeks. I got divorced after thirty years of marriage first wife, Betty, and then I met a a women online, Carol, and we married in Las Vegas. This was streamed live on the internet. We had only known one another for six weeks, but it lasted fourteen years. We bought a house in Grand Forks, and while Carol stayed there working in dental, I stayed in Maple Ridge working for eight-plus years, coming home every three months.

Once in 2007 I went to Tim Hortons in Maple Ridge at 1:00 a.m. on my lunch break. My daughter Shelly worked with me at the leisure centre in Maple Ridge, and that night my granddaughter Chelsey was there. There were some words said to Chesley, who was fourteen at the time, so I went to speak to the person and we exchanged some words. He called his friends, although why I don't know— he was six feet tall and around twenty years old, and I was sixty. They surrounded my car as I stepped on the running board to get a bit higher. Shelly and Chesley were trying to hold the guy on my left who had started all this in the first place, and the others were screaming at me. I was wondering how this was going to end and my daughter dropped her cell. As I looked down I was hit by the guy on my left and I was knocked out, slumped over my car door. When I came to they were gone and Shelly and Chelsey were crying and took me to the hospital, which I don't suggest people do. It pays to call an ambulance in these cases so there is a investigation by the police.

It's safer to turn and walk away

EDITOR, THE NEWS:

Re: Alleged assault a 'consensual fight' (*The News*, March 28).

I would like to respond to the letter by the liaison for the Maple Ridge-Pitt Meadows RCMP department.

As a young adult, 31 years old, I am disgusted at the one-sided, bias investigation by the police department.

This was not a consensual altercation by my dad. After my statement to the police, it has come to our attention that the constable in charge of the investigation is well known to the staff of Tim Horton's, as he is a regular patron.

Also, the police media liaison has informed my dad that he knows the youths involved very well. This, to me, is a conflict of interest.

All my dad wanted in the beginning was an exchange of apologies by both parties. But due to the neglect of proper procedures, things have changed.

This is no way to teach the younger generation, that because you have friends of authority you can get away with misbehaving.

The RCMP also informed us that the media's information was not correct. I guess to the police and their friends it was not, but to the victim and his family it is correct – except that there was five men, not 10.

The police said that these men "showed maturity well beyond their years." I don't see a man grabbing himself and making obscene jesters in front of a 14-year-girl as mature.

The police questioned all five men, who claim that they were coming down to stop the fight. That is not the case. They came down to join in the altercation that one young man, about 6'0" and 20 years old, was having with my days, 5'7"

and 60 years old.

I also wonder why the police did not question my niece, who was in the middle of the altercation, or why it was never mentioned the hit to the back of the head that I received, the car being kicked, the taxi driver in the parking lot, or why it took them a week to interview my dad.

I would also like to make the community aware that this was an isolated incident and if my dad ignored the obscene gestures and verbal insults towards myself and my niece and drove away this would never have happened, but if we did not make it public it could happen to someone else.

Because my dad chose to do the right thing by us, he was the victim and

Storrings

the young men are the innocent. This situation is becoming more common in society and we, as a law abiding society, have to be aware and more careful of our surroundings.

Maple Ridge, as any other larger community, has serious problems and we, as a whole, have to stand up for our rights and protect our loved ones.

In this day and age, many young people do not have the respect towards their elders, women and children. What my dad did was the right thing to do regarding protecting us, but today it is unsafe to do that. As the police have said, it is safer for us to turn around and walk away.

SHELLY STORRINGS
MAPLE RIDGE

Police didn't ask for granddaughter's statement

EDITOR, THE NEWS:

Re: Alleged assault a 'consensual fight' (*The News*, March 28).

My grandpa, aunt and I went to Tim Horton's to get something to eat. As we were eating, some guys arrived in Tim Horton's. I heard one of the boys mention to another something about a party. They left a short while later.

We finished up our meal and went outside to leave. As we were about to get in my grandpa's car, those same boys started grabbing themselves and saying stuff. As we were about to leave the parking lot, they kept on saying things.

My grandpa then got out of his car and asked, "'What's your problem?'"

My aunt got out of the car, as well as me. She then got in the middle of my

grandpa and the boys, trying to get him back to the car. As she did that, they circled the car, not to break the fight up, as there wasn't one. They wanted to hurt my grandpa. My aunt's phone got knocked out of her hand from being hit on the side of

Murray Storrings

her head. My grandpa was then telling her to call 911. So my aunt bent down to grab her cell phone. As she stood up, my grandpa was punched and knocked out for a bit, slouching over his car door. I was screaming with anger and sadness.

Then the boys took off.

My aunt got the car license plate and I got the van license plate while she was on the phone with 911.

I would have never thought in my life this would happen to my grandpa or anyone. Where has people's love and respect gone nowadays?

I'll never forget that night. I was so scared and angry, not to mention disgusted by how some young boys would do this to a 60-year-old man, being my grandpa, Murray Storrings.

The police seemed to not want to believe anything we said, but believed everything the boys said and never bothered to ask me for a statement, which seems strange.

CHELSEY STORRINGS
MAPLE RIDGE

Paper clipping of event at Tim Hortons in Maple Ridge, 2007.

Murray after brain operation from Tim Hortons attack, 2007.

At MRH, the doctor put a Band-aid on the cut near my swollen eye and said not to sleep more than an hour before having someone wake me. We went back to work and I did my shift and went home. The next day I went to Grand Forks. My brother Dennis drove my car, and on the way, we hit a deer. I was off on sick time on my other job and I stayed in Grand forks for a few days to get better. The following week I came back to work, but in the next month something was just was not right. My balance was off, and I'd sleep a lot and had trouble staying awake driving. We went to Grand Forks Hospital and they gave me a quick check and said I was fine, but something was not right. When my doctor, Elizabeth Zubek, came back from a trip on her honeymoon, she saw the article in the paper and said maybe I should get a CT scan, which was set up for Friday. I worked a double shift Thursday night, but on the second shift I had to lay in the sick bay as I was turning grey.

The guys at work told me that something was wrong but I finished my shift and went home and slept a few hours till my appointment at MRH. I went in and halfway though the scan they stopped it and put some dye in my vein, at which time I thought something was wrong. Once it was finished they asked me to wait in a room, and after a tense few minutes the person came in and said, "Murray, some not so good news; first, your brain is bleeding and you have a subdural hematoma under the skull and outside of the brain itself. As blood accumulates it increases pressure on the brain and we need to operate today. The other news is you have a golf-ball-sized tumour on the thinking part of the brain."

Shelly and Chelsey picked me up from MRH and took me to the brain ward in Royal Columbia Hospital in New Westminster. That night I had my operation. They drilled a hole in my head to relieve the bleeding, of which there was lots, and then I spent five days in the brain ward and was released home to recover. In six months I had my head cut open to cut out the tumour, and to this day I do everything in order. Before, I could not do things in sequence.

Of course, nothing was done to the young men; the police said it was a fair fight, as one may expect them to say nowadays. I had to try and forget it, as it made me hostile toward the police. I stayed in Grand Forks until I was fully recovered with my wife Carol, who looked after me as best as she could. Then, after months of recovery, I went back to my two jobs in Maple Ridge until I retired in 2015 and came to our home in Grand Forks.

I made stained-glass windows to keep busy and worked around our house until we sold and parted company later in 2015. I then went to Summerland to help a grade-school chum, Eleanor Nyhus of Haney. Back then she was in my class for a few years at Alexander Robinson in Haney. She lost her husband and needed some help around her home until she sold, and we bought a place in Osoyoos, BC, where we are today.

So even with all the turmoil my brothers and I went though from infancy, we survived, and we hope this story inspires someone. That would make writing it worthwhile. One wonders if foster care has changed to much. Our files showed us we were moved much too often to have a proper, normal childhood life, but we did the best we could with the help of many social workers and people that made difference in our lives. We were grateful to them. I did see when I was in Yale as a child that the Native kids were taken away from their homes like we were, and they were put in residential schools, which the government has apologized for. They should have, because it was a black mark on our country as well as the Japanese being taken from their homes. Canadian foster children were also taken from their homes and sometimes moved so many times. When this happens, the children are mixed up forever and will never forget what has happened to them for the rest of their lives. It is easy to say, "move on, forget it," if one has not been though such a experience.

So where is the government on this issue? I never hear much. We are the forgotten children who are left alone once again. What my brothers and myself lost as foster children in the system that we never had a chance at a good education. We were moved from place to place and put in many different schools. Our relationships suffered as we could not seem to feel safe, among other problems. We were hostile in our foster homes from many moves, and later in life it followed us until we finally could try to move on and try to be normal in life.

It also it hurt our job outlook, although I managed to have success in retail business, become a supervisor with the custodian department for the school board and a stained-glass artist. I studied genealogy to find most of my family members all over the world, including a dear cousin Denene Colton Wright who lives in Albuquerque, New Mexico, and many more cousins. Jean Gaw Buckley in the US is another cousin that has helped me in my genealogy a lot over the years. My cousin Denene has a foster child of her own and is a great mother to this child.

Without our beloved grandmother's influence, we may not have survived, and our lovely mother tried during difficult times in the 1940s with a husband that was not interested in providing for his children. This is now called a deadbeat dad. At times our mother had alcohol problems, but she always remembered our birthdays and always wanted a home for us with her—that was her dream, which ended up being only a dream. I can say today that I forgive her and love her for ever.

Most of all, I have my daughters Marie and Shelly and Chelsey, my granddaughter, who I love dearly, as well as my newfound daughter Charlene. You will always be in my heart. Thank you for putting up with me at times when I wasn't myself and didn't know why. And to my two wives, Betty and Carol— thank you for the good times we had and forgive me for the actions that were not as nice as they should have been at times.

> To all the foster children in the world: don't ever give up hope. There is always someone that loves you even though at times we think were all alone.

~Murray Kenneth Storrings

This was written from memories and Welfare files from the Privacy Act CFD files. We had many social workers that tried to help but because of government rules, they could only do so much.

The book was completed in 2019 after many years of work. Thank you for everyone that helped me to carry on when I didn't want to but knew I must. There are lots of pictures in the book, but the pictures are part of our lives.

Shelly, Chelsey and Murray, 2007 in Osoyoos, BC.

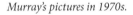

Murray's pictures in 1970s.   *Murray's wedding, 1972 in Maple Ridge, BC, with Betty (wife), Glen (brother), grandmother Gladys Chrane.*

Dec 4, 1971

Newlyweds Piped into Church

The newly-married Mr. and Mrs. Murray Kenneth Storrings were piped into the reception at the Eagles Hall by her uncle, Pipe Major Malcolm Nicholson, following their 5 o'clock wedding Dec. 4.

The bride is the former Betty Ann Nicholson, daughter of Mr. and Mrs. John Nicholson of Haney, and the groom is the son of Mr. Doug Storrings and the late Mrs. Eleanor Storrings. Rev. F. J. Wylie officiated at the double ring ceremony at the home of the bride's parents.

Given in marriage by her father, the bride wore a short white dress of chiffon over satin with lily point sleeves and a bouffant skirt. The fitted bodice featured beadwork trim at the neckline and a matching crown held her short veil. She carried a cascade bouqet of orange roses.

Matron of honor for the bride was Mrs. Janice Chequis. Her yellow and orange dress was complimented by a bouqet of yellow and bronze chrysanthemums.

George Sigouin was best man.

Mother of the bride wore a green and yellow suit with a corsage of yellow roses. The groom's grandmother wore a navy blue dress with pink and white corsage.

Toast to the bride was proposed by Jerry Whiting. Malcolm Nicholson was master of ceremonies. Out of town guests came from Quesnel, Yale, Hope, White Rock, Vancouver and Surrey.

The bride's going away outfit was a pink dress with corsage of pink roses. The newlyweds have made their home in Maple Ridge.

Engagements

Mr. and Mrs. John D. Nicholson of Maple Ridge are pleased to announce the engagement of their eldest daughter, Betty Ann, to Murray Kenneth Storrings of Haney, son of Mr. Doug Storrings and the late Mrs. Storrings.

Newspaper clipping of our wedding in Haney, Dec. 04, 1971.

Murray and Carol just married in Las Vegas, 2004.

Chelsey Storrings in Maple Ridge.

Granddaughter and friend Fallon at their grad in Maple Ridge.

Daughters Marie and Shelly in the late 1970s.

Chelsey Storrings as a baby.

Daughters Marie and Shelly in 2000 in Maple Ridge.

Marie, Shelly and Murray with Van.

Murray and daughters Marie and Shelly on tracks in Yale, 1979.

Family picture in Maple Ridge at Murray's house in 1991.

Murray's daughter by Kathy S. (1970-1971). Charlene as a young child.

Murray and sister Penny and her daughter Erin in 1992 in Maple Ridge.

Penny, brother Murray and sister Kim, 1992 in Maple Ridge.

Betty, my wife from 1972-2001.

Betty and Murray's home on 236th Street in Maple Ridge.

*Betty Storrings (Nicholson), Grandmother and mother-in-law
Betty Nicholson at Grandmother's home, 1970s.*

Betty and Marie Storrings, about 1975.

Our cousin Gary Doern.

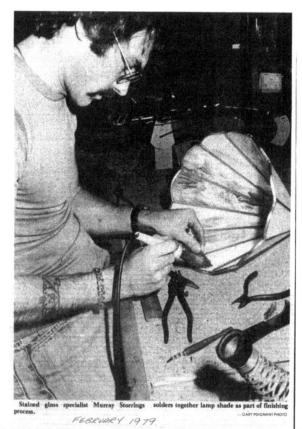

Stained glass specialist Murray Storrings solders together lamp shade as part of finishing process. — GARY POIGNANT PHOTO

FEBRUARY 1979

Through the looking glass — carefully

Newspaper clipping of stained-glass story.

by GARY POIGNANT
Gazette Staff Writer

The front of the store is cluttered in an assortment of stained glass creations and electrical equipment but devoid of people.

Behind the counter at the end of the room is an open doorway. Seated at a table, working under a couple of chain supported fluorescent lights, is the craftsman behind a large number of the stained glass creations up front.

He's Murray Storrings, a man who traded in his paint brush and paint for a glass cutter and plieable lead six years ago following a casual suggestion from a friend.

Ironically, Storring was working on a 12-sided lamp similar to the first one he made

People

after entering the field from the profession of wall painting.

"Care for a coffee?" Storrings asks, putting down the glass cutters on the chipboard table and moving over to a kettle tucked in among a grouping of stained glass equipment on a rear shelf. The visitor nods his head, glancing at the large, refurbished television screen pouring out sound and pictures on the end storage wall.

The visitor, returning to a bench to lean against, notices Storrings is meticulously placing the lead and the white stained glass into a neat, circular order. A bell, from the store's front door rings, and Storring's wife Betty puts down the piece of glass she was working with and tends to the customer.

"Stained glass work hasn't changed," said Storrings, not looking up from the piece he was marking. He said that the practice has been around for thousands of years, with only designs changing.

The lamp he was working on, one of two which would eventually be placed in a purchaser's bedroom, was laid out in semi-circular fashion in front of him. Each piece of stained glass, cut from a master plate made out of tin, is joined by thin strips of "fairly soft" lead.

The lead, which is purchased by Storrings in bulk, has grooves on either side for the glass to fit in. He pointed out that the space in the grooves is wide enough to enable the lamp to be formed into shape.

After each piece is fitted in, the lead is hammered in snug to the glass with a lightweight hammer. A horseshoe nail is hammered into the table to hold the lead in place. The process continues through all pieces in similar fashion.

The glass shape is etched in with the cutter, and snipped off with a unique pair of cutting pliers.

Once the pieces are all together, Storrings grabs either end of the lamp shade and pulls them together. While holding the shade in place, he switches on the soldering gun. Each of the joints, both inside and out is soldered.

Storrings, halfway through this project when the visitor arrived, said working with stained glass "can be quite time-consuming".

"I never get bored," he said, "because I usually have three or so different assignments going at the same time. I could get bored doing just one thing for a long time, but I don't with stained glass."

He recently completed his biggest project to date — a 1000 piece, 5½ foot long, pool table lamp.

"It seemed to take forever," said Storrings, who worked on the lamp off and on for a month. The other smaller projects on his list were used to give him a rest.

The glass used — exactly like typical window glass except that it's colored — is machine-rolled and shipped in a variety of colors.

These colors, says Storrings, are the key to successful work in stained glass. "You have to make sure they fit in," he said, pointing to a window his wife was working on.

"Usually you go light, dark, light," said Storrings, who works from basic moulds and designs and adds extra pieces or colors for custom finishing.

His own impressions of what can and can't be added to a particular design are gathered after visiting the home and checking the color in the surrounding area.

The work — which also occassionally doubles as his spare time hobby — is more challenging than painting the walls of houses. "This isn't that easy to do," said Storrings, adding that "I'm always learning."

He said the fact he owns a store forced him to learn "much faster than I liked to."

Despite the continued exposure to his work and hobby, six and seven days a week, Storrings can't see himself doing any other kind of work.

"There is such a potential of things you can do in this work," he noted.

Storrings puts down the lamp shade next to the one he's already finished and conducts a mini-tour of the crowded facilities to outline the purposes of other tools in the shop. Two grinders and filers clean off edges of glass or reshape them slightly. Another neat little unit which resembles a small table-top vice, etches circles into glass. But, he adds, the unit doesn't "cut" the glass for you.

The knife-shaped glass cutter he was using earlier goes to work and snips off the excess glass to eventually form the circle.

"I very seldom break anything," said Storrings, adding the reasons for mistakes like that would be due to too much pressure on the glass.

Working with glass can be dangerous, as Storrings has discovered.

A thin slice of glass, that came to a razor sharp point, had just been cut into shape by Storrings on a project a few years ago, when he accidently turned and knocked it off the table. Instinctively, because he didn't want to see it shatter on the floor, he stuck his foot in it's path.

The thin and sharp end went through his shoe and sock and into his foot, breaking a tendon and forcing him to take an unscheduled visit to the hospital. But, he adds, the piece didn't break.

If he would have stayed in his old job, errant paint tins were all he would have to worry about.

Stained-glass story, 1978.

Stained-glass window I made for a couple.

Murray Storrings near Sechelt, BC.

Afterthoughts of Murray's Story

A memo from a social worker in 1957 states:

Murray's birthday is on the eighteenth of May this month and we asked him while he was in the Haney office what he would like for his eleventh birthday. He got quite interested and said that he did not really know, and we teased him and said he must have some idea what he wants for his birthday. He thought for awhile and finally said he would like something for his new bicycle his mother bought for him. I asked him if he wouldn't like to go and look around in the stores with me and he smiled; we had never seen him smile before, and he said he would like that. We therefore agreed to one day next week. It was said Murray rarely smiled. Valerie Garstin, social worker.

Valerie Garstin follow up on my birthday gift in 1957:

Murray picked some decorations (streamers) for his handlebars on his bike. I think it will take quite awhile to get to know Murray, as he has had so many changes in workers and foster homes.

We received in this office a birthday card from his mother for him and enclosed was five dollars. As there seems to be no other alternative, we will be giving it to Murray for his birthday. All these three boys are anxious for family but his mother, his Auntie June and his grandmother are the only ones that seem interested.

The Five Lots

Grandmother Gladys Chrane's Five Property Lots in Yale above Her Home on the Mountain

One subject that has bothered us brothers for years is the question of who got the lots that Grandmother said that would go to her five children: Uncle Walter, Uncle Glenn, Aunt June, Aunt Norma, and our mother, Eleanor Storrings. In 1965-66, my brother and I were staying for a few days at our grandmother's house and she talked to me about the five lots up the mountain. There were more lots but they were sold to pay the taxes on her property over the years. She told me that because our mother had passed away, us boys would have our rightful share. A day later, Grandmother told her son Walter that when she passed away, one of the five lots would go to Eleanor's kids.

Our Uncle Walter told us to leave, but before we did, I got into a argument with Walter and was hit behind the ear and knocked out. Dennis got Walter to stop what he was about to do, and we left after Walter gave me forty dollars, which I declined. That was it; I didn't talk to him for a few years, but I always went to see Grandmother before her passing. By then Grandmother had signed over the property and the lots to her son Walter. He was saying he was not going to do all this work on the property and share it, so she was bullied into signing it over. He then gave his brother Glenn his lot, as Glenn would not stand for this, but the two sisters and our mother did not get the lots that Grandmother promised them.

I checked with Victoria and found that Gladys Chrane did not have a will and there was no probate in her name. Family members told me that Aunt June and Aunt Babe, as well as Grandmother, were upset about what Walter did with the lots. I believe that Walter was fined in court at this time in 1966 and needed the money to pay for his fine of $2000, which was a lot of money in 1966. Then, in the 1970s, I would go to Yale to see Grandmother and she was very upset about Walter's marriage. She knew she made a mistake signing the property over, as now the property would not be in the family eventually, which is exactly what happened. This heritage property was in our family for over a hundred years. family members were not asked or given a chance to buy this property, although we knew it was going up for sale. If Walter had sat down with the rest of the family and offered us the chance to buy it, that would have been the correct way to honour his mother and his grandparents who put their lives and memories into this home.

If offered, I was in a good position to buy, and I now regret not being given the chance. This was not the way to treat his sisters by selling there lots. I am my mother's voice, and this is what my mother would have done—spoken up, and her brother would never have gotten away with this type of family greed, which happens often in families. I will continued to check into when Walter got the property in his name, but really it does not matter now.

Some thoughts on the death of Grandmother—we three brothers were asked to come to her home to pick some thing from her possessions and when we got there we were showed a cup from a family member. Before the person let us look at it, they looked on the bottom of the cup, thinking I'd better check in case it was worth something. In the end, we got nothing of importance. Uncle Glenn only wanted the family Bible, and as he was leaving, he was asked by a family member if he wanted to sell it. Uncle Glenn said in an angry voice, "That's all I wanted, and no, I don't want to sell it."

This book is to show what happened to us a child, but also later in life. It was like we never existed in the family, but Auntie and Grandmother always tried to be good to us as much as they could. They did not want to say anything to cause friction in the family. Also, the small home was sold but then bought back by Walter and his wife Clare so they would have complete control of the property. Nothing was offered to the rest of the family in case they wanted to keep the heritage home in the family, as many residents thought they should.

Our grandmother would be disgusted and heartbroken that her home and property were sold out of the family.

GLEN DOUGLAS STORRINGS

As written by Murray Storrings, with the help of Dennis and Glen, from Glen's files and memory.

Glen Storrings in 1950.   *Doris Storrings (our aunt, Dad's sister).*

Alex Storrings, our grandfather   *Alex's wife (Maggie Kearns), our grand-*
on our dad's side.   *mother from our father's side of the family.*

Cousin Reta Sutton and her dad.

Cousin Reta Sutton.

Cousin Lennie and his dad.

Aunt Phyllis and her sisters Joyce, Pat and Jo.

Back row from left is Pat, Jo, Charlie, in the front are Reta and Lennie.

Aunt Phyllis Storrings.   *My mother.*

Glen, Murray and Dennis, 1951.

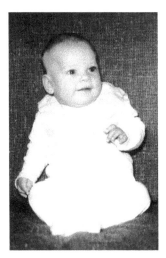

Glen's son (Glenn Jr.) as a baby.

Glennie Chrane, our cousin killed on her motorcycle in 1989 at the age of nineteen.

Glen and Murray, 1980s.

Teague and Chrane home in Yale.

Cousin Wally Doern in Yale with his beloved dog Lady.

Wally behind Dan's car in Grandmother's driveway where Dan backed over Wally playing marbles behind the car. the car knocked him flat, running over him, but the wheels missed him and he was not hurt.

Yale garage.

Murray and baby Marie, 1972.

Murray and cousin Wally Doern have a snow day in Yale.

Glen on left and his cousin Wally Doern at Lake of the Woods in Hope in the 1950s.

Jew's Nose as they called it then, above Grandmother's house in Yale.

Wayne Hahn from Yale and Murray at Wayne's home on Island, around 1980s.

Yale graveyard where some family rests.

Glen was born August 16, 1942, in Agassiz, BC. Before he was committed to the Ministry, he was moved for six years from aunts to grandmothers, friends and neighbours and back and forth to his mother and father so many times one does not know to this day how this child survived.

Some of Glen's foster placements in Sardis and Haney were the Crawford's home, where there was no running water, in 1948, then to Mrs. C.R Newby in Sardis and then the Pryor home in Sardis. He was also in the Bourelle foster home in Haney in 1948, where he was sent to St. Mary's Hospital for an operation. In 1951 he moved to Mr. and Mrs. J. Madsen's on Lorne Rd. in Hammond, BC. On November 15, 1951, he was sent to Mission Hospital because of a chest condition, and five days later he was sent to Abbotsford Hospital. In 1953 he moved to the Langston home on Callaghan street in Haney, where he learned how to box and fight to look after himself and two brothers.

In 1952 he moved to Mrs. Gladys Chrane's home in Yale while waiting for a new foster home. They found him a home in 1954 with Mrs. L. Thompson in Haney, but four months later there was another move to Mrs. Elsie Nelson in Hammond. Then he went back to the Volker's home later in 1954 but in 1955 he went AWOL and was returned by the RCMP in Grand Forks, BC. He moved to the Slagers foster home in Haney, then moved to Mr. and Mrs. Carl Nelson's in Hammond in 1957. He went back the Volker family and then to Brannon Lake Reform School on the Island. After that he went back to Volker's once again. He was with the Noel foster family in 1959, then with Mrs. Anderson in 1960. Then he was moved to Oakalla. He was released on parole in 1961 and moved to Mrs. June Doern's (his aunt) in Yale c/o his grandmother again. He was sent back to Oakalla while awaiting transfer to the Pen after being sentenced by Judge Barry of Yale to two years in the BC penitentiary in New Westminster for breaking and entering in Hope, BC, with Pete Dentling, his friend of a few years who was deported back to Germany several years later and eventually died there in middle age.

2676 East 1st Ave
Vancouver BC
March 11th/60

Dear Glen

I would like to come out & see you this month. That's if you are not expecting a visit from some one else. Should you drop me a few lines & let me know if it is okay.

Hope you received the tobacco, tooth brush & paste, hair oil ect. I ordered for you on my last visit. I was told some one had put in an order for some tobacco for you before me

2.

I am feeling much better than I did when you saw me. I have been under doctors care for over a month with my back

You were right about your father. I phoned & found out about him. I'll leave all news untill I see you

Love
Mom

PS.

I'll order some thing for you when I see you, which I hope will be soon. Let me hear from you as soon as possible

Letter Part 1: to Glen from his mother.   *Part 2 of Mom's letter to Glen.*

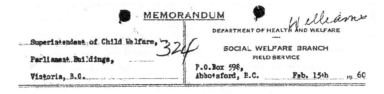

MEMORANDUM

Williams

DEPARTMENT OF HEALTH AND WELFARE

Superintendent of Child Welfare, 324

Parliament Buildings,

Victoria, B.C.

SOCIAL WELFARE BRANCH
FIELD SERVICE

P.O. Box 598,
Abbotsford, B.C.   Feb. 15th   19 60

Re:- STORRINGS, Eleanor & Douglas
       chi. Glen Douglas - b. 16.8.42.

Further to our memo of December 29th concerning the above-noted child in care.

You will be sorry to hear that in the meantime, Glen has been involved in a serious incident at the Haney High School. He refused to leave school property when he turned up to a school dance. He struck a teacher using a weapon and later in the evening returned and struck the teacher a second time. He was sentenced on February 9th to one year definite and nine months indefinite. Mr. McLean, former Haney worker prepared the pre-sentence report. It is reported that the magistrate wept following the disposition of this case.

We are hopeful that this lad will be transferred from Oakalla to Haney Correctional Institute.

A. E. Bingham,
Regional Administrator.

AEB/dm

Hitting Teacher at MRSS in Haney, Feb 1960.

Trial adjourned after collapse

The trial of Glen Storrings was adjourned Friday when Storrings collapsed in county court and was taken to hospital.

Storrings, facing a robbery charge, was in the prisoner's dock at the time. He was given emergency treatment by inhalator crew.

The trial, which had just started, was adjourned by Judge Ladner to March 8.

Glen at fifteen, late 1950s, taken at Brannon Lake Reform School on Vancouver Island (Nanaimo).

Glen, newspaper clipping of trial (charges were dropped in 1967).

Glen

Our mother was killed in a tragic accident in 1961. It was devastating to all of us and still haunts us to date. In 2018 I asked for and received the coroner's report and inquisition regarding this accident with Taxi Company. Miss Joasalu was the welfare worker from Haney who knew my mother, and I saw in this report that they never got the spelling of her name right. Also, there was no lawyer for our mother's side. They said she was on welfare at one time so there was no money for her children, as they were in foster care. In other words, the taxi company got off free because Mother had no one there to speak for her except one social worker. There were no family members there, and all three of us brothers wish we were asked to attend. We were disappointed with the family's decision not to be there for our mother.

Standing at attention, taken at Yale in 1951.

Glen's placement slip.

Glen's placement slip, 1948.

```
Attention: Mrs. Moscovich

            re:   STORRINGS, Gladys and Douglas
                  Chn.:  Glen, b. 16.8.42
                         Dennis Raymond,b9.2.44
                         Murray,b.18.5.46
                  Restmore Auto Camp, Near Hope, B.C
                  PROTECTION  17545
          ────────────────────────────────────────

            On April 15, 1947 the Storrings children were
      accepted as non-wards and placed in the Abbotsford area.

            On May 26, 1947 the Storrings were getting re-
      established in a home at Restmore and had been requesting the
      return of their children.  Glen and Dennis were returned to the
      parents on this date.  Murray went to his own home on June 3,
      1947.  We quote from the summary on our running record at this
      time:-
                  "In view of the acute nature of the situation ex-
                  isting at the time the children were accepted as
                  non-wards, we feel that a considerable amount has
                  been accomplished by the move.  The parents are
                  showing much more initiative and sincerely missed
                  the children.  The children seem much happier and
                  better behaved, showing the benefit of a good home
                  environment as opposed to the effect the atmosphere
                  of tension and marital discord was having on them."

            However, by August the Cultus Lake situation was
      repeating itself.  Despite our efforts to encourage the parents
      in a more rational and normal way of living,
                               husband was refusing to work and had
      been beating her regularly.  He spends every weekend drinking.

            Bills for rent and groceries were rapidly piling up.
      She said that the several weeks previously Storrings had not
      returned home from Emory Creek Logging Camp where he had gained
      employment and as she was without food, she came to Chilliwack
      to look for him.  She found he had been purchasing liquor but
      could not locate him.
```

Social worker's comments on the three brothers.

Before Glen's sentencing, Judge Barry told Glen's uncle that he would be lenient on the boy, who was eighteen years old at this time. His sentence to both boys was two years in the penitentiary. This began another prison term. His prison number was #718. After his release he was twenty-one and living in Hope. He went back to Haney and got in trouble once again in 1963. Once again he went before the courts and was sent to the penitentiary again, this time for two-and a-half years. #2390 Glens prison number . This time his father was serving two years for drugs, One day Glen's two brothers came to see him in prison and to their surprise they saw their dad in the visiting area with their brother. That was one of the very few times the younger brothers can remember seeing him in person. Glen's face was beat up, and when they asked what happened the guard on the loudspeaker said, "No talking about prison rules."

This stretch in the Pen was more violent, as Glen was in Warden's Court. He swore at the warden and got thirty days in the hole. On the way up to the hole in the elevator, they stopped the elevator and beat him with a brass key. When he was in his cell in the hole, they entered and beat him with black jacks. After his thirty days he was returned to population. Glen was released after a few years, and that was the last time he was in prison.

I have missed a few more ward placements and many more moves in his childhood. I was not aware that our brother Glen had endured so many moves, as he was not in the same foster home as Dennis and me, who were in the same home until 1953. The three of us applied for our trust fund, which was sent to us in the amount of about $300 dollars for the twenty years of misery we had to endure. A footnote in Glen's foster care is that he was placed back and forth to our grandmother's home in Yale at least ten times in his childhood. This would have been so depressing for him to have to leave his family home to go to another stranger's foster home.

Miss Joasalu of the Haney Welfare Branch went to see Glen every week in Oakalla in 1960, and she brought him tobacco and a couple of magazines so he could see that we cared. She wanted him transferred to Haney Correctional Prison so he could receive counselling services and be in a better atmosphere but that did not happen with Glen. It did with Dennis, who went there twice, and me, who went there three times.

Feb. 15, 1960, re: Glen Douglas Storrings
From A.E. Bingham to the Superintendent of Child Welfare, Parliament Buildings, Victoria BC

You will be sorry to hear in the meantime Glen has been involved with a serious incident at the Haney high school. He refused to leave the school property where he had turned up at the school dance. He struck a teacher with brass knuckles (which he made himself) and then later in the evening he returned and struck the teacher a second time. He was in court and sentenced to one year definite and nine months indefinite. It is reported that the magistrate wept after the disposition of this case with Glen.

Signed A.E. BINGHAM, Regional Administrator

To the Child Welfare Branch:

NOTIFICATION OF CHANGE OF PLACEMENT

	BH	Wage Home	Free Home	Ad. Home	Hol. Home	Inst.	Hosp.	Unk.

This is to advise you that *GLEN STORRINGS* *Aug 16 1942* was moved
(Name of child.) (Birthdate.)

on *OCT 10/47* from *MRS HELEN PRYOR* to *MRS GLADYS CHRANE*
(Date.) (Previous placement.) (Name.)

YALE B C
(Address.)

Reason: *Moved To home of maternal grandmother*

This child is a ~~ward~~ non-ward and is a responsibility of *Prov of BC*
(Mun. or agency.)

for maintenance. CAS CWB is responsible for collections.

Agency *SWB CHILLIWACK* (Signed) *V. Vincent*

1M bks. (25)—542-7720

Placement slip.

---

153 ● MEMORANDUM ●

DEPARTMENT OF HEALTH AND WELFARE

SOCIAL WELFARE BRANCH
FIELD SERVICE

The Superintendent,
Child Welfare Division,
Court House,
Vancouver, B.C.

Chilliwack, B.C., Jan. 14, 48

Attention: Placement Section

RE: STORRINGS, Gladys Eleanor & Douglas
Child: Glen, b. 16.8.42
c/o Mrs. David Crawford,
Gill Road, Chilliwack Mun. (org.)
PRO.#17,545

We are enclosing "Request for Placement" and Placement
Slips for the above-named child placed in foster home on January
13th, 1948.

(Miss) N.Hollingsworth,
Social Worker

NH:KD
Encls.

Placement slip for Glen.

Photo insert of Glen as a child, with Dennis on the left. Notice Glen is standing at attention like he was in the army.

Holding little Glen, with his Auntie Babe, Norma (Chrane) Dalstrom, in Yale around 1944.

Aunt Babe with Glen. She looked after him from time to time.

Mother with her favourite dog at home in Yale.

Jan. 19th/61

Dear Glen.

I went over to Haney that morning with Miss Joasale. He found a house to rent. Has to get my cheque on Monday I stayed over night in Haney Thursday with Miss Joasale & was to go back that night at eight o'clock with her. I wasn't in at that time. So when I phoned her Monday she seemed to have changed her mind about me going over there.

So phone me, when you

To Glen

To wish a fine
and thoughtful son
A merry Christmas Day
And then
a year to follow
That is grand
in every way!

Love
Mother.

Letter to her son from our lovely mother.

Glen, Maple Ridge, 1980, by Donald Waite Photography.

Glenn Jr., Glen's son, as a baby.

Glen and his long-time partner Anne Banks. They were together since 1978 until she passed away in 2011 (Glen stood by her side when she was in care for years).

Glen and Anne Banks in Maple Ridge, 1980s.

Reason for placement for this child taken into care 1947: unable to locate parents. Apprehended until court hearing in 194. The type of home required is a home that will show affection and understanding and one that will allow him the opportunity to enjoy children's simple pleasures.

From a Ministry memo in 1947. The length of placement was three months.

Before 1947 Glen has been with Grandmother and some aunts but as a free placement, meaning no one was paying for Glen's care. the social workers wanted Glen to be with his brothers in the Pryor foster home. At that time Dennis was two and a half and I was six months old. The whereabouts of our parents were unknown at this time. The welfare office wanted to know if it was practical to have a Vancouver radio stations put a call out for both or either of the parents and said they would ask the BC Police Department to look for them. The memo says:

We wonder if the mother is available and can get rid of her husband if she might resume care of these three boys. Perhaps if she is paid social allowance, provided the husband would not endeavor to eke out a existence off the family rather than work and provide for his family.

Glen

I was given up as an infant to my grandmother and also to my Aunt Babe, who cared for me at times. My mother went back to Vancouver to my father in 1942 and left me with my grandmother in Yale. I'd be moving well over fifty more times in my early life in foster care and in non-ward placements. Before 1947 I was in non-paid care, but in 1948 we all were wards committed to the Government of Canada.

Glen Storrings bio in 1948

At six years old he has blonde hair, blue eyes, good complexion, husky. His behaviour is as follows: very active, is afraid of heights, stubborn, self-willed, takes personal pride in cleanliness, seems to have an unusually mature reasoning and outlook and is a very attractive boy. He likes toys such as blocks, trucks, wagons and a sleigh.

Eleanor Nyhus, a young girl, would come over to get Glen so her mother could feed him when he was staying at the Thompson foster home.

Photo above is Eleanor Nyhus. Murray and Eleanor were in grade one and most of elementary school in Haney BC at Alexander School in Haney BC together . They spent several years in Alexander Robinson School together. Eleanor now lives in Osoyoos.

In 1954 Glen was with the Thompsons on Lougheed Hwy East, near the Nyhus home. He had to stay in a barn if the foster parents were not at home and the next-door neighbour Mrs. Sarah Nyhus would ask her daughter Eleanor, who was about eight years old, to cross the field to the Thompson home to get Glen to come to her house. Sarah would feed Glen and let him have a bath, as she knew he was in the barn around suppertime.

Eleanor Nyhus (Brooks)

Glen

In 1950 the files say that my mother was to agree to have me adopted but this never happened to any of us. My mother said I was headstrong and I'm thinking maybe that was the case. At times they dressed us up in nice suits and took pictures of us and sent them to Victoria to show how good the Ministry was looking after us. We got back a few pictures, but they were photocopies and not good quality. At times certain foster parents such as the Volker's near Websters Corners seemed to go out of their way to help me and drive me to Yale to be with my grandmother for a holiday. Then they had to ask Welfare to pay them for expenses, and in all our files it says they seemed very slow in paying.

Glen was also at camp in 1955 and on the ball team. The manger wanted him to play, as he was a very important player for them, as stated by Mr. Mclean, a social worker and later a probation officer. They all thought he was a fair person at the time but was a quarrelsome boy at his foster home and had trouble with the other two wards. On a few occasions in 1954 the foster parents said he should be removed from the home unless Welfare came up with extra money for the job, in which case they would keep Glen in their home and give them time to work through some of the difficulties.

Glen

What saved all three of us was our grandmother. We went on trips by car but mostly train to Yale, getting there at 5:00 a.m. My grandmother would walk to the train station to greet one of us (we hardly ever went together to Yale). Those were the best times in our young lives, and I have memories of our times with Grandmother right up until she passed away in 1981 at ninety-three. We still miss her a lot.

Living in the cabin

I remember being close to six around 1947 when our parents were living above the cemetery in Yale near Fred M.'s home in a cabin that had a waterfall. It is owned today by Queenie Conrad. Her mother was my grandmother's best friend. Anyway, our parents left us alone up in that cabin in the bush. Murray was about eighteen months, Dennis was close to four and I was close to six.

Dennis pointing to the area where the cabin in Yale BC was where we were left for a weekend alone 1948

Our parents went to Vancouver, so I looked after Dennis and Murray, but I was mad at my dad, so I poured the bottle of milk in his bed. In those days they left the milk at the door. One day, as my brother Dennis has written, the big black car came up the long, high driveway with a government seal on the side. They had to get us to come out from the bush area into this car, but we would not go at first until they offered us some thing to eat. We were taken away, as someone called the Ministry on our parents. The only way we got out of the cabin was that I knew how to open the locked door and get out to play with my brothers. I thought the parents had left three days before the car came, and I had to feed Murray, as he was too little and suffered from malnutrition as they say in the files. Also, if there was a fire, we were trapped inside but it was summer. Murray took pictures at the site last year with the okay of owner Queenie Conrad. Our family graveyard was just across the highway from the cabin, which was scary for me. A lot of our family is there in the gravesite.

In Murray's memory he still sees that big black car with the government sticker on the side door but I think that's because Dennis told him what he had seen. Murray finds it creepy to this day, but we don't think he would have any memory of this event.

I see pictures of my aunt Babe with me. She looked after me at times, as well as Auntie June and Grandmother and neighbours of our parents. It seems to us three that the Bourelles on 17th Ave. North where all three of us were living was at times one of the best places. For a few years we lived there together, which was the last time we were all together. They shipped me off by myself to many more places in the years to come. Our parents sent us to the aunts on our father's side of the family, which we did not know until a few days ago as we are finding more information.

The welfare workers report that as we get older it was harder for them to place us in a permanent home. Grandmother's health was in question so she couldn't accept responsibility for me. I went off to an aunt and then to the Bourelles. The social workers felt us children should move on to a younger family, as they were getting elderly, the file states. It seems that Grandmother was interested in me then, as she spoke to privately to the social worker. She seemed reluctant to care for me, and as the files say, these plans went on indefinitely. There was a tug of war with our mother and the Ministry, and the three of us are the ones that suffered for most of our childhood. But more importantly, we all three survived to be good-standing men.

In grade 3, Glen belongs to the school library and his reading is becoming more advanced. He is bringing home one to two books each week and Dennis has handed his books down to Glen, which helps his reading. Their mother has once again sent Christmas gifts to her three sons.

The social worker in one file said they also found it strange that both my grandmother and my mother seemed prepared to give me up in 1950 when I would have been eight years old (part of the memo is blanked out).

The workers feel that it would be damaging for Glen to have his two brothers remain in the family while he is sent away among strangers once again. It seems financial, and we offered to pay for a regular foster home for one child. However, we must be sure how deep and sincere the mother's interest is with Glen, as Glen has been with the grandmother more than the other two brothers.

In another report Grandmother was concerned about us boys and said she would be capable of caring for us. Reading these reports, my brothers and I think about what a mixed-up affair it was and wonder how we ever survived all this back-and-forth drama. My mother would not consider adoption for Murray and Dennis, and in 1950 she thought they should rescind the wardship and place Murray and Dennis with the relatives once again and send me to Williams Lake to Rosa and Fred Hinsche, a foster home. This plan never happened; it seems.

Glen has resided at the Bourelles home since 1948 and his two brothers have joined him in 1950. His mother has remembered Glen at special holidays, sending him candy, toys, books and novelty clothes such as a cowboy shirt and baseball cap and has asked the welfare department how Glen is doing. Our workers have asked Glen his feelings towards his mother, and the boy has shown there is not a strong tie or affection to his mother. He appears to associate her with being a provider of gifts. Glen has mentioned a reference to a black (Chinese) man with whom his mother is living, and his father is never mentioned.

I was teased at school at Alexander Robinson that my dad was a "china man," as my mother would come to school. She would come without permission, and I expressed fear about him. It stated in my file that I was harder to manage than the two other brothers.

Later Murray found the child that our mother had with the Chinese man around 1953. Murray also found our two sisters that were born in 1957 and 1959 from our mother and father. After our mother was killed, they were adopted out to different parents.

Glen is well mannered and likes school when with the Bourelles. The way it stands now with these three boys every female person is "Mummy" to them, and they don't know what security means. This is a difficult situation in that the mother is interested in these children, as she sends them parcels and comes to see them, but she does nothing about setting up a decent home. We feel we cannot sacrifice these children while she makes her mind up. In 1949 Mrs. Storrings was sentenced to thirty days in Oakalla (blanked out). She was twenty-six years old at this time.

Glen spent part of his early childhood, for the first couple years, with his grandmother in Yale. Then he was moved from home to home for the remainder of his childhood to well over forty-one placements since 1957, possibly more. Some were for only a few days, months or years, and it is safe to say Glen had more than fifty moves in his childhood. Before going to the reform school, the boy has had few satisfying experiences from life.

Except for a short period of time, he has been in care, as have his brothers. He looks at adults as being no good. Up to a month ago, Glen was in no serious trouble. He is only fourteen and he sticks up for his peer group. When his friends were sent to Brannon Lake,.Glen thought he should go too, as he could have stayed on probation.

Glen standing in 2019 in from of a home that was his foster home in the 1950s
(Volker's foster home on 22nd ave in Haney BC)

Just released from Oakalla, Glen is pictured below at nineteen years old. He was serving prison time for assault on an MRSS teacher in Haney,

The community felt this boy should be put behind bars, but his worker did not feel the same and said that Glen should receive every help possible. His file in 1957 shows many pages blanked out, so one never will know the whole story. So, in 1957, Glen packed his belongings and moved out of the Volker's foster home and stayed with his friend Gary Nelson at Fifth Ave. in Hammond. The welfare worker said Glen could stay at Gary's mothers' home, and Glen seemed happy, but his school was not going well, as Mr. Draper was once again on the verge of expelling Glen.

Gary got into trouble with a teacher Glen and came over to help Gary. Mr. Blois came into the room as Glen was going to fight with the teacher, but he was allowed to stay at school where he met a girl that he liked and sat behind in class. That lovely girl was Sandra Macpherson, and Glen and Sandra went out together for a few years, but Glen was in and out of prison, so it was hard for Sandra to have any type of a steady relationship with him. But they liked each other, and her parents allowed her to go to Oakalla to see Glen when he was in trouble. Before Sandra was remarried she came to see Glen and they spent a few hours talking and having lunch. That was twenty years ago.

Murray found Sandra recently on a Haney site and talked to her on the phone and asked her about Glen as a person. She told Murray that Glen was at times a pussycat, and he respected her and treated her well. Murray knew her in the 1950s, but he was younger than them by a few years. It seemed Murray finds everyone once he makes his mind to do so, but their aunt would say to him, "Don't find any more relatives!" That didn't stop him, as he found more every year.

Glen

Then there was the school dance at MRSS when a teacher handled my brother Dennis and Dennis came and told me. So my friend Pete and myself went to the dance. I had brass knuckles and I took on a couple teachers. One was Dan Buss and another we left, with the teachers getting the worst of it. The police picked us up a short distance from the school in our car, and I received nine months in jail for that fight.

The three brothers were mostly loyal to each other and that helped them survive, and they also seemed to put others before themselves to show loyalty in certain situations. The courts and welfare workers tried to help Glen in his teens but by then the damage was done; help should have been given as a child with that many moves from one home to another. They seem fond of their mother and ask about her practically every time we see the brothers in our office.

They took lots of pictures of us, and this made it seem like we were for sale. It was to show to people who may want us, but it was hard to find a foster home to take all three of us. As a child I had a bad case of asthma and eczema, and later on I had epileptic seizures as a teenager. Around 1978 they stopped with medication and no drinking; I have not had a drink since 1978 .

In 1949 I was seven years old and had a visit with my mother, as I had not seen her for some time. This was arranged as they felt this would help me. I had taken the attitude of not belonging to anyone, and after seeing my mother the files say I appeared happier. I thought no one really wanted us; it wasn't normal to be going from one home to another. It breaks our hearts even to this day.

I was in Abbotsford with Mrs. David Crawford in 1948, but then back to Haney to the Bourelle's. I was going to be moved to Vernon but because of my health it was advised I not be moved to the interior, so all three of us moved to Abbotsford to a foster home in April 1947.

We were put in protective custody at times during our young lives. My mother stated in 1947 that she had found a house and intended to take us on either May 20 or 22. Murray would have just turned one and I was five. Dennis was just about three, and it seemed our parents were paying money to their account for Welfare to look after us, but this did not work with our mother taking us three boys once again. Mrs. Tolmie looked after me in 1947 for awhile; she was my aunt, my dad's sister.

In 1944 Mrs. Glen Chrane, along with a little girl named Dawn, offered to look after the two children as Murray was not born yet. Dennis was only nine months old and our mother could not look after us, it seems. In the fall of 1946, we were with our parents and were in poor health. In 1947 we were deserted.

Glen in Maple Ridge Park with Grandmother Gladys Chrane.

Mother and baby Glen in 1942.

In March 1957 they did a guidance examination on me and found I had always been a hostile, aggressive youngster. I had lots of fights in town and out of town.

Glen states that adults let him down and he felt they were no good, as one could expect with what the child had gone though in early childhood and from the decisions the adults made for these three brothers. But Glen and his brothers made their choices as young adults and know they were not in the best interest of their well being.

A letter in Glen's file from the guidance clinic reads as follows:

Glen's loyalty to his friends has got him in trouble. He wanted to go to Brannon Lake with his friends who had committed the car theft but the judge deferred his sentence. Glen followed this up with stealing another car and was this time sent to the reform school with his friends on April 23, 1957. Since October 1953 when Glen was seen at the clinic, he has spent most of the time with foster homes in the Haney area. All three Storrings boys have had difficulty accepting their status as wards in the welfare system. Glen's two brothers, Murray, aged eleven, and Dennis, aged thirteen, are in separate foster homes in the Haney district. All three have tried desperately to cling to family ties. Unfortunately, there has been little in the family situation that is positive, although the paternal grandmother, Mrs. Gladys Chrane in Yale, BC, has kept in touch with Glen and his two brothers and this has been very helpful. Glen's mother at this time has not seen Glen for over two years. The whereabouts of the father is unknown, and the boy is very aware that his mother has always rejected him.

We are asking Mrs. Chrane to contact us to bring us up to date on the family history. Their grandmother is up in years and cannot look after the children on a long-term basis, but we understand there are aunts and uncles on both sides of the family living in and around the Yale area that may be found to take Glen.
Signed by District Supervisor Bruce Mclean, May 14, 1957.

I worked up until I was hurt in the 1990s. In 1978 I met Anne Banks from Maple Ridge and was with her until she passed away in 2011. I still live in Maple Ridge, in the same apartment block for forty years, and I still see my two brothers when they come to town. We are still loyal to each other after all these years. I had one son, Glenn, from Marlene Sloan. I also worked doing stained glass at times for Murray's store in Maple Ridge.

I don't really know how all three of us survived this life, but we did, and I hope others do the same. It is our hope that this story helps other children that are in care or have been in care to speak out about what has happened, good or bad. We have a voice as well as what the Native children are doing by speaking out that they were treated badly by the Canadian

Government. It is a healing process for all of us in foster care in Canada, and for the Native people that suffered too. As foster children, we three brothers think we were forgotten by our government, and our history in foster care seems not to be very important. We like this book to change this for the foster-care children who are still suffering and the ones that never had a chance at a normal life.

By Glen Storrings, as written by Murray, with help from Dennis in 2019. Thank you to my two brothers for their help writing this story. I did not want to think about what happened to me; it is too painful to put it in writing.

I must say, the social workers I had in care mostly all treated me well. It was not their fault we were moved so much—it's the system. The system let us brothers down.

DENNIS'S STORY: PART ONE

These are memories from Dennis's life in Haney and areas in the Lower Mainland. This is the story of his family history and life in prisons and in many foster homes. He had over forty-three moves in foster care and many more early placements before being a ward in 1948.

DENNIS

I know I have not moved on from this life, as I am still in foster care and prison in my mind. It seems it will never leave me, no matter how I try to block it from my mind. But here is my story as best as I can remember, with the help of my files.

Social History (in triplicate for CWD)

#5	April 17/47	Own home to Hatzic B.C.	Non Ward
	May 26/47	address changed	
	14.4.48	Pryor to Storrings 3 mo. probation	
	9.10.47	home to Pryor	Non Ward
	9.7.48	Committed to Clark SCW	
	2.11.49	Pryor to Odell	fo. m. ill
	19.11.49	Odell to Kendall	fo. m. Care
	2.2.50	Kendall to Dartnell	fo. m. ill
	5.4.50	Dartnell to Odell	fo. m. not well
	6.6.50	Odell to Bonelle	— Honey unable to keep him
	6.5.53	Bonelle to Fulljames	— ill — further
	5.7.54	Fulljames to Kendall (Honey) Unsatisf. adj.
	— 12.55	Kendall to Chrane - Yale - holiday
	30.12.55	Chrane to Kendall
	22.12.56	Kendall to Slager (for painting)
	31.12.56	Slager to St Jean (for painting)
	15.3.57	St Jean to Hemminger
	18.4.57	Hemminger to Chrane
	27.4.57	Chrane to Hemminger
	28.6.57	Hemminger to Goodskelch Camp
	7.7.57	Camp to Hemminger
	8.7.57	Hemminger to Kendall for tr. pa. zeg
	5.9.57	Kendall to Yurko
	1.11.57	Yurko to Walters
	13.2.58	Walters to BLS
	25.7.58	BLS Caldwell holiday
	27.8.58	Caldwell to BLS
	28.8.58	BLS to Torgerson
#	1.1.59	Change of rate -
#	29.4.59	Change of address
	12.8.59	Torgerson to Chrane
	20.8.59	Chrane to Torgerson
	29.8.59	Change of F.P. same Drade
	5.10.59	Drader to Cheghie
	4.1.60	Hogues to Evans
	9.5.60	Evans to Cheghie
	3.8.60	Cheghie to Oakalla
	16.11.61	HC1 to Cheghie
	1.3.62	Cheghie to Oakalla
	16.11.62	HC1 to Vancouver

BORN 9 FEB 44

List below of Dennis Storrings's moves while a ward of Welfare (not including moves from age one to four)

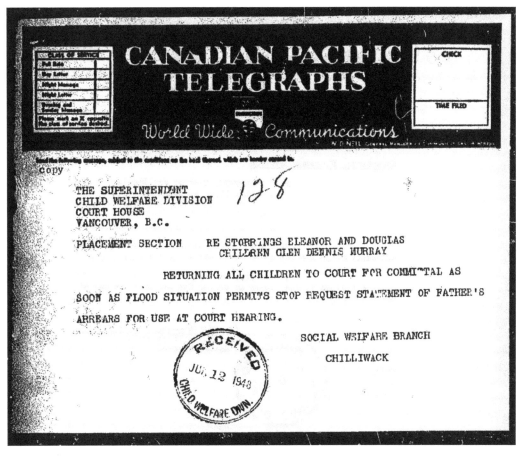

Committal 1948 for three brothers.

STORRINGS, Gladys and Douglas   October 15th, 1947

By October 9, 1947 we had been informed that Mrs.
Storrings   has given up the ghost as far
as looking after the children is concerned

Parents' information.

Photos of our family

Dennis and Murray with our mother in Maple Ridge Park, 1950.

12 450 10 Ave
Nancy B.C.
May 12, 1956

Dear Mom,

How are you? I am fine.

I've got a paper route now with 31 papers. We changed our house number to 12 450, I am on the baseball team now we play every Monday and Friday. I am doing better in school. How is the weather in Vancouver? It is sunny out here Our cat had four little kittens and they're cute. I hope you will be up at Grandma's in the summer time. Please write soon. Happy Mothers Day. Love Dennis

Dennis's letter to his mother.

THE CHILLIWACK PROGRESS
WEDNESDAY, FEBRUARY 20, 1946

Child Saved From Drowning

Mrs. R. Armstrong, Cultus Lake, saved the life of Dennis Storring, four-year-old son of John T. Storring, when he tumbled into Sweltzer creek near Cultus Lake Saturday.

The child was brought to Chilliwack hospital where he received treatment for shock, is reported in good condition.

Dennis near-drowning at Cultus Lake, late 1940s.

It has been alleged that the burn looks as though part of the rubber melted into the skin. Apparently subject is extremely sensitive about this wound, so that he considers himself a freak. He will not swim without a T shirt.

Dennis was attending Grade 8 at Maple Ridge Junior High School when he was dismissed from school for persistent disregard to teachers and general rules of conduct, and disobedience. Obviously he was not interested in school and has failed at least once. He was frequently in conflict with the authority of the school, and often defiant to school teachers. He was expelled from school on September 29, 1959.

One of his foster parents took Dennis fishing with him, but found that he was very impassive and lacking in initiative. Dennis seems to have no idea of what he is to do unless he is constantly directed and told.

Protestant.

Subject does not have any organised interests or belong to any groups, nor does he have any known hobbies. He is content to wander about the community although he enjoys swimming, and likes to attend a show as often as he can.

Subject presents a pleasing conforming appearance although at times it is difficult to get him to respond, however beneath this veneer he is an aggressive, hostile boy. He is persistently in conflict with authority; seems to be mistrusting and suspicious of adults. He seems to find it difficult to relate to adults except superficially. This conflict seems to be manifested in recurring anti-social behavior.

Subject has never been able to take root in a foster home, probably because he still maintains a loyalty toward his mother. He has stated that he could only stand a foster home for a short time, and that when he feels he is becoming too involved with the family he deliberately provokes the situation so that he is asked to leave. He has been in 3 or 4 different foster homes in the Haney area, in the last 2 or 3 years. However, he has returned to one of these Homes (Chequis) on a couple of occasions when he has been involved in further difficulty and threatened with committal. Apparently he has been moved at least 10 or 12 times since he came into foster home care, July 8, 1948, together with his brothers Glen and Murray.

CFD files from Victoria.

informed Srt.Anderson that Murray was suffering from malnutrition.
During September Mr. Storrings held three jobs and the family
barely got along. They made no payments on their rent. On September
27, the children had been without food all day, so Mrs. Storrings
was given a second emergency order. The baby had had pneumonia
and was not in a very good condition. Dennis had fallen into a
Lake some time ago and when he was brought out nearly drowned, a
neighbour had put a too hot water bottle on his stomach, which
resulted in a bad burn. This refuses to heal and the Doctor had
told the mother a skin graft would be necessary.

The father has frequently promised to have these
conditions seen to, but never fulfills his promise. On December
31, 1946, Mrs. Storrings was again destitute, and her husband had
gone off to Vancouver. It is this man's habitual pattern to
desert leaving no food or money at home. We subsidize the home for
the sake of the children, but before we can take any definite
action, Mr. Storrings returns home and things drag on as before.
This time the Community Chest supplied the family with necessities.
At this time Glen
Dennis' burn was bothering him and the baby had a bad cough.
Mrs. Storrings again said she was
through and added that it seemed to make no difference to her
husband to see his children go hungry to bed. He has made no
effort to find employment and support his family. During January
the situation dragged on as before. The children were always
clean. At our request Sgt. Raybone had a talk with Mr. Storrings
whom he found eating a large meal of bacon and eggs at his
mother's house, while his wife and children starved at home.
The Sgt. warned him, as we had previously done, that should anything happen to the children due to inadequate food and housing,
Storringswould be open to a criminal charge. Shortly after this
Mrs. Storrings reported that things were somewhat better, although
her husband still did not have steady employment.

In March, 1947, the Police phoned that Mrs. Storrings
had been out on a party and had refused to go home to her children.
They had been left in charge of a girl, whose mother had come and
taken her home, leaving the children alone. Mrs. Storrings Sr.
who lives next door had filled in for a time, but finally Mr.
Storrings went home to look after the children. His wife arrived
at ten o'clock next morning. When we called the next day Mrs.
Storrings said she had taken all she could and was going to leave
him, that she was unable to care for the children herself, but
that she felt that as their father had said he would put them in
a boarding home where they would receive better care than she
could give them, that if she left and forced him to do this they
would be better off. As she seemed undecided still as to what
she should do, although she said she was leaving, we asked her
before she made any definite move to contact the office and we
would try and make some plan for the children. She phoned and
left a message on the night of April 3rd, but we did not receive
it until the morning of April 8th.

The resources available among the relatives of this
family are extremely limited. The paternal grandparents, who
live in the next cabin are a very poor type of people, and the
paternal grandmother states she wishes nothing to do with it.
She lies to protect her son, and has done nothing in the past to
encourage him to look after his family, other than to feed him at
her place while they go hungry at home.

As a temporary measure on April 8th,
we urged Mr. Storrings to contact his sister Joyce, who was living
with a family of rather low standards, but not working, and she
consented to come in and look after the children temporarily. We

CFD files.

In Maple Ridge. Dennis, Murray and Glen with grandmother Gladys Chrane, 1952.

The Teague and Chrane home in Yale where the three brothers went often for holidays to visit our grandmother. Those are our best and happiest memories.

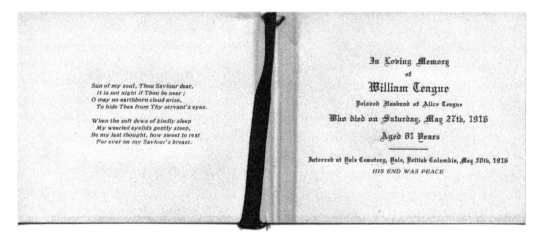

Sun of my soul, Thou Saviour dear,
It is not night if Thou be near;
O may no earthborn cloud arise,
To hide Thee from Thy servant's eyes.

When the soft dews of kindly sleep
My wearied eyelids gently steep,
Be my last thought, how sweet to rest
For ever on my Saviour's breast.

In Loving Memory
of
William Teague
Beloved Husband of Alice Teague
Who died on Saturday, May 27th, 1916
Aged 81 Years
Interred at Yale Cemetery, Yale, British Columbia, May 30th, 1916
HIS END WAS PEACE

Card printed for the death of our great-grandfather William Teague of Yale.

Our beloved Rusty, Grandmother's dog, who we would see on our holidays at Yale (Rusty lived to be fifteen years old).

MRS. ALICE TEAGUE, PIONEER OF EARLY DAYS IN YALE, DIES

✦✦✦✦ ✦✦✦✦ ✦✦✦

Husband Held Responsible Jobs in Cariboo Gold Stampede

The outstanding connecting link with Yale of the early days, Mrs. Alice Teague, died Thursday morning at the home of her son-in-law and daughter, Mr. and Mrs. R. L. Chrane of Agassiz. She had come down from Yale to spend Christmas with her relatives when she was taken ill with a severe cold. Being 83 years of age and not very strong, she was unable to resist subsequent developments.

The name of Teague has been associated with historic Yale almost since its establishment, for the late William Teague, a Forty-Niner in the California gold rush, came there in the early years of the Cariboo gold rush and, after returning from the Cariboo, settled there. Before doing so, however, he went home to the little Cornish village of St. Day, and married his fiancee, bringing her out with him to Yale.

Trip Lasts 53 Days

The voyage on a sailing ship occupied 53 days. Later Mr. Teague occupied most of the chief posts in the government of Yale, including those of justice of the peace, Indian agent and clerk of the court. It was at the old court-house, where Chief Justice Begbie of Cariboo fame often used to officiate, and which is now surrounded by fine old trees planted in those early days, that he and his wife lived for years.

Later they moved to the fine old house built by Sir Joseph Trutch, one of the contractors for the Cariboo Road and a lieutenant-governor of British Columbia, and it was on the spacious verandah of this house that, of a summer's evening, the present writer has at various times talked of the pioneer days with Mrs. Teague. With gentle voice and sweet smile she would recall the stirring scenes she had witnessed in the early eighties—when the C.P.R. was being constructed through British Columbia and when Yale was seething with life.

Tablet Unveiled

The late Henry J. Cambie, pioneer railway builder and explorer, and Judge F. W. Howay were among her friends and it was not surprising that, when the cairn in memory of the historic happenings in Yale was erected a few years ago she should be invited to perform the unveiling ceremony.

All her daughters, except one—she had five, the survivors of a family of seven—were born in Yale and went to school at beautiful All Hallows, the elaborate Church of England school.

The last gathering of pioneers which Mrs. Teague attended was in Stanley Park a year or two ago when the guests of honor were pioneers who had been in the province for more than 50 years. Mrs. Teague is survived by Mrs. W. W. Bailey, Mrs. W. A. Nunan of Tacoma, Mrs. E. C. Johnston of Seattle and Mrs. Chrane of Agassiz. Another daughter, Mrs. F. W. Mackenrot, died last year. She is also survived by 10 grandchildren. The funeral will take place at 2:30 Saturday afternoon at the cemetery at Yale, where the remains of her husband are resting.—N. R.

MRS. ALICE TEAGUE.

Of the news of the death of Alice Teague, wife of William and our great-grandmother from Yale.

Allen Storrings, World War One.　　　*Burton Storrings (Allen's father) in World War One, from New York area.*

Glenn and Walter Chrane, our uncles, with Aunt June and Aunt Babe and their father Raymond (Robert) Chrane in their home in Yale.

Family photo taken in Quesnel. From left, Murray, Aunt June, Glen, Cousin Wally, Gary, Cousin Ryan Doern.

I was born in Mission, BC, on February 9, 1944. I eventually went home to Yale; my mom and dad had a little cabin in the bush up from the old pioneer cemetery where all our family is resting in peace. My great-grandfather came to California, USA, from Cornwall, England, in 1854 at nineteen years old then travelled to Yale. He later sent for his wife, Alice Michell, who was still in England and came around the Horn, which took over a month by ship. They had six girls and one boy. The boy, Cundy, was born in 1877 and died August 6, 1888, of the scarlet fever. One girl, Charlotte, was born 1871 and died July 27, 1881, of the fever, as told to me by Grandmother.

Grandmother and her daughter (our mother) stand next to Grandmother's sister's Packard. Her sisters would come to small-town Yale in their fancy cars to show how rich they were, as they owned property down in Seattle.

I remember one Christmas when I was taken to my grandmothers by a social worker from Haney to Yale BC and dropped off. My grandmother said Dennis come in and I will make you a sandwich before we have our Christmas dinner, and I was hungry also, so of course I said yes to her as I loved her cooking , I played outside with my two brothers and cousin ,and we saw two cars coming down the driveway and we knew who it was the rest of the family ,I was so happy to see all our family members as it was so lonely at Christmas without family .There was my grandmother ,Uncle Walter, Uncle Glenn, Auntie June, and Uncle Mike , Uncle Dan, Auntie Babe, and Uncle Vic. I called Dan Uncle Dan but later in life found out he was grandmothers boyfriend much younger than she and she told us it was her handy man around the property. Dan had a nice old car and worked on other cars in the garage on the property. We all gathered around the table and had a wonderful Christmas dinner as I was so hungry from the trip there . These memories will last a lifetime as there was not many good ones mainly only at grandmothers' home if it wasn't for her, we may not have survived to tell our story.

Our great aunt with our grandmother, looking like she didn't want to be in small-town Yale with her new Packard.

William Teague knew people in Yale. Yale was named after James Murray Yale ,and a employee of the Hudson's Bay Company and Port Moody was named after Colonel Richard Clement Moody, the man in charge of the Royal Engineers. They took a lot of gold out of the Hills Bar strike, which was across the mighty Fraser River; the Fraser was named after Simon Fraser. It was wild in spots, but I loved the Fraser, and I grew up around it.

I feel proud to be the great-grandson of William Teague. He also had a gold mine in Yale called Queens Mine above the town, plus other mines around BC. Our grandmother often said he had a glass jar with chunks of gold in it, plus there was a gold nugget in the Teague house over the fireplace. I think at his mine he was in pursuit of veins of gold as he was panning the rivers and creeks for flower gold or nuggets or digging down to bedrock. There is a picture in this book of my great-grandfather with two other fellows standing in front of his mine, and you can see the opening in the side of the mountain. One of my brothers and a friend, Gordy, went up there years ago, but I never got the chance.

When William Teague and wife came to Yale, they had a chance to buy Governor Trutch's home, which they did in the late 1800s, and it is still there today. My great-grandfather died May 27, 1916, of old age, after going to Seattle to see his daughters. The Stonemasons and

Victoria paid for the granite tombstone in Yale, as he was a government agent for BC, and other influential townspeople gave him a grand burial in the old Pioneer Cemetery in Yale.

William and Alice Teague's daughter Gladys (our grandmother) eventually married Raymond Chrane (Robert), and had three girls and two boys. The first girl was born on April 23, 1923—our mother Eleanor. My mother went to a small school across the tracks in Yale, as did her two brothers and two sisters.

My mother met Douglas Storrings in Yale at a dance. Grandmother always said that he was no good, and she was right. My father never worked or worked very little, but he was persistent and won my mother's heart. So, in 1942, my brother Glen was born, and while my mother worked in Vancouver my grandmother looked after him. As for my dad, he was usually in Vancouver drinking.

In February 1944 I was born in the Mission hospital in BC. When I was four or five days old my parents took me home to a small cabin. Murray was born in 1946. He was a delight to be around, even though he was hurting inside and wondering why his mom wasn't coming to get him. Murray loved to joke around. It also hurt Murray when they split us up in 1953. When we were together, we would help each other, but when we were apart, we suffered a lot.

You seem to roll with the punches. Our brother Glen was a godsend; he was the oldest and was very protective of us. He later became a street fighter in the 50s. Guys came from all different towns to take his reputation, but they mostly lost. He was like a bull; you couldn't stop him. Plus, he had all that anger in him from growing up the way he did.

While at Cultus Lake in 1946, my mom and dad and a couple of others were drinking in the one-room cabin across the lake (Cabin 3, I think). There was no food but there was booze. I was playing outside by the creek that flows into the Cultus. Well, I fell in and of course I couldn't swim, being two years old. There was an article about it in the Chilliwack newspaper. When everyone came from the cabin, I was lying face down in the creek. Someone pulled me out and a woman ran into her cabin and got water right out of the hot water tank, which was really scalding hot. She put the hot water bottle, without a towel, on my stomach and chest. I found out years later that the woman asked my mom why I was wiggling and squirming; well, I guess I would be, as the rubber from the bottle melted right into my skin. I don't have any recollection of the tragedy, but for years I had a complex about the burn, which is still there. I wouldn't go swimming around other people, or if I did I would wear a T- shirt. Usually I would go to a secluded place on the Alouette River. I was a good swimmer after the near-drowning, and I learned to swim on that river.

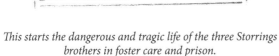

This starts the dangerous and tragic life of the three Storrings brothers in foster care and prison.

Dennis Raymond Storrings.

Pryor's Foster Home in Sardis, BC

My memory is very good. Over the years I go over situations that happened in the past and keep it all in my mind. Before moving to Pryor's, our first foster home, as a ward in 1948, us boys went back and forth to Pryor's, then back to our parents in Yale and other areas. They would lock us three boys in the cabin in Yale near the graveyard where former resident Fred Mclinden and his wife lived and then go on a three- or four-day trip to Vancouver.

I was around three or four and there was nothing in the house—no food. I remember my brother Glen pouring milk in my dad's bed out of anger for leaving us alone. Glen, age six, let us out of the cabin by finding a way out of the door to play outside. Murray was about eighteen months old. I was playing in the driveway and near the waterfall until almost nighttime. Before our parents came back, someone had reported them for leaving us alone, so one day a black car (real black) came with something on the door that caught my eye. It was a big star with writing on it that said Social Welfare Department. It made no sense to me as I couldn't read, but years later I knew the full meaning of the words. I can recall a woman and man who got out of the car and said to us boys to come to them. They said if we were good boys and got into the car, we would get a chocolate bar. Well, I was first in the car and then my brothers followed.

When we were finished our candy, we looked out the window and we were away down the highway. But before that, as we got into the car to eat our candy and pulled out of the driveway, we looked back to our little home and began crying. As we were going down the highway, I thought we are going on a big adventure, but little did we know it sure would be a real adventure and not fun at times. Well, we were on our way to the Pryor's foster home, one of many foster homes as wards of the government.

We read in our files that the Pryor's had to let us go due to ill health. I liked them; they were kind and liked us boys. This would have been around 1948 or so. We were going back and forth to our parents before then. Our next foster home was the Odell family in the Chilliwack area. I don't remember too much about this family, and we didn't stay too long, as usual. We moved to the Kendall's foster home in the Chilliwack area and they said Murray and I were the best two boys they had ever seen. I asked Mrs. Kendall if we could stay with her for a long time, and she said she hoped we could but it never happened. I don't recall too much of this family.

I was in a foster home later in Haney with the same name—the Kendall's. I sure am glad I wasn't alone; the three of us did get strength from each other, and of course Glen, being the oldest, was the boss and protector.

One of the social workers wrote in my file:
We saw the boys playing in the yard, and Dennis said, "You are not going to take us away again, are you?" We assured him, "We just came to see how you were. And you will be staying where you are."

But things changed every few months, it seemed. I can't remember moving from the Kendall's to the Darnell's. I really don't know much about them, but it seems that when it's a negative part of your life you mostly remember those parts and some nice parts also. I think the other early moves were with aunts, grandmothers, friends and neighbours but were less significant, until I got a little older. When we moved to the Bourelle's in Haney in 1950, it was like verse "I was lost, but now I am found." They were in their sixties, a warm and loving couple, it seemed to me. Glen and Murray were with me and two other foster kids, Sharon and her little brother, were there. I felt good about that. After the homes before the Bourelle's I was tense and stressed out, but as soon as I entered the Bourelle's home I felt relieved and lighthearted that is how wonderful they seemed in my mind. I also felt safe with my two brothers. Glen was very protective of me and Murray. He missed his mother, as we all did. He might have missed his dad, but I don't think so.

The Bourelles had a big old house with a lot of property, and it didn't take us boys long to start exploring. There was so much to see on the old roads in the forest, and it was a real adventure. We started school at Alexander Robinson School, which I didn't like too much. Our bedrooms were upstairs, and we were always scared of the boogie man. I don't know who put that in our mind, but we were sure that the boogie man was really under our beds. There was one room upstairs, and we were scared to go in. Once, we peeked in and saw an old metal bed, and the room was cold and scary. We wondered why no one slept in there, and we called it the ghost room. I also started walking in my sleep, and I just about fell out a window.

At mealtimes sometimes we had stew with dumplings. Well, Murray and I hated it, so what we did was, when nobody was looking, we would put the dumplings in our pockets and give them to the dog. The dog's name was Shep; he really liked us for giving him the dumplings and other food we didn't like.

On all the roads in the fifties there were orchards, and you could find apples, apricots, cherries, pears, plums—you name it. We had lots of stomach-aches. One day the three of us were coming home from school on our bikes, and we came upon the old road leading into the orchard, we had plans of eating some fruit but changed our minds once we saw the big black bear coming out of the orchard. We had already got off our bikes, and in the confusion Glen and Murray took off on two of the bikes. The only bike left was Glen's, and I couldn't ride it, as it was too big for me. So here I was looking at the bear, and the bear was looking at me thinking *I don't need this kid. I'm full of apples, pears and cherries*, so off he ran, which was fine with me. I pushed Glen's bike home.

I found out that Murray had a nervous breakdown and his first asthma attack, which put him in Royal Columbia Hospital, as there was no hospital in Haney at that time. He thought the bear had eaten me. The Bourelles and their son shot the bear a day later and hung it on the pole outside the house, and we ate bear meat for a while. I didn't like it, as it was too greasy. I kind of felt sorry for the bear, as he did give me a break; that's the way I thought in those days. I still like all animals, especially the elusive wolverines.

I really liked the Bourelles. They had a way of comforting a young guy who was hurting inside with the loss of both parents but did not like the way our dad treated our mother. I don't believe in treating anyone like that. It's funny how things come back to haunt a person.

The principal at our school was a Mr. P., and I didn't like him very much. He was always picking on me. One day I had to go to the bathroom and I couldn't hold it and I messed my pants down in the bathroom. I took my shorts off and got cleaned up, but now I was stuck with the dirty shorts, so I stuck them behind the old steam heater, which created a bad smell with the heat. What a smell. Well, the principal got wind of it and put two and two together and figured it was me. Instead of just confronting me alone, he had a plan. While I was in class he held the dirty shorts up so everyone could see, and he told the class what I had done. I was never so embarrassed, and I cringed in my seat while everyone was laughing hysterically. Well, I left the room and the school. They called me poopie pants for a while until I got mad at them. What a mean thing to do. It went away after a few months.

While we were at the Bourelles their other foster child, Sharon, was there, and her brother. She was always crying. I don't blame her, with being taken away from her home and put in a strange place. Across from the school was a grocery store, and we boys went in there often and that's where we started stealing a few chocolate bars here and there. After getting caught we learned to do it right. I loved candy and would do just about anything to get it, as we never got any in the foster homes.

One day the Bourelles told me to go out to the road on 17th Avenue because my mom was coming to see me. While waiting on the road I saw a figure a long way off. It got closer and closer and it was my mom. She was pushing a bike; imagine pushing a bike all that way, just for me. I thanked her and I was looking the bike over and talking to her, wondering why she wasn't answering me. I turned around and she was gone. I couldn't believe it. I had so much to tell her, and her she was gone just like that. I pushed my bike home and cried all the way. I never saw her again for quite a few years and then we moved to the Caldwell's for a short stay as Mrs. Bourelle took sick. We moved back to them in 1953.

I never got good vibes, not even when I first set foot at the Caldwell's. Not like I did at the Bourelles'. They had lots of chicken sheds and lots of property, and a scary basement with spiderwebs. I think the year would have been late 1952. Mr. Caldwell was a bit of a bully, and Mrs. Caldwell told everyone at the bus stop in front of us that we were bad boys and orphans. Glen said, We are not. Our mom's coming back for us." Mr. Caldwell said he was the general in the household. He was nice with the older boys but could bully the smaller kids.

They had another boy who was in his teens. He was from England, and Eric B. was his name. He only stayed for a while and I never saw him again. Well, once we settled in and started school, the adventure started. We all had chores to do, mostly working in the chicken coops and collecting eggs. I used to fool around with a 1930s Studebaker truck; it had the starter on the floor, or you had to use the crank, which could be dangerous and could fly back at your thumb. I would drive it all over the place, and I was only eight years old. It wasn't that far to school.

By being in so many foster homes, I became a people pleaser. I learned to try and please everyone. As I'm writing this I get emotional, because my foster mother was a good person at heart. Our favourite thing was to go to Davidson's pool. It was just up the road from the Caldwell's, and it was part of the river. It was a beautiful river and still is. I spent a lot of my young life on the river, fishing, swimming, and just exploring. I felt at peace when I was near it or on it. Because of the burn on my stomach I wouldn't go swimming around other people; I felt like a freak.

In the files it says *Dennis should get a skin graft while he's young* at the time of the near drowning. I felt embarrassed when girls were around. I had pretty good looks, but the scarring bothered me with girlfriends. So off I would go on a hot day and swim in a pool where there were no people. And I knew all the secluded spots. I learned to swim when the Kendall's threw me in the river, and I started to dog paddle. I'm still a good swimmer.

So off to Caldwell's again. We did a lot of chores, including picking fruit and you name it, we did it like slaves. We were only young, so Ken did the real heavy jobs. One of our tasks was to work in the egg room cleaning eggs etc. There was quite a few laying hens, and some got out of the chicken coop and they laid in bushes and fields and in grass under sheds. So, Ken said, "You boys will get two pennies for every egg you find in the wild—not in the chicken coops but in the wild."

Glen said okay, and he made himself the boss of us boys, which I didn't mind. We picked up all the eggs every day, and well, after a few weeks we had cleaned everything up. There were no more eggs and no more pennies. So, Glen comes up with this scam: instead of collecting the eggs outside the coops, since there were so few left, we would steal eggs from the egg house and put some dirt on them and say we found them outside the chicken coops. We started his little plan and tells Mr. Caldwell he found six eggs. And, "Oh yes, Mister Caldwell, Dennis also found four."

"Well, that's good, Glen," he said, and he started to go into his pocket to get a few coppers.

"Oh, I almost forgot," Glen says. "Murray found four also."

"Okay, Glen," he said, "That will be twenty-five cents."

"Oh no," said Glen, "twenty-eight cents."

Well, the look on Ken's face. He didn't know whether to hug Glen or strangle him. So down to the store we went. It wasn't far, and you could get lots of candies for a penny, so off we went to Davidson's pool and ate the whole lot. Well, we were happy this plan was working, and we had the taste for more candy. Ken said, "Boy, those hens sure are laying. I should put them all outside," but we didn't pick up on what he was saying; we just wanted more candy. So, he set Glen up and caught him coming out of the egg house with eggs.

Glen was only ten years old, and Ken was mad because he was duped by a kid, so his anger started to boil over. He put Glen down in the basement. He told him, "You're getting it now," and proceeded to work him over with his fists and anything that was lying around, swearing all the while. I was watching from a window, and I got it for that also. After the beating Glen took, he never cried once, and that only made Ken mad. So, he said, "I will fix you," and he yelled, "Mabel, bring me the bar of soap." Glen was wondering what his fate would be. Murray watched for a while but couldn't watch his brother get abused. He cried, which made me cry also. I had to see what was going on, so back to the window I went, just as Ken was forcing the bar of soap down Glen's throat and in his mouth. Glen was spitting, coughing and yelling, or trying to.

A few weeks later I got it too, a couple of times. So, after Ken was finished, the sweat was pouring off him, he had a strange look on his face, and he said to Glen, "You will be locked in the basement till you have learned your lesson." I can always see Glen's face looking through the panes of glass with cobwebs all over. He had a look of sadness and anger, and he cried, trying to get out of the basement. He liked it when Murray and I would come and see him at the window. It was like a prison, with the threat of a spanking or worse hanging over our heads. He must have been down there for a while with very little food, if any. I don't know what Mabel thought of it, but she didn't say much; she was probably too scared.

After that, things were never the same. One night I wasn't feeling well and couldn't eat anything. After she made a peanut butter sandwich for me, Ken caught her and he said to me, "Well, my wife made you a nice sandwich and you don't want to eat it. You little bugger." He took the sandwich and smeared it all over my face and said, "Now you will eat it, you little sissy." I didn't care for peanut butter for a long time, and all the time I was saying, "Sorry, Mr. Caldwell." I sometime lived in fear of Ken. One time I stole some nickels from their bedroom, and he got me to confess after a few slaps.

I went into the basement for my punishment while my brother Murray watched from the driveway. I screamed and was scared to be down in the basement alone. One time I did something wrong and he took me outside and gave me the switch. I learned to act like it was really hurting and then he would stop. Just before they were thinking of getting rid of us, all three of us were thinking of running away and going back to our lovely grandmother's home in Yale. When Ken found he could no longer hurt us, that was the last straw; we were on our way back to the Bourelle's where Glen had already been sent.

The next move was just as bad as the Caldwell's, if not worse. We were sent to North 25th Avenue, or Webster's Corners, in Haney to Mr. and Mrs. Fulljames. They ran their home like a business, and at times there were thirteen kids in the summer. They got a cheque every month for every foster child, and there was very little for the children for food. It seemed to us that we had to steal food at night. We would get one full meal a day, but we would get porridge and johnnycakes for breakfast. And if you were school-age, after finishing the porridge you went to school.

Murray and Dennis in 2019 standing in front of the Fulljames Foster home
that was our foster home in 1953 in Webster Corners as it stands today in Maple Ridge 256th st.

I didn't like school. The only thing I enjoyed about it PE class. I would tell the class teacher I had an ailment and he would let me go. Well, what I would do was, while the teacher and the whole class was in PE, I would go into the room where they kept the lunch kits and where you change your clothes for the PE class. I would open the lunch kits and take only cookies and pastries, but I wouldn't take all the cookies. I would take what I liked, such as cinnamon rolls. Then I would go and play hooky and enjoyed my sweets.

This stemmed from having to wake up and crawl past a door to a room where Mr. and Mrs. Fulljames were sleeping. I would try not to make the floor squeak, because if you got caught it was a switch on your bottom and elsewhere. Plus, their door was open. My mission was dry bread to eat, but once I saw those chocolate balls with coconut strings in them, and macaroons etc. I would put them in a little bag and go back through the scary part of sneaking back to our room. But I thought it was worth it. It seemed to us foster kids that we got none of the good pastries; they went to her own kids.

I know it's just something I went through, and I don't think I'm smart for doing some of the things I did. I was just trying to survive, as I missed my mom and was always looking for her to come back and take us home, but she never did. I was mostly started stealing out of necessity, and after I got a sweet tooth there was no stopping me. At the age of nine I started stealing out of grocery stores. It was small stuff at first, like candy and gum etc. and then it was cigarettes.

Murray and I had a bed up in the attic, and Glen was not with us from the Bourelle's foster home on.

Murray and I sort of stuck together; we didn't talk much or play with the other foster kids or the Fulljames kids. It seemed that every foster child kept everything inside and didn't trust anyone, including adults in power like foster parents and welfare workers. You learn fast when it comes to spankings and beatings, and I learned to only trust my brothers. We were close and relied on each other; there was a strong bond between us. Even though Glen wasn't with us at the Fulljames house, we always found ways of seeing each other. Of course we were devastated when Glen was separated from us, as he was our saviour in hard times. It was heartbreaking for Murray and me. But we carried on.

We were always hungry, and the Fulljames home was one of the first foster homes where we took stealing to another level; we started stealing dry bread because we were extremely hungry. Then we stole pastries as a treat, then watches, rings and all the change we could get, starting with pennies then quarters then fifty-cent pieces and the odd silver dollar.

I remember when the Fulljames got their first television set; it was the summer of 1953. A lot of neighbours heard of the event and came running to see something they never saw before. It was quite an event. As time went by, after putting up the antenna etc., we could watch a bit of TV each night, such as the *Lone Ranger* and *Star Cinema Time*. They could only get two stations, channel 12 and channel 2. But if we were bad, we were sent to our room without dinner and no TV. I loved the westerns with Hopalong Cassidy and Roy Rogers.

We had the social welfare department workers come to the foster home every couple of months to see us and to check if everything was okay. But usually the foster parents were pre-warned, so Mrs. Fulljames would give us a big bowl of ice cream and cookies just before the visit. In our little minds we thought *boy they're nice to us*, and we told the worker, "Yes, they are nice to us." But after the worker left, it was back to normal.

One time Mrs. Fulljames came into our room and said to Murray, "I know you're stealing cookies" and pulled him out of the bunk and split his head open on the metal rim of the bunk bed. Murray was screaming and I was terrified watching this happen to my little brother. He needed stitches in his head, and the scar is still there today. Then the workers came to Haney to question us. Before they came the foster mom told us if we said anything, we would not get an ice cream cone. When they asked us how things were going, we said fine, as we were scared to say what had really happened that day. But I learned to cope and was starting to learn the system.

In October 1953 Murray and I were up in the barn where they kept the bales of hay in the loft. One had to climb eighteen steps to the loft, and there were bales of hay stacked twenty high. Early that day while at school I got a penny pack of matches. Murray and I were up in the hay loft and I was showing him how light a match. Once it burned down it burned my fingers, and I dropped it. It fell between the bales, and we could not put it out. Murray and I saw it just burst into flames and we ran for the ladder that would take us out of the barn. Murray went first but lost his grip on the wooden ladder and fell to the hay on the barn floor and it cushioned his fall we ran out of the barn. I ran to where the goat was tied up and I thought if I was with the goat, they wouldn't think I had anything to do with the fire. By now the whole barn was in flames. They were getting all the animals out of the barn, and they had a lot of machinery that was totally gone from the heat of the fire.

I feel sad about the whole thing. Murray and I didn't set out to burn the barn; I mean, it was an accident, but I shouldn't have been playing with matches, and I take full blame for the tragedy. I'm saying this now, as Murray wasn't the one who started the fire, even though he was blamed for it. I was scared to death of the Fulljames, so as a nine-year kid if they would have said the queen lit the fire, I would have totally agreed, no disrespect intended. And to a young boy, with the switch Mr. Fulljames had in his hand, I think I would have even said the goat did it.

I made sure they saw me with the goat but my brother and I were marched into the house and separated. All Mr. Fulljames said was, "Well, you're in big trouble now so you had better own up," and all this time he had that dreadful switch in his hand. But he had to be careful, as the whole place was swarming with police and a lot of neighbors trying to help. *This is no good*, I thought, *I will try lying, as that's what worked before*. So they got the fire out, and then came the investigation. I was sitting in a corner in the house, and I could hear them go into where Murray was. "Well now, it's Murray, isn't it?"

"Yes," said Murray.

"Now we know it wasn't you who lit the fire, it was your brother, wasn't it?"

I could hear the door open and I guessed Murray and I weren't getting any supper. Even to this day I don't know why I blamed my brother Murray for starting the fire; that's how scared of Mr. and Mrs. Fulljames I was. And I had good reason to fear them. Anyway, I told everybody concerned in the matter that Murray lit the fire, and I never lived it down. It haunted me for years. I badly wanted to move badly from the Fulljames home and so did Murray, but by blaming Murray I stayed and Murray moved.

I must have cried for days; not only did I lose Murray, but I had to stay where I didn't want to be. I was sad to see my brother go, as we were close. He moved to the Cameron family. After all that happened, I would keep to myself. I would go off into the forest or down by the rivers. I became a real loner, but I liked being alone because I could handle my own feelings but didn't like being involved in other people's problems. And I had a lot of excitement. In the fifties people had sheds they used as storage for jars of pickles and fruit and other things, with a big padlock on the door. There were a lot of summer homes also, and most of them were deep in the bush or by rivers. I couldn't go by one without trying to get in and see what goodies were inside.

When I was still at the Fulljames home I would walk miles, returning with my booty, which I hid before going home. I continued walking to school after Murray left, and I also continued stealing pastries. It wasn't the same after Murray left. I started thinking of ways to move, and the final straw was when I was doing my homework. Math wasn't my favorite subject. Mr. Fulljames was watching over me as I did my math, and I was scared stiff to make a mistake. When I did make a mistake, he would cuff me on the back of the head, and the more he hit me, the more scared I got and then it turned to anger. I finally started to yell and swear at him, which led to a good beating. Well, so much for the math. The next day I ran away and stayed in the bush for a day or so. When I came back, the Welfare lady was waiting for me. I told her what happened and that I wanted to move. Of course, they always believed the foster parents rather than the child. So, in my case, they were going to move me. I moved from the Fulljames home around the first of January, 1954.

Kendall's Foster Home in Haney, 1954

Then my next foster home was the Kendall's when I was just about ten years old. Jim and Doris Kendall were in their forties. Jim worked for Eaton's and Company. He drove truck and delivered goods to the public. I liked Doris but not Jim; he was a bully. They had one child of their own, and he was the same age as me. His name was Bill, and he was a nice enough boy. We lived down 10th Avenue North in Haney, or as they call it today, Maple Ridge.

They had a lot of land, with outbuildings, chicken sheds and barns. There was a big field in the back of the place, then forest that went all the way to 11th Ave. Doris was the one who taught me my table manners and other manners. She treated me good, but that's more than I can say for Jim. They took me on trips, and I got myself a paper route. The Alouette River wasn't too far from the Kendall's, and I used to go to the river constantly to go fishing and swimming, or I would just go there because I loved the place. The Kendall's taught me to swim in the river. Mr. Kendall said. "Well, in you go," and he threw me in. They were looking out for my safety, or at least Doris was. Jim sort of got a kick out of it, seeing me thrashing about. I started off by dog paddling and learned to be a good swimmer in time. The Kendall's had a lot of fruit trees, and I used to sit up in those big Bing cherries trees and stuff myself till I was green in the face and a big stomach-ache. They also had a big garden.

I went to school in Haney; I think I was in grade 2 or 3. I also continued my pastries habit. I wasn't interested in school. I only went because I had to. I had a good bike for my paper route, and all along 10th on the side of the road were apple trees. I used to go on the farmers' fields and pick them. I had to watch out for the farmer's bull; when he saw me, he would come charging after me.

One of my jobs was to collect the eggs in the egg sheds the hens would peck me when I put my hand under her to get the eggs. This one rooster would always wait for me to come from the house to the chicken sheds, and when he saw me, he would run after me and jump in the air and spur me. I was pissed off but also scared of him. Well, one day I'd had enough of his antics. I went to the shed with I had a stick, so when he started his little game and was in midair, I used the stick to trip him and he landed on his back. Well, he was humiliated and he wandered off to the shed past all the hens who were watching the episode. The strange twist to this was that before that, he was the boss. After what happened he was ignored by the hens and was on the bottom of the roost. Funny how they are; that is the pecking order of chickens. I felt sort of bad for him, because I treat all animals good. Two months later he died, probably from being treated so bad by the hens.

One of Jim Kendall's favourite things was to get his son Bill and me to put on the boxing gloves and start boxing, all the time yelling, "Sock him, son, hit him, that's a boy." Me, I was more passive, and I didn't like to hurt people, so his son had a field day with me, to Mr. Kendall's delight. One time we were boxing, and Bill was distracted by his yelling. I hit him a good one on the chin and he fell down. Well, so much for the boxing—we never did it again, and he sort of looked at me different after that. Mr. Kendall, I mean, but his bullying didn't entirely stop. I guess it was in his makeup to do what he did.

Mrs. Kendall was a nice woman and I can't say enough about her. If all the foster parents were like her, I would have had a delightful time. Now, don't get me wrong, I was in some cases at fault for the turmoil in the foster home, but the constant moving was too much for us. I used to go down 10th Avenue to the river and spend the whole day there fishing and exploring to my heart's content, and I enjoyed it by myself. I must say, the Kendall's was good at times, as a few homes were. Every home had its good and bad parts.

A huge forest area in the back was where I used to collect the bark off of cascara trees; you had to cut the bark with a knife and pull it off the tree, but you should leave a bit of bark so it will grow back. Most people didn't bother to leave any bark on the tree, and the tree will die. That's why you never see the cascara tree, as it died off. Once I had a burlap sack full. I would take it to Buckerfields, and they would give me a dollar or so, not too much as I remember it, as they used it for medicine. So, with my paper route etc. I had enough to satisfy my sweet tooth.

Christmas was a wonderful time with the Kendall's, and sometimes they treated me as good as they did their own son and bought me gifts also. Then 1954 came and went, and 1955 came into view with the Kendall family. I knew a boy my age who lived on 11th Avenue. A friend of his who was our age wanted in on our little "run away from home" plan. So, we set a date and waited, careful to not tell anyone of our plan.

The day came, and we met in a wooded area. I didn't like the kid; I could tell he was very nervous and was having second thoughts, but he said, "No way, I'm going," so we left on our trip to Yale to my grandmother's house. We headed east towards Mission. I knew the area well, as I was born in Mission. We went walking all the way, which is about twelve miles. Once we got there, we headed for the train yard, and we found a freight train headed east. It started up, so we grabbed the ladder and got on board. We found a spot where we could sit and be out of sight. So, we waited till the train was ready to roll, and as it picked up speed, we thought, *this is the life for an eleven-year-old*. We felt better once we got out of Mission; we went through Agassiz, then Hope and next was Yale, fourteen miles past Hope. When we were coming into Yale the train slowed down and we jumped off, making sure no one saw us. The train took off and we walked up to the Canyon Hotel in Yale, which was just what we wanted. We had plans of getting some cigarettes and chips and bars from the cafe.

I took it upon myself to be the burglar; I pried the window open and went in. I gathered up everything I needed and passed it out to my friends. They had never done anything like that before, but I had so it was easier for me. I found a bag to put everything in and I took the bills and change from the cash register. I figured I was a big-time pro, and after that we found some bushes and proceeded to eat the chocolate bars etc. Then we smoked a few cigarettes, getting dizzy. The two boys with me didn't mention the money, so I kept it. I hid it in a spot where I could get it another time. Plus, if I got stopped and had all this money on me it wouldn't be too good.

We stayed out of sight till it got light and then around 8:30 a.m. we walked down the tracks towards my grandmother's place, to the back way. It was a nice old house. We go there and knocked on the door and I said, "It's Dennis, Grandma."

"Oh, it's you, Dennis, and who are these two boys? How come you're not in school?" I made up some story, but my grandma never believed a word of it. She was a kind woman, and she said, "Well, sit down and I will get you all breakfast." She served us up some bacon and eggs. While we were eating, Grandma went into the where the phone was, and I could hear her talking to the social welfare department. She was on the phone for quite a while. When we were just about finished eating, I saw a pen and paper on the table, and I wrote down *Sorry for lying to you, I will be fine, Love you, Grandma* Then we bolted out the door and headed down the tracks heading east. We stayed on the tracks for a few miles then went up to the highway and started hitchhiking. After a while a guy decided to give us young lads a ride; myself, I think he had interior motives.

After a while we went through Spuzzum, and we were just about near Boston Bar when the results of drinking out of the Fraser River started to take effect. It started with stomach cramps then vomiting, and, well, the driver started to wish he had not stopped and picked us up. He pulled over and after a few minutes of standing outside we started to feel a little better. Just as we were about to get back in the car a police car pulled up. "Hello," the policeman said, "are you boys all right?"

Now the driver really wished he hadn't picked us up. I said we drank some bad water but were all right now, and he asked us where we were going. "Oh," I said, "my brothers and I are going for a ride with our dad."

Now the driver really didn't want anything to do with us, and he said, "They are lying. I picked them up just past Yale, they were hitchhiking."

Well, my two friends were really scared. The policeman said, "You three boys stand right there." He talked with the driver and the driver took off, probably so happy to get the heck out of there. The policeman asked Sid what his name was and Sid was so scared he blurted out everything we did He told the we broke into the hotel and café in Yale also Tony confessed right away, and added, "Dennis made us do it. It was his idea to run away."

I thought *oh yes, blame it all on me.* I was glad I hid the money and was hoping they wouldn't mention it, which they didn't. So the cop said we were runaways and Tony asked if we were going to jail. The policeman said we were going to jail until our parents were informed. He took us to Boston Bar, and they didn't have a police station; they used an old ranger station.

He took us down to the basement and they had a big cage made of steel with a big door. Well, when the other two boys saw that they started to be upset, but even at my young age I was sort of used to it. Moving around in foster care was like jail at times so it didn't bother me at all. In the cell we went, and the cop slammed and locked the door. We was down there for about two or three hours—just enough time to let it sink in.

The cop came and got us and on to Hope we went. We arrived at the Hope Police Department and inside we went. Sid's parents were there and Tony's parents also The cop said, "Where are Dennis's parents?" and they said Dennis didn't have parents.

Sid's mother said, "He's the one who talked my little boy into this mess."

"Yes," said Sid's dad, who was looking at me like he wanted to throttle me.

It did hurt in away, seeing them leave and being comforted. I stayed in the cells until Welfare came to get me. I was thinking, *well, at least I have the money put away.* After that night I was returned to the Kendall's, and well, the looks I got…

All Doris said was, "Oh, here's the bad penny." Eventually I was charged with breaking and entering and got probation. So ended my experience with hopping freights. I thought I had better settle down and stay out of trouble for a while, and I still had hopes of my mom coming to get me, so I didn't want anything to mess it up. This was around 1955. Little did I know it would be a long time before I'd see her again, in 1958 at Brannon Lake School for Boys on the Island.

By now I was wearing my welcome out at the Kendall's. I was good hearted, even though I had all this anger built up in me because of all the foster homes and beatings and always thinking my mom was coming back for me. Then one summer I was sent to a summer camp for welfare kids, but I took off after a week. They found me breaking into a summer home for some canned food. I was taken to the police station in Haney and given probation again. I was only twelve years old, and I was on probation several times. I was also thought to have stolen ten dollars from the Lutheran Church, and they suspected I had been involved in several other B & Es. This information is all in my files from Victoria.

They wanted to send me to Brannon Lake Reform School, but the magistrate thought he would give me one more chance and put me on probation. So, in 1957, after court, they moved me to Mr. and Mrs. Yusko in Pitt Meadows. Right away I didn't care for the home. I had conditions with my probation, and I had to come into the police station every Saturday and talk to an officer about my weekly activity. It sorts of helped. The files say:

Dennis is having trouble at grade seven in MRSS school with stealing, and the principal, Mr. Draper, is at his wit's end to try and control this youngster.

Yusko Foster Home in Pitt Meadows

The Yuskos lived quite a way out of Haney in a little place called Pitt Meadows. They were a Dutch couple. I took the bus to school. I didn't like all the rules there; it seemed like an army camp. He told me not to dress and look like a hoodlum or a punk, and he said there wouldn't be any of that in his house. He said to turn my collar down; they would say the same thing in school to the students. He said, "If you read the Bible more, you wouldn't have all the troubles you got. In my country, they have no welfare; you had to work and work hard. During the Second World War, the Germans starved us... We had to eat tulip bulbs."

From the files

During this period Dennis remained at the Yusko farm home, but he was reluctant to commit himself whether he liked it or not … He complained that it was too far out of town and he was out of touch with his friends etc. Actually, Dennis has few friends, although he does have many acquaintances. During this period also we tried to help Dennis by imposing external controls in the person of RCM P Sgt. Culvert who agreed to see Dennis every Saturday. Dennis faithfully turned up at the police station each Saturday and reported on his activity for the week. It seemed to help him, but we learned later he was still up to his stealing and there was continuing trouble at school. The teachers were fed up with him.

In September 1957 Mr. Draper said that I would become quite violent when cornered, but all the foster homes and beatings and missing my mother more than anything would likely be the cause of my outbursts.

Dennis has been watched closely by the RCMP and his pilfering has continued into 1958, so today he appeared in juvenile court. We had no alternative but to recommend Brannon Lake School for Dennis. The courts wanted to give him one more chance so they put him on proba-tion. Dennis had admitted to not showing up at school on November 10th but refused to do detention or take the strap. We talked to Dennis on the phone and pointed out that these were school regulations and that if he did not abide by them, he was told he would be expelled. And if so, we would expect that he would be ready to earn his own living …

Even though I was in trouble and unruly, I was very shy, and I had good manners. I learned them from my grandmother in Yale. She was a wonderful lady, my grandmother.

So, as 1958 moved along I was still going to school and getting ready to move to a new foster home. I didn't like living in Pitt Meadows and wasn't getting along in the Yusko home. Mrs. Yusko liked me, and she had compassion for me. I remember a fad at school where everyone wore shoes with blakies on them. I never had a pair, so I borrowed Mr. Yuskos pair. They were ugly shoes, but they had blakies on them. Shows you how fads come and go, and it seems a person just has to have what's in fashion. It was the same as keeping our collars up and the different hairstyles. Living in Pitt Meadows I was too far from my brothers and I missed them both. In 1957 Murray was living with the Hovis family, one of many foster homes for him. He had been with the Hovis family for a few years, from 1956 to 1958. Murray helped me a lot when I was down and out, such as with food when I ran away from different foster homes.

Dennis around nine years old, 1950s.

Dennis at Maple Ridge Park, 1950.

Dennis at Grandmother's house in Yale.

DENNIS'S STORY
PART TWO

Walters family Foster Home in Haney, 1957-58

The Walters family lived down old 8th Avenue. They had a house right next to the Alouette River, and I loved the river and spent a lot of time on or around it. I liked the Walters family; they had a boy about my age. I was going through a lot of trouble at school and played hooky a lot. The men in the family were into boxing, and they were quite good. I believe I was thirteen when I moved to the Walters' home. After a few months I got a big idea while walking to school on my road. I saw these milk bottles on the porches of a few houses, and in the bottles I saw one- and two-dollar bills, and maybe some change. It was to pay the milkman and then he would leave more milk.

So the next day on my way to school I emptied all the money out of the milk bottles at three places. I forgot about going to school, and I headed for the forest and the river, but first I went to a little corner store and spent all the money on candy. I loved sweets, as I never got much from the foster parents where I lived. The owner of the store gave me a strange look, wondering why I wasn't in school and probably wondering where I got the money for all the candy. Well, then I headed for the deep forest where I felt safe. I climbed a tall cedar tree and sat up there and enjoyed my candy.

Mother in Yale.

Murray and Dennis, Yale.

Grandmother in Stanley Park, Vancouver, BC, on right with friends about 1910.

Well, this went on for a while, with me taking the money out of the milk bottles, but the milkman must have known after a while that something was wrong. Also, the owner of the corner store reported me to the truant officer, so he was on the hunt for me. Anyway, I tried it again one day, and I was just shaking the change out of the milk bottle when I heard a voice say, "Hold it right there." It scared the hell out of me, and I think I dropped the bottle. I looked over to a bush area and saw the two big sons of the man that owned the house. "You stay right where you are," they said, "The police are on their way."

I thought of running, but they were in good shape and would have caught me. They got a hold of me and one of them slapped me with his open hand across my face. Then they pushed me to the ground and sat on me until the police came. I knew I had been caught in the act. By now there was quite a crowd around me to see who the milk-bottle thief was.

One said, "Is he the little thief? I hope they throw the book at him." I felt like the kid caught with his hand in the cookie jar. In the crowd was my foster parents, who were mad at me and a little embarrassed by all the commotion.

Mrs. Walters said, "I am phoning the welfare and the police have already been called." I knew I had been caught in the act and they seemed happy that the milk-bottle thief was finally caught. The police officers came and took me to the station, which was behind the Super Value in Haney. It was a small place with two cells, I believe. They searched me and found a few fifty-cent pieces in one of my pockets. When asked where I got them, I said that I had found them on the road, which didn't go over too well—into the cell I went.

Being in a cell didn't really bother me. It might have in a small way, but I had already been through so many moves and foster homes by now. There were steel bunks with no blanket till night time, and there was a window you could see out. It had bars and wire mesh. They warned me not to do this again but then at school I pickpocketed a wallet from a classmate and was charged and sent to Brannon Lake.

At this time the magistrate was Willie Hope, and I always remember him with kindness. He was a small man who drove a little black Hillman car. He gave me as many breaks as he could before he had to send me to Brannon Lake Reform School at fourteen. In February 1958 I went to court for theft under fifty dollars and was on my way to reform school.

We finally come to Jingle Pot Road. I will never forget the name; that road led to the reform school. After a bit we came to the grounds and set back on the left were the main buildings. On the right was the young offender's Unit . Some kids were as young as ten years old, and there were also teenagers in for murder. There were all different cases. A common offence was incorrigibility, meaning acting up in their homes and meanings like liar, unruly, uncontrollable not easily changed, bad beyond correction and change not able to be corrected, not reform able are some of the meanings.

I could feel myself going into the mode I had gone into in the foster homes. They took me into the main building to a place they usually called R&D, meaning receiving and discharge. After stripping down and getting my institutional clothing, I put on my joint gear. I was then assigned my living unit. As I was young, they put me in Unit 8. My brother Glen was in the Lake the year before in 1957 and was well known and liked, so I mostly never got bothered by anyone, although there was always someone who didn't care who you were and was eager to fight or try to molest you. But I always stuck up for myself and wouldn't take any crap from anyone.

So over to Unit 8 I went, and I got my bed and bedding. I was making my bed when this older guy came over from the main building. He said, "How is your brother Glen doing?" He knew my brother.

I said, Oh, he is in YOU, the Young Offenders Unit in Oakalla, doing eighteen months."

He said, "Glen is solid, and we are good friends." Solid meant he was a good guy and lives by the code. Then he said, "I want to tell you about the code; always live by the code. The code means never rat on anyone, never steal from another con, such as tobacco etc. Don't be friendly with the bulls. A bull is slang for guard; don't talk and be friendly with them. Never rape a woman or fool around with young kids, as it is a killing offence amongst inmates. You don't last too long if you're a skinner, meaning a child molester. Always stick up for yourself, otherwise you will be picked on and it could escalate into something bigger. Don't fool around with queers, meaning guys that are gay. While committing a crime, always get away with what you are doing, such as wearing gloves, so you don't leave fingerprints. Don't be a braggart, stick to yourself, but at the same time be courteous to those who are solid. And if you fool around with another guy old lady, it's not a killing offence but usually you get punched out; guys that do that are called Joe the Grinder. Also, selling things for money is a no—you get called a jailhouse merchant, which gets you a knuckle sandwich (punched out) so you barter instead of charging cash for drugs etc." There were always drugs in every jail I have ever been in.

This code changed over the years to the point that they threw the code out the window and now it's just no code at all. In the early days you knew where you stood but now it's haywire and anything goes. The code was stuck in my mind, and I still live by it even after all these years. Anyway, in the upcoming days I was assigned to work in the kitchen. I got up at around six or six-thirty, made my bed and it had to be done right—all tucked in, army style. Then we all walked over to the main building and went into the dining hall to have breakfast. If you were sixteen and older you got a cigarette at meals, but the younger guys couldn't smoke. Then we all went to the gym and they raised the flag as we stood at attention. Then we were assigned our work placement, and off to the kitchen I went to peel potatoes.

The kitchen boss was a real mean bully, and I never did get along with him. He was from my hometown of Haney, and my brother went to school with his brother. His dad was the Haney bootlegger so he knew me and my brothers. He was always on my case, and I always swore at him and that got him going, and off to the cells I went.

One time when I was in the Hole, three guys got the idea to escape. Well, they got a winter sock, took the heavy shower nozzle off and put it in the sock and one of them got out to use the shitter, as they did not have cells with toilets in them; the toilets were together in one area, not in every cell. So, this day there was only one bull, or guard, on shift. This inmate—I won't mention names—he took the sock and hit the bull over the head a few times, knocked him out and darn-near killed him. Then he got the keys and let his buddies out of their cells. I always remember him saying, "Storrings, you want out? Come with us."

I said, "No, that's all right," and he said okay and they got outside and went over the fence and off they went. Well, finally more guards came and saw what was going down. There was blood all over the place, and they got the guard to the hospital. He just about died, but he survived. There was a lot of anger on the part of the guards, which I can't blame them for as he had family. I never did try to hurt people in that way, as they were just doing their job. Sure, I used to swear at them and sometimes get into a tussle with them, but it wouldn't go that far.

Well, they got away. I can't remember how long they were on the run, but they were finally caught. The boys couldn't get off the Island as the police were watching the ferries. Then they caught them, and they really gave it to them in more ways than one. The boys went in front of Beaver Potts, the magistrate, who was well known to give out heavy sentences to the Pen. He gave these guys the harshest sentence he could. I think he had to stay with provincial instead of federal, which meant the Penitentiary. He handed them the most he could under the provincial system and they got two years definite and two years indefinite, and they were shipped off to Oakalla Prison in Burnaby. I knew them well throughout the years, and they are all gone now; many of the guys I knew are dead.

This is an insert from a page that a social worker posted in a memo in 1957, just before I went to Brannon Lake Reform School:

This young boy has been given numerous chances in the Haney Juvenile Court. When his older brother Glen was in Brannon Lake Reform School, Dennis told the police that he got into trouble so that he would be sent there too … After his brother left he was sentenced to that institution in February 1958 for theft of a wallet from school. This officer recalls that there have been numerous complaints about Dennis's behavior which were overlooked by the police in view of his depraved history … The Department of Social Welfare at Haney would have additional social history information on this youth's court records …

Getting back to the reform school, one day I was down in the gym and I went to the boot room to change into work boots. I went up to the double door and the guard was inside handing out boots. I believe it was Mr. Bishop, and he was big and in good shape. He said something smart to me and I swore at him. Well, he reached out and pulled me right into the boot room and started to punch me all over the room. Instead of cowering I fought back and well, that made him madder. All the inmates out in the gym were clapping for me. Off to the hole I went, and after I got out I sort of settled down and did my time. But good things never last …

I was at my unit and I went to the bathroom and blood came out, so off to the Nanaimo Hospital I went. They cut me open and took out the kidney stone. Today they use another method, but in 1958 it was done differently. After a week or so I was getting ready to go back to the lake. I made a false bottom in a box of chocolates and hid cigarettes to take back as I was underage and couldn't smoke at the reform school. I was taken back to "the Lake" and put in the reform school hospital but first they searched me and my belongings. Lucky for me they didn't find the cigarettes. I shared them with other guys.

After I healed up from the operation, I was back at Unit 8 and me and a friend of mine decided we were going to escape. In the back of Unit 8 were the power lines that lead away from the institution, so off we ran, knowing there would be a count in about an hour. Once they found us missing there would be RCMP looking for us. We ran for quite a while until we came to the water; it was rough and there were whitecaps. So, we found a boat and started to push it towards the water, and well, it was too big to push. We got tired so we left it and headed into the bush. I'm glad we deserted the boat as we probably would have drowned. In the bush area we found a summer cabin, and we broke in and got some canned beans to eat. We stayed in the cabin overnight and the next day we walked for quite a while and then we came to a road. My friend and I went up on the road and just then a police car came along. He really surprised us, and we didn't have time to run.

He handcuffed us and put us in the police car. They knew who we were—escapees. We made up a story that didn't work, and off to the Lake we went. We were taken to the hole, and later I could hear my friend getting the paddle; he was screaming but he got it good. Me, I was lucky because I had that operation and they didn't want to cause any damage. The guard said, "You're lucky, Storrings, but I will get you next time."

This set my release date back a lot and they tacked more time on me. After I got out of the hole, I settled down. It was now August 1958. I stayed out of trouble and they gave me a pass to go to a foster home, the Caldwell's. Now, I don't remember if it was on a pass or when I was released, but the Second Narrows Bridge went down while I was on the ferry. On the pass I saw my brother Murray and stayed at the Caldwell's. After the pass I went back to the reform school and stayed out of trouble. I was released and I went to my new foster home, the Torgerson's. I had to get ready for school too.

My dad and my aunt (his sister). Looks like he is smoking.

In August 1958 I was released from Brannon Lake and taken to Mr. and Ms. Torgerson. They had no children of their own. I met Mrs. Torgerson first, and I met Mr. Torgerson later that night. They seemed to be nice enough, but I was always on guard from previous encounters. I stayed busy getting school supplies; I was going to Haney Junior High for in grade seven.

Brannon Lake Reform School in Nanaimo as it is today.

I went MRSS in Haney with a lot of people I grew up in Haney with I learned when I was young to stick to myself; you could say I was stressed out a bit, but I could handle it. Around the first week into September, I was ready to go to my first day of school. That morning I had breakfast and went down our road to 17th Ave. and caught the bus to the junior high. Murray was two years younger than me so he would have been in grade 5, and Glen was the oldest. I think Glen got kicked out of school for fighting.

1958 was a good year, and the girls, well, they were just beautiful, and they caught my eye. It was a wonderful time for a teenager like myself and I liked living close to my brothers. I just had to walk up 17th Ave. south and I was at Murray's foster home. In 1959 I had to watch out for the foster dad, as he was mean. I believe Murray's foster father was in the Second World War; a German soldier. When Murray and I were outside picking plums, he would come outside and grab me by the ear and twist it hard and say, "I know you're stealing those plums." I would pull away and swear at him, and then he would chase me off his property.

I often asked my brother if he ever hit him. There was also a boy living there who had medical problems, Ronnie McCrea. They treated him badly verbally, and he was in a wheelchair. I met him a few times, and I liked him and knew some members of his family. My brother did not like the foster home he was in, and by this time Murray would have been around twelve going on thirteen. We saw each other quite a bit while I was at the Torgerson's home, but that was to change. I believe Glen was just getting out of Oakalla or still had time left to do, and I believe my dad was in Oakalla in 1959 also. My mother was living in Vancouver at that time. While at the Torgerson's I would go out at night with two brothers I knew who were of couple of years older than me who lived on the same street. I was only fourteen.

The Chilliwack Progress

The Chilliwack Progress (Chilliwack, British Columbia, Canada) · Wed, May 24, 1967 · Page 19

http://theprogress.newspapers.com/image/77133595

Printed on Nov 24, 2014

Brothers Elect Trial By Jury

Dennis Raymond Storrings and his brother Murray Kenneth elected trial by jury Thursday at their preliminary hearing into break-in charges.

The pair are charged with break-ins at Saan Stores Limited, Woolworth's, and Chilliwack Dry Cleaners. They are in custody and made no plea last week.

Their county court case opens May 31.

Murray and Dennis Clipping.

We would go down to Dewdney Trunk Rd. and go into the basement or root cellar and steal a gallon of strawberry or blackberry wine from this guy that made it. You see, in those days they had Bootlegger, Booz Cans etc. You could buy after hours, and I used to go to the bootlegger with Glen. It was down close to Webster's Corners, and the house was old and spooky. My brother and I would knock on the door and the old man would let you in, if he liked you. He knew Glen, so in we went, and he asked us, "What it will be?"

My brother would say, "A mickey of rye and a case of Lucky lager." Glen would pay him and off we would go; we would jump into this other guy's car—he had a license and a nice '49 Ford. My other brother and I had three '49 Fords over a few years; they were nice cars. When I started drinking beer it was ten cents a glass. I was usually quiet and shy, and I wouldn't change that much when I drank. I would just talk a little more, and the shyness would go away a bit.

But at times I would get into fights. One day the Torgerson's went out with friends, and I got the big idea to take Mr. Torgerson's car up the road, as the keys were in it. Another guy and I thought we were big shots driving the little Austin. Well, I lost control and ended up in the ditch and couldn't get it out. Now we were in for it. We were standing by the car when up drove Mr. and Mrs. Torgerson and their friends. They started to give us hell, yelling at me. They thought better of hitting me as by now I became quite angry if I was hit. They finally got the car out and drove it home and they told me to walk along with the other guy. They said Welfare was going to know about this.

As it went, I stayed at the home for a while more. I roamed the countryside, and there was a beautiful creek just up from my foster home with high canyon walls. I enjoyed getting out by myself or when I could my brother and I would travel together. Us three brothers stuck together because we helped each other. Don't forget, we were taken from our parents at an early age and all we had was each other so we stuck up for each other. But the social welfare department thought different.

One file read:

Murray is somewhat concerned about his brother Dennis (This is when I was in Brannon Lake) *and they have been corresponding apparently. Dennis may present some problem to Murray on his release. Dennis has the ability to upset Murray to some extent and may try to involve his younger brother in future delinquencies...*

This may be somewhat true, but we just had each other, and it was comforting to have the support from each other. I was in the homes and the workers were not. Don't get me wrong; Welfare did try sometimes but we fell through the cracks in most cases. I knew my brother didn't like it at Mr. Stephanie's home; he was a bully and enjoyed tormenting Murray.

The foster parents are concerned that when his brothers return to the district, he will be influenced by them and perhaps cause a lot of trouble. We tried to reassure Murray's foster mother on this point, but Mrs. Stephanie is still apprehensive. In any case, Mrs. Stephanie promised to keep Murray at least until the end of the school term of 1958 ...

I would do well for a while at the Torgerson's but stealing was a way of life to me by now. It started when I was younger, and I would do it in a lot of the homes. In later years stealing became quite easy and a way to get what we wanted. Murray was still up the road from me, and one day he and I were walking from his foster home to my place and we saw Mr. Torgerson walking towards us. When we got close to him, we could see that he was crying and had his head down.

I said, "Where you are going?"

He said, "I am leaving. My wife was having an affair with the neighbour. I asked where he was going to live and he said, "I am going back east. I can not take what she did to me." He had sadness in his face and he said, "You're a good boy, Dennis, I will miss you. All the best to you both." And he left. I never saw him again.

Walking towards my place with my brother, I reached in my shirt pocket and pulled out a package of Black Cat cigarettes and lit one up. I can't remember if Murray smoked, but if so I would have given him one. I used to steal or buy them in stores, and I believe at the time they were thirty-eight cents a package. It's not like now when they lock them up; in the fifties, they had cartons of cigarettes left out in plain sight.

Glen was charged with breaking and entering and car theft in February 1958, and he was sent to the young offender's unit in Oakalla for eighteen months. Approval was given for a payment of four dollars a month to Glen from his family allowance trust account. The check should have been sent monthly to the warden of Oakalla, who I believe at the time was Christie, a stern man. He ran things like the army. They still had the death penalty in at this time; the gallows were up in the south wing, and old-timers told me when they hanged a person it was dead silence and then all hell broke out, with prisoners banging their metal cups on the bars etc. Doctor Richmond was the doctor at the time, and he checked the person that was hanged to make sure he was dead. A wonderful man, the doctor was. I knew him well over the years while I was in and out of Oakalla.

While I was still at the Torgerson's another Welfare boy that I knew, I will call him D.R., came to live with me there. I knew him and his brother. Murray was in school one day and Welfare came and got him, along with his belongings, and said, "You are moving to Yale to live with your grandmother." He didn't like the way they did it; he didn't have a chance to say goodbye to Ronnie, who was living at the same home, and to classmates, but he didn't like the foster parents and he wanted to move anyway. So off to Yale he went, and I was sad to see him go.

After Mr. Torgerson left it was just D.R. and I living at the home with Mrs. Torgerson. I was having trouble at school and playing hooky a lot. I was attending grade 8 at Maple Ridge Junior High School when I was dismissed from school for persistent disregard to teachers and general rules of conduct and disobedience. Obviously, I was not interested in school and had failed at least once. I was frequently in conflict with the school authority and often defiant to teachers. I was expelled in September 1959.

My mother, Eleanor, taken in Vancouver, BC.

My lovely mother.

My lovely daughter Emilee.

Mary Burrage, a lovely girl I met in Haney.

Rare picture at this age of me at Grandmother's home in Yale.

Our first cousin Aaron Tolmie on our father's side of family.

From my files:

Dennis has never been able to take root in a foster home, probably because he still maintains a loyalty towards his mother. Dennis was always waiting for her to come back.

Some welfare workers did realize the heartache we went through…. Anyway, back to the Torgerson foster home. In September 1958 I was charged with theft of a coin collection from foster parents, and they let me off with probation so then I could stay at home. One day this man picked me up in his car and took me up to a wooded area where he tried to do things to me in a sexual manner. I freaked out and pulled a knife on him. Well, he got scared and drove me home, and I never saw him again. It reminded me of Brannon Lake and I just reacted.

1958 came and left and the foster mother met another man. We moved to a house on old 10th Avenue with D.R., the other boy. I was still at school and I met this beautiful girl, M.S. We was both shy, and she went away on holidays and I started dating this other girl, G.T, who I met at school. The girls seemed to like me. I always remember 1959 because that's when Buddy Holly, Big Bopper and Ritchie Valens died. It was a sad day. Well, I stayed at the new place for a while more and then I moved just a mile away to the home of the Chequis family in late 1959-60.

From the files:
Recently Dennis had a perm so that he would have curly hair like his brother Glen.

A year ago the police had said I had black hair, so now it was quite reddish to change my appearance. The home of the Chequis family was alright. They were from Neepawa, Manitoba, and were Ukrainian people. I just loved the meals they made and the woman did all the cooking, like cabbage rolls, borscht etc. They really liked their tea, and there was a lot of tea drinking during the day. I really liked the family. Mr. Chequis worked for years at the Hammond Mill in the little town of Hammond. When I first moved to their home it was 1959 and I was in grade 7 in junior high.

The foster parents had five children of their own, plus me and one other teenage boy called Fred. For a while I settled into school but I always missed my mother, and I was almost losing hope of seeing her again. As it turned out, that was the case. I worked on weekends at the bowling alley setting pins. It was all done by hand, and I got hit on the shins a few times. I hung around with Fred, and he and I started getting cars. I got a 1940 Ford and had it parked in the driveway. Fred bought an early Volvo and we took out girls in it; those were happy times. I was having problems at school, but just the same I loved the late 50s.

In October 1959 Glen was released from Oakalla and he was living at the Volker's foster home . They were concerned that Glen would get into trouble, as he took off to Vancouver three or four and got charged with driving without a license.

Mr. Chequis had a shed that he kept budgie birds in. He was a very decent man and treated me good. I found it hard to get along in most foster homes, as I had a lot of anger inside of me and expressed it a lot of the time. In school I never got along with the teachers or the principal, and they had the strap and the paddle also used the pointer. I got the strap quite a few times and the paddle once. When I was in the principal's office to get the strap, I would put my hand out and just when he was going to strap me, I would pull my hand away. Well, this went on a couple of times but in the end, I would get it.

I knew two brothers that were in foster homes, Gordy and Doug. Gordy had really nice cars and I got along with him. I was sad to see him go. I knew another family they were really good to me, and I hung around with one of the boys, Carl McCrea, in the late 50s and walked to school together. Eventually we went up to Whitehorse together. I will come to that later.

In school there was a lot of fights, and in those days' guys fought with their fists and got reputations, including Glen. But there was a guy in school that nobody wanted to scrap with; he was just tough and knew how to fight. This female music teacher was always on my case; she was mean—real mean, and she would see me in the hallway and hit me with her pointer for having my collar up. I would tell her off and always kept my collar up and I would end up in detention or the principal's office, or I would flee out the side door and head for the forest and the river down old 10th Ave.

I had my 1940 Ford and I managed to get a James Dean jacket; actually, I had a red one and a blue one. They were big in the late 50s.

From my files:

Dennis is now working at the bowling alley and earning approx. seven dollars a week there. He pays some of this each week to Mrs. Chequis on his car… We feel that this is fine as long as he continues to make the payments, and we are in hopes that perhaps we are on the way to forming a relationship with Dennis and may eventually help him to become settled somewhat in this home.

But that was not to be…

Xmas 1959: Mrs. Chequis was in the welfare office today, quite concerned about Dennis. She states that over Christmas he stole a jar of Noxzema from her sister's family and he later returned it. Later, he was seen going out with Fred's shirt on, and they felt that he had taken this and was going to sell it … After being told to take the shirt off, he later appeared in Fred's T-shirt. He also took this off, but he has become quite hard to handle. They stated that he was wrecking his car because he was annoyed and had smashed one of the doors and Mr. Chequis is quite concerned. Because of these things they feel that they can no longer keep him. They will, however, keep him until his probation period is over, about the middle of January 1959, but they do not want him in the house after that.

Christmas came, and what a beautiful dinner we all had. It was now 1960 and I was getting into music. There were some good singers, especially black singers, at that time, such as Jackie Wilson; he did a good job of "Lonely Teardrops." Sam Cooke did "Working on The Chain Gang," Otis Redding did "On the Dock of the Bay," The Coasters did "Charlie Brown." It was a great time for music, and Elvis was coming along just great. I loved "Hound Dog." We had the early radios and record players and we had A.M. radios in the cars. I started to go to dances, and I really liked Buddy Holly and Buddy Knox. It was sad to see Buddy Holly pass away. Later there was Ricky Nelson and Bobby Darren, Mack The Knife, Little Frankie Lyman and the teenagers….

From my files (early 1960s):

Mrs. Chequis phoned at 4:30 today to ask us to please remove Dennis immediately. In the background we could hear a fight going, with Mr. Chequis and Dennis arguing. He has evidently exasperated the family beyond all bounds and is now upsetting the other three foster boys in the home. Dennis has been accused of stealing three shirts of Fred's. He denied this, but the plastic bag from the shirt was found in his pocket. As a result, we went over and got Dennis from the home, took him to the local police station, and the corporal there talked to him at length to try to get him to see that what he was doing was wrong. He was first sullen and belligerent and then tearful but continues to deny that he took the shirts.

We then arranged for Dennis to go to Mr. and Mrs. Evans on Dewdney Trunk Road for a few days. Mr. and Mrs. Evans were both formerly nurses at Essondale. Mr. Evans also has several fish boats and knows Dennis quite well as he acts on occasion as an auxiliary policeman. Dennis was aware of this and not too happy with the placement. However, Mr. Evans did show good judgement, we felt, and greeted Dennis with, "Let me take your coat, son, and we will have some dinner. The rest have eaten, but I am late too," with that we left until the next day.

Dennis appeared in juvenile court and was charged with a breach of his probation and put on a further six months' probation. The judge talked to him at great length. He has maintained an interest in Dennis for some time and tried to hopefully help him. The plan now is that Dennis will stay with the Evans family.

Mr. Evans was strict, but he did try to help me. Mrs. Evans was very good to me at times, and they had a boy also called Dennis. He was about my age, and I liked him; he was good to me too. also, two girls, Overall the family was kind, but I had a lot of anger in me. Mr. Evans used to take me out on the Fraser River on his fishing boat and show me how to make ribs for the boat by steaming them and forming them to fit the boat. I can never say anything wrong about the family; they tried their best to help me, but I was sad and angry, and I clashed with Mr. Evans.

I remember one night I was up in my room, which faced the street, and I heard someone calling my name. I looked out the window and it was Murray. He told me Glen got into a fight and while fighting Glen had a seizure. In the heat of the fight the other guy kept on fighting, probably not knowing Glen was having a seizure; I won't mention the other fella's name. It upset me, as Glen meant everything to me. That took a lot out of Glen, but he still fought for a few more years.

One day I got mad at Mr. Evans, swearing and carrying on like I did, and they wanted me gone from their home. I was moved back to the Chequis's place.

From my files, re: the burns and scarring on my chest from childhood:

Dennis has recently been medically examined and is evidently doing well; he has decided not to go through with the skin grafting at the present time.

Well, of course I didn't want to go through with that again. They should have done that years before. I was around four when that happened so why did they wait so long? The scar made me feel insecure all my life.

At the Chequis' home things were going good until the stealing started again. One time in 1960 I was put in a cell to think things over. The police eventually charged me with breaking and entering and theft in August 1960. I went in front of magistrate Hope and was sentenced to one year definite and one year indefinite in Oakalla Prison Farm in Burnaby. A police officer drove me from the station in Haney. I went through the old gatehouse with the big sign on top that said in big letters "Oakalla Prison Farm," and we went through and down the hill, passing the west wing. I saw inmates walking around, some playing hand ball. At this time there was just wire mesh around the yard in the west wing area.

As time went by they put up tin sheets and wire because when visitors walked past the west wing there were a lot of tennis balls being thrown over with treats inside (drugs). Then the visitors would be let in and go to the visiting area. You had a long bench or chairs where you sat and had to talk on phones and look at your visitor on the other side of the glass. A lot of inmates used sign language as the phones were bugged.

The west wing was for those awaiting trial and the south wing was where death row was located for inmates already sentenced. The east wing was the kitchen and work gangs, which was shovel work, mostly. They had gangs of inmates working in the fields, and they grew their own vegetables. I remember one day when a gang was working near the fence overlooking Burnaby Lake. We were working on the mud stick and a couple of guys I knew put on double coats that were heavy, as they wanted protection from the shotgun pellets. There were two guards with shotguns watching us as we worked, and well, these guys started to run for the fence. One inmate made it over the fence but his friend got hit by the blast and thanks to the double coat he just fell to the ground and was overpowered by the guard.

His friend got away but was caught the same day. I might add that when the guards would shoot at inmates for escaping, they weren't using double-odd buck, which would kill you; they would use a less powerful shot.

When I was in the east wing waiting to be classified, I went in front of the board and they told me I was going to New Haven Prison on Marine Drive. All the buildings were quite old, and I was put on the farm to work. One day two inmates tried to escape, they were running as fast as they could down the back forty, as they called it, and the warden told a bunch of us to chase them down. He looked at me and said, "Come on, Storrings, get after them." I said that it wasn't my job to do that and I refused.

Well, he got mad at me and said, "I am sending you to the Hole for disobeying an order." I got days in the Hole, but it didn't bother me as I had been in the Hole before. One day my friend and I got the idea we were going to escape. We were working on the farm and made a run for the fence. It wasn't that tall, so over we went and crossed Marine Drive. We waited in a wooded area until dark, and by now they knew we were missing. Once it got quite dark and we were a few miles from the institution, we started looking for a car to steal. We spotted a car in the driveway of a house, and we didn't want to start it so close to the house as the people would hear the noise and come out and capture us before we even got started on our little plan.

As the car was unlocked, we put it in neutral and started to push it out of the driveway and down the road a bit. Once we had it far enough, Wayne D. got in and hotwired the car. It started up the car, which was a '52 or a '53 Chevy. I had a lot of the old ones, so I know my cars. We took off, but what we didn't know was the owner had been watching us all along and had phoned the police. We were going east, and I happened to notice a police car going the other way and before we knew it, he turned around and came after us. W.D. started to pick up speed but the police car was a little faster than the old Chevy we had. W.D. said he would find a driveway to turn into and shut all the lights out and the police officer would go by.

Well, it sounded good but after pulling into a driveway and shutting all the lights out W.D. forgot to take his foot off the brake pedal. I was just opening our car door and getting ready to run, same as W.D, when I heard the officer say, "Do not move." I was looking down the barrel of his gun. Well, that did it. We froze, not wanting to get shot, and another couple of police cars showed up, and that was the end of our escape plan. They handcuffed us and took us to the Burnaby RCMP detachment. We went to sleep that night, as we were tired with all the excitement and running around. In the morning we got a little breakfast and then we got ready to go into court.

As we went into the courtroom Judge Bell said, "Well, if I could I would send you both to the Penitentiary, but under the law and because of your age, I am giving you six months for the escape and six months for auto theft." I was already doing one year definite and one year indefinite, so now I was doing eighteen months definite and eighteen months indefinite.

We were both returned to Oakalla and were sent to the east wing again, awaiting classification. I thought I would be sent to Haney Correctional Institution, and I wanted to go to H.C.I. It was a brand-new institution and Haney was my hometown. I would get visits rather than being far away and no visits.

They called me in to get classified, and wouldn't you know, they sent me back to New Haven. I couldn't believe it. So back I went. I don't know where W.D. went; I never did see him again. It was like so many guys I knew; I would get to know someone, and they would get lost in the penal system. There were so many lost souls. Well, it was now October 1960. I hated New Haven and knew I wouldn't be there long. I was back working on the farm, and I was going to escape again but thought better of it.

I was doing a lot of weights, keeping in shape. Murray and Mr. and Mrs. Chequis come in to visit me at New Haven and brought me tobacco, toothpaste etc., and it was good to see everyone. I stayed out of trouble for a while, but one day I got into an argument with another inmate and started to fight. I was sent to the Hole. A friend, N.E., sent me cigarettes and matches in the mashed potatoes. After I got out of the Hole they shipped me back to Oakalla. I went to classification again and finally I was sent to Haney Correctional Institution. I was lucky, in a way, because I had my family on my mom's side who helped me in times of trouble, such as my grandmother. I loved her so.

On the day of the transfer to H.C.I. we got into a large truck or van. There must have been about fifteen of us. They called it a Bun Wagon. We were all shackled together, and finally we came to the Haney, and I felt a little sad as it was my hometown. As we went down Dewdney Trunk Rd. going east, we came to 21st Avenue and we turned left and went past the high school. We went up to the long Axis Rd. and there was the new prison, opened in 1957. They said they wanted me in a closed prison because of my escapes.

In 1960 they were still working on the gate house, but for now they just had a gate across as you went in. Into the main prison we went and proceeded to R and D, receiving and discharge. A few years later an inmate who worked on the warden's car beefed it up and got a lot of horsepower out of it. Well, one day he decided to take the car and escape, and he went crashing through the gate house. I believe they shot the car full of holes. He crashed the car and they took him to the Hole. Too much horsepower…. Anyway, the escapes were just about the same— a car used from the prison.

One day in May of 1961 while in HCI I was watching the news in Unit Two and I saw a picture of a taxi accident. They said a thirty-eight-year-old woman was killed at Fry's Corner in Cloverdale and they gave her name. Well, I couldn't believe it. I was sent down to see the padre and he said, "I have some bad news for you." I said I already saw it on the news and he felt bad for me and got the nurse to give me a sedative. In the next day or so I was let out with a guard to go to the funeral. It was a sad day for me.

I was working one day on the mud stick, digging a hole and filling it in again and racking stones etc. I was mad at something and the guard told me to get busy. I just threw down my shovel and refused to work. I was upset about my mother's death in May 10. You see, in all those foster homes when I was young, I was taught to not show my emotions, so when my mom died I kept everything inside. Anyway, the guard got two other guards on the radio and they took me inside to the warden's court. I went in front of the warden, deputy warden and a guard. The warden asked why I refused to work. I swore at him and he gave me thirty days in the Hole.

I was taken up on the elevator. It was a bad Hole; even though that institution was a couple years old, it was well known they had a bread and water punishment in the Hole (three days bread and water then one regular meal then three days again). First, they take all your clothes off and they give you a set of coveralls. They put you in a cell and close the door. The door was solid heavy wood or metal with a small opening at the top, so if you were standing you could only see straight ahead. The cell was about five feet by eight feet and had no bed, just concrete. You got one blanket at night. They had a light on twenty-four hours a day, and in the ceiling they had cold air coming in the cell all the time. It got quite cold.

I did a lot of push-ups and other exercise. There was a round hole with a nozzle and if an inmate got out of hand, they would press a button from outside and the whole cell would be soaked with water. You got a haircut once a month from inmates that were taking the course from Mr. Craigie, whether you wanted it or not. When you wanted to go to the toilet you had a big white bucket in your cell, and when it got full you asked the guard to empty it in the toilet outside of your cell. I know of inmates who were mad at a certain guard and when the guard opened the door the inmate threw everything on the guard. I would never do that to any guard, and the guards respected me for that.

When you were given your bread and water or the full meal the guards wanted you to eat everything. I used to save a sandwich for later, and it helped, but they would come in and take anything they considered contraband. Sometimes I would get mad and have a tussle with them, but then you would go to warden's court again, and usually they would take good time away. Say you were doing two years and you stayed out of trouble—you could do eighteen months and you were released. But if you got into trouble, you could do the full two years. While in HCI I was in the hole many times.

In November 1961, the parole board gave me my parole and said I would be going back to the Chequis foster home. I was transferred to pre-release camp. This was a place you went before getting out. I always remember getting out and being driven to my hometown of Haney and going to the Chequis's home. They took me to a clothing store to get new clothes. Murray was living in a foster home with Mrs. Chequis's sister, not too far from me, and I saw him the first day I got out. I believe Glen was in the BC Pen, but Murray and I would go see him soon....

While in HCI, I was so happy when they called my name for a visit with my brother Murray. We had quite a long visit with each other. Also, there was Mr. And Mrs. Chequis, and according to my file, after the visit while they were driving away, Murray turned back and said, "I miss my brother." Mrs. Chequis said he had a few tears running down his cheeks. As I said before, we always looked out for each other....

Well, I was out again, and it felt good.

From my file:

Talked to Mr. Prasse today, Murray's foster father. He says Murray and Dennis spend many an evening at home in his place playing games and having coffee and cake or just plain watching TV. He was worried about the fact that Dennis chums around with undesirable characters.

I had a good Christmas at the Chequis foster home in 1961. There were bottles of all different types of liquor –wine, rum and whisky, and they had men or women that played the fiddle, violin, guitar and the spoons. I had my share of the liquor, even though I was young. I didn't like it much, and I just woke up not feeling good. I bought another 1940 Ford, and I parked it in my foster parents' driveway. I would work on it and I got it running well and the body was in fairly good shape.

One day a couple of guys really wanted the 1940 Ford, and they wanted to put a nice paint job on it and take out their girlfriends. What a great time; for five dollars, one could get a package of cigarettes, lots of gas and a case of beer. What a blast. A five-dollar bill nowadays can't get you much. I was going with a girl from Haney, and she was a real beauty. I lost her when I went back to HCI.

Well, we had a small riot in HCI in 1962. We gathered bars of soap and when the guards come into the different units in riot gear and started down both sides of the unit I was in, Unit Two, I believe, we let fly with the bars of soap. Well, the whole place exploded into yelling and banging lockers with our metal cups. If you didn't participate and sided with the bulls, you could run into trouble and even a severe beating or in some cases death. They rounded up the inmates they saw throwing bars of soap or they sometime just picked out certain inmates. They called us troublemakers, and I was one of the troublemakers, but I was a loner.

I used to keep away from the bulls. I was on my bed when they came for me. There was four of them, and of course I put up a fight. I was wiry and had done a lot of weightlifting. Anyway, they got the cuffs on me and off to the Hole I went. One had to watch out not to lip off to the guards because they would lay a beating on you on the way up in the elevator, but I did it anyway. Other than that I kept to myself, and I think they respected me for that. I wouldn't bother anyone as long as they didn't bug me.

I had to strip naked and they checked for any contraband on the inmates. "Suit casing" was a way of smuggling things in and out of the institutions. It was a slang word for inserting things in a body cavity. Anyway, they gave me a pair of coveralls and put me in a cell. They usually give you a blanket around 7 o'clock, but tonight they thought *you want to act up you got nothing in your lockup* tried to sleep but after all the riot and such I couldn't get to sleep right away, so I did some exercise, push-ups mostly. I finally got to sleep, and with no blanket I had to curl up into a ball as it was cold.

I woke up around six in the morning as I could hear the trays being put into the cells. It was our morning meal, which consisted of four slices of dry bread and a mug of water. I received thirty days in the Hole and the warden took ten days of good time away, which meant I had to do ten extra days along with my original sentence, which was eighteen months definite and one year indefinite. All this was for my part in the riot. You know, I never forgot that cold air blowing in the cell twenty-four hours a day... something about it stuck in my mind all these years.

After my time in the Hole I went back to my unit. I stuck it out in the landscaping shop. It was now November 1962, and I was ready to be released from HCI. I was sent over to the pre-release camp, which was not far from the main jail. Around this time everyone thought there was going to be a war, but Kennedy never relented and things cooled down. But for a while, whenever a plane went over everyone thought *this is it*. I am glad it never happened.

I couldn't sleep much the night before I was getting out, and finally the morning of November 16, 1962, I gathered up all my stuff, gave away all my tobacco to friends of mine etc. and changed into my street clothes. I had a few dollars in my account, about eighty or so, and I was thinking about having a beer in the Haney Hotel. I was underage, but my brother Glen knew the owner well and he would let me in. I was really excited about seeing my brother Glen. I couldn't see Murray because he was in Brannon Lake Reform School. I will get back to Murray in just a bit. My two brothers went through a lot of hardships also.

So down to the gate house I went. The guards always patted you down just in case you were smuggling letters out for other inmates etc. I had the idea of taking out my ID, card which had my picture and number one it. My number was 2579; I will never forget it. But if I got caught, they would have taken me back in and I would have gone to warden's court and lost some good time. They frisked me and never found it. I waited for a while and they put me in a vehicle and down the road I went towards my hometown of Haney. On the way down Dewdney Trunk Road I was getting a funny feeling, as I always did when I got out of the many prisons I was in over the years. They took me to the welfare office and this is what they said in a report from the files:

On November 16, 1962, Dennis was released from Haney Correctional. Institution.… He did not make parole, as no other recourse was available, and Dennis was placed in the worker's home, Mr. Vanderveen. He was unable to return to the Chequis home, and while in the worker's home Dennis remained out of trouble with the police. He seemed to become less withdrawn and after a month would participate in conversation freely.… His posture improved, and at mealtimes he was more relaxed that when he first came. He was quiet, tiptoeing around the house, and he seemed to have difficulty looking directly at one when speaking or being spoken to. He kept his room and personal things in perfect order, with institution-like neatness. When asked, he was willing to help with some household chores, chopping firewood for the fireplace. He did take an interest in the car, and several times spontaneously decided to wash it. He brought his friends to the house, and later in his stay seemed sufficiently at home to make a few demands, transportation etc.

Even though I spent a lot of time in different jails I still had good morals. I was always kind and polite to women and others. Morals were something I stuck to, and I am glad for it. I saw some rapists in jail get killed for being a rapist. I wouldn't even fool around with other guy's old ladies, as they called them, even though I had a few come on to me. That's just the way I was and it worked for me. It saved a lot of trouble.

I was only sexually abused once that I remember by a foster parent. He was a bully of a man, and he not only beat me with a stick but also made me do things sexually. I do not like to mention names, but he was a brute of a man. I always kept it inside. He was an upstanding figure in Haney, and I believe he is no longer with us. Some foster parents took it to a level of cruelty, and all I could think was I wished my mom would come and take me home with her, and my brothers also. If I didn't have my brothers, I don't know how I would have coped with the situation. I have two sisters also, but I have never seen them; they were adopted out to different families. I hope to see them before I go.

I am writing this story so people will get an idea of what it was like for us three boys in the foster homes and institutions, and I write the whole truth of what we went through. I know it sounds brutal in some cases, but that is the way it happened.

In February1963 I was in one of my favourite homes and the last one in the care of the Social Welfare Department. This home was different as the foster parents were both social welfare workers and they both had their master's degree in social work. I went there when I got out of Haney Correctional Institution. God bless them both.

I eventually decided to go to Whitehorse with my friend Carl, his dad and Carl's sister Shirley. The road was pretty rough in those days, and Carl had a blue 1958 Chevy Impala convertible. We stayed at a trailer park in a trailer that Carl's dad owned right beside the old paddle wheelers. So after getting settled in, we went into town in Carl's car and as we were sitting in the car four gentlemen dressed as bobbies, English-style, opened the car doors and pulled Carl and me out of the car. We didn't know what to think. There were a lot of people around, and they put us in a cage on the street.

After a few minutes they opened the cage door and took us in front of an older gentleman with a big white beard. He said, "I am charging you fifty cents for not having a beard." Well, everyone was clapping, and I was red in the face as I was shy with all the crowds. He then gave us a certificate. It was the Sourdough Rendezvous that they have in this town every year

It was quite a scene, especially for just coming into town. But I must say, it was an experience. I liked Whitehorse in those days. I believe it was close to the time that President Kennedy was killed, or shortly after, as they had a walk in his honour.

Carl and I had no trouble getting girls to go out with us; we were both young and good looking and had a beautiful car. I finally got a job at Northland Beverages, a pop factory. I stayed working there for about six months. I was going with a girl named Rita S., and she was a real beauty. She was part Native and I liked her a lot, but it didn't last. Then I started to go out with a Spanish girl. Her dad was in the army and they lived on the army base. I liked her somewhat but the relationship didn't last. I always treated my girlfriends with respect and kindness.

I used to go to a small place near Whitehorse in a lodge there. I would go in and get a soft drink, and they had a parrot there, a bird with beautiful colours, but boy he could swear. Tourists would come in and say *what a beautiful bird* and boy, some of the foul language he would use. I got a kick out of him. I would say to him, "What a pretty bird," and he would say to me, "Don't give me any of that lip, I am not your pretty bird."

I left Whitehorse with Carl and his sister and their dad. They stayed in Revelstoke and I started to thumb a ride to Haney. I got a ride from a guy in a '57 Chevy and he had been drinking. I did not like the way he was swerving all over the road, so I asked him if I could drive as I wasn't drinking. He said okay and he left me off in some small town … I forget the name. It was dark out, so I spotted a church and the door was unlocked. I went to sleep on one of the benches and woke up in the morning. I never touched anything, and I closed the door and started to thumb a ride again. I finally got to where I was going in Haney, which was my foster home with the Vanderveen' s.

While I was with them I met a girl who turned out to be the love of my life, Mary B. She was a beautiful girl with blonde hair. She was sixteen and I was eighteen. I got a job at Rose Croft Nurseries budding and grafting miniature roses, and I was getting seventy-five cents an hour. Mrs. Vanderveen worked not too far from the nursery so I would get a ride with her. We would cross the Fraser River on the Albion ferry and back after work. Mrs. Vanderveen was a great lady, and she always treated me good. I didn't have a car yet so sometimes she let me use hers, and I would take Mary out for a drive. She was beautiful girl who I loved.

After I worked at the nursery for a while, I spotted this 1952 white Chevy. The owner let me make payments. I felt good to have a car of my own.

Behind us on Volker Rd. Haney lived a girl who used to come over to babysit for the Vanderveen's Later she was in a group called the Poppy Family along with Terry Jacks. What a beautiful voice she had.

I would often go over to Gibson's to split and pack shakes, which was hard work, especially packing bundles of shakes out of Haney. Glen took me to Vancouver to get a tattoo, and I got a bird with a ribbon and Mary's name on my arm. It was only five dollars; now it would be a hundred and something. I got the tattoo off an old guy called Captain Ted. He had a shop on Hastings just before Pigeon Park.

While I was away working, I would let Mary use my car. When I got the car I was in Haney away up Dewdney Trunk Road, just past Webster's Corners and I had Murray in the car with me. I was going down a steep hill and I put it in second gear and the motor blew apart, so I told the guy I got it off of and he put another motor in it and it ran good after that.

Years later I saw Mr. Vanderveen in Matsqui Penitentiary. He was a counsellor, but later he became warden of Mission Pen. I miss them both; I think they are gone now. I had a nice room downstairs at their house and Mrs. Vanderveen was a good cook and she fed me well. After a few months I was starting to miss work and losing interest in the job. And I must say, I was deeply in love with Mary. I was her first love and we would go off together in my car and enjoy our time together.

But with my reckless ways it was just a matter of time before we could no longer keep our love for each other together. It started one night when we were at the Swing Inn. After a night of dancing, I was going to take Mary home in my car, but I ran out of gas so instead of using the phone and asking Mary's dad to come and get her we walked to Glen's place. He had an apartment down old 8th Ave. and we stayed there for the night. In the morning we heard a knock-on Glen's door. It was Mary's dad. He knew Glen and suspected we were there but Glen said we weren't. That was not a good thing to do as he was concerned about his daughter and lying like that was an insult to him.

He was downright mad. Anyway, he told me, "I don't want you seeing my daughter anymore," and it really hurt me as I loved Mary so much. Anyway, we saw each other on the sly but it had to end. And I had just got a job with Winter Works in Haney, and so did my two brothers. We were working at a park racking and cleaning up. One day I saw the police car came driving up and I knew that was it. The officer came right over to me and said, "You are under arrest for breaking and entering," and he put the cuffs on me and took me to the police station in Haney.

Mrs. Vanderveen came to see me and she was really upset. She started to cry. The next day I went into court and they read out the charges, and I had no chance of beating them as they had my fingerprints inside the house. I pled guilty, and the magistrate gave me six months definite and nine months indefinite. They had funny sentences in those days.

So off to Oakalla I went, and you know, I never left my prints again—gloves were the norm. I was sad that I had to leave my brothers and my foster parents. The next day I was put in a police car and driven to Oakalla where they put me in the east wing. Then they sent me down to Westgate A, which was still on the Oakalla grounds. They had Westgate B as well; I was there the year before and I worked in the license plate shop making plates. As I was assigned to a tier, to my amazement who did I see? My brother Glen. He was doing a small sentence for theft, and I didn't know he was there. As I got settled in, I ran into a guy I knew. He was angry at me because he thought I was going with his girl, which I knew nothing about. What happened was Ray was going by Garibaldi High School in an institution van and he would throw out love letters to Mary. That was just before Mary and I started going together, and she stopped doing that when we went together but Ray thought she was his girl.

As expected, Glen stuck up for me, and guys knew of Glen's reputation. He was tough as nails. Anyway, Glen and I and Ray got together, and Ray finally said, "You're right, Dennis, I believe you," and that was that. We became friends. Years later I bumped into him in the BC Pen. He said to me, "You know, when that thing happened with Mary, I was packing a shank," and I said I was too. We both laughed. He since has passed on.

While Glen and I were still in Westgate A this guy came onto our tier and right away I knew something was up. After about an hour all these guys started to gather around him, and he was a giant of a man, a weightlifter named Woody... I won't mention his name. I knew most guys but had never seen him before and everyone knew he could handle himself. So anyways, about six guys from our tier started to fight with him and, well, he knocked two guys right out. But my brother had enough, and he said to the guy, "It's not right for all these guys ganging up on him." Glen said to the guy, "Just you and me," so they went at it. Glen was no easy guy to take on, and he was a good street fighter. Well, they were evenly matched and then my brother grabbed a metal weapon and started to wack him with it.

Finally, the guards come rushing in and broke it up. As it ended up, many months later, just about everyone got out of Westgate and we were on the street. Just about all those that were involved in swarming he got them later and they were definitely scared of him, except Glen. One night at a dance hall in Haney my brother and I spotted the big fellow.

He was also at the dance and he spotted me and Glen. He came up to Glen and said, "Glen, I respect you for the way you told the mob to cool it and just the two of us went at it, but I didn't like the way you clobbered me with the metal object. But," he said, "it's over now," and he shook hands with Glen. He said, :I got just about all of the ones that swarmed me," and that was that. I could tell Glen was ready for any action, but it turned out okay. I never saw the big fella again. I heard he is doing fine and living on the Island.

My friend got me a job in Calgary. He was working at West Steel Products, a steel company. Gordy was in Calgary with his wife and he knew I was going up for parole so he asked the boss at West Steel who said, "Tell your friend to come and apply for a job and I will see how it goes."

Back at Westgate, after they had turned me down for parole about an hour passed and they called me back in front of the board and said, "We have decided to grant you a parole." Well, I was happy. Glen was out by now and living in Haney. After a few days I got out and went to Haney until I was to go to Calgary. I still had my car at the Vanderveen' s'. After staying in Haney for a day or two I went to the Coquitlam train station and said goodbye to Mrs. Vanderveen, who had driven me there. I boarded and got a seat, and as I was looking out the window I could see Mrs. Vanderveen waving to me and pointing to someone. It was Mary and her girlfriend. Just as the train was pulling away, I saw Mary and she was crying.

I found out later that she drove at a high speed to see me but it was too late; the train was picking up speed and left the station. I was so upset I put my face in my hands and cried, but I didn't want anyone to see me crying; I was on my way to a new adventure in Calgary. I saw Mary a couple of times years later, but sadly it was over.

On the trip to Calgary I mostly sat in my seat and thought of Mary and our good times. I was sad and also in shock about all the events that happened. I came out of it by thinking I would get a job and do well, and I guess I thought we would see each other again but that was just wishful thinking. Finally, the train pulled into Calgary and I got off with just one suitcase to my name and the start of a new adventure. I had never been to Alberta before. After looking around a bit I saw Wendy, Gordy's wife. She was happy to see me, as I knew her from Hammond when I used to go to her place with Gordy, who was going with her back in those early years

I had a room by myself in the same big house I used to go to at their place in the morning for breakfast. The first day Wendy took me around Calgary as Gordy was working. After I got settled in my room, Gordy come home and was glad to see me. I thanked him for all he had done. He said tomorrow he would take me over to West Steel Products and see the boss. They took me out for dinner and I came home and got some sleep. In the morning I went to West Steel Products with Gordy and I was introduced to the boss. He asked me if I ever worked making culverts and riveting. I said no but I could learn. He asked me if I could start tomorrow or start now, and I said I could start right now and he liked that.

He said, "You're hired," so I punched in with my card and started to punch holes in metal hinge pieces. As I was punching the holes in the hinge with the foot pedal, I didn't take my fingers out of the way fast enough and it come down on my fingers. Boy, did it hurt, and as I was sitting on the stool looking at my fingers from the pain of it I fell over backwards and landed on the concrete floor. Workers came and helped me to my feet. The boss came and said, "You better go home and rest," but I said "No, it's okay," and I went back to work.

The boss liked that too, and that was my start at West Steel Products. After that they put me on riveting culverts on day shift. My first payday I went over to the Shamrock Hotel and they cashed our checks for us, and we had a few beers. It felt good to be working. I was still on parole and had to report to the parole officer once a month. After a few months they put me on night shift, and I kind of liked it. I stayed at West Steel for about six months. I used to walk all over Calgary on my days off. I felt so happy, and I was young and dressed well. I went out with a few girls but nothing serious.

One thing I used to do was go down to the east end and go into a place called the Chicken Inn. They never sold beer or hard stuff, but I could bring in a micky in the inside pocket of my jacket. When I walked in all dressed up in a good suit, the people in there all took a good look at me; they were all negro and they liked my style. I would sit at a table and order a pop and a package of cigarettes. They had good music playing, and I would secretly pour myself a drink. I went in there a few times and they always treated me good. It closed a bit later.

I really liked Gordy. He was a year older than me and had been through a few foster homes, as well as his brother Doug. While I was still at the same rooming house as him we went to the Shower of Stars in Calgary. There was Bobby Rydell, Fabian and Brian Hyland, to mention a few. The Beatles were just coming along with their music, as this was 1964.

I had been coming into work late, and one day I said to the boss, "I had better get a new alarm clock," and he said, "Yes, you had better get a new job," so that was that for West Steel Products. I went to the office and got my cheque and I was gone. I moved out of the rooming house and moved into a place down on 17th Ave. and 11th Street with Gordy's brother, who was working at Barny's Kentucky Fried Chicken. He got me a job there. I started on the pots etc. and worked my way to the grill.

Gordy sold me his '52 Chevy, and it was a great-looking car and I kept in good shape. I enjoyed working at Barny's. It was hectic at times, and one day I had so many orders. I shouldn't have got mad, but I let it get to me, and anyway, I just up and quit. I regretted it after, but it was too late. Gordy's brother wasn't too happy with me, as he got the job for me. It was getting close to when my parole was over, and I wanted to go back to my hometown of Maple Ridge.

I was starting to go back to my old ways of making money, and by now I was quite up on what to do and what not to do in regard to burglaries or B&Es. Gloves were now very important, as I got caught by leaving my prints behind before. People often would ask me how I would get into different places. I had a few ways: one was to get up onto the roof and go in the skylight or vent. It was dangerous, as you wouldn't want to fall off, and you had to not only get up but you had to make it down also, or once you were in you could go out the main door.

I did not really like doing family dwellings; it just didn't sit right with me, and you could get shot or really beat up. I am not proud of doing these things, but that's the way we were brought up, as hunger has a way of getting one in difficulty. I could and did fall back to crime when I needed money. Anyways, the day came when my parole was over, and I decided to go back home to Yale and Haney. On the day I was leaving, I took some money that was in the house where the two of us stayed, and it didn't belong to me. I took my suitcase, bought a case of beer, went to the bus station and got a ticket to Haney.

In those days you could bring beer onto the bus as long as you didn't open it. There were ashtrays on the arm of the seat and one could smoke on board. I quietly opened a beer and had a cigarette, but I made the mistake of drinking too much and I went to sleep. I woke up to a police officer saying, "Wake up." He took me off the bus, along with my suitcase and some remaining beer.

So off we went to the police station in Banff. They took everything off me and put me in a cell. I still had some of the money left, so in the morning, me and a couple of other guys were marched down the street, handcuffed, to the courthouse. They gave me a fine for drinking in a public place— I think it was thirty-five dollars. Back at the station they took the fine money from my effects and I was put out on the street. I still had my bus ticket and I had to wait for a bus. I met a woman on the bus who told me she owned a motel in Kamloops. I think she wanted me to come with her. But they had a bus change, and those going to Kamloops had to get on a different one. I stayed on the one I was on.

I looked at her as my bus was leaving, and she had the saddest look on her face. I never forgot that. I did see her a few years later in the Haney bus depot and said hello to her. I thought about it later and I guess that was the way she met younger men. You see, all my life I respected all woman, and I was very shy, otherwise I would have gone with her.

I went to Haney and went back to the last foster home I would ever be in. I stayed at the home till early 1965. After I finished with all the foster homes, I went and lived with Murray at the Morse home on St. Ann Street. We rented a room upstairs, and it was quite comfortable. Murray and I shared the rent. It was only about $175 a month, and in those days one could go into Super Value and get a buggy full of groceries for twenty-five or thirty dollars, but not now.

At this time Murray and I had a 1949 Ford, and you could get a car for $100 or less. In May of 1965 I started to go with a beautiful girl from Silverdale. Bernice Taylor was her name, and she had kisses sweeter than wine. I liked her a lot. Murray and I met a guy we knew from the joint named Ben, and he loved his beer. One day the three of us got the big idea to go to Prince George. Well, we loaded up the '49 Ford and off we went. We had credit cards that we had got illegally, and we used them for gas and tires etc.

We stopped at our grandmother's to say hello, and she made us something to eat. We stayed overnight and were on our way in the morning. She was a grand lady, that's for sure. We took turns driving and ended up in Prince George at around two in the afternoon. Ben was eager to get a few beers in him, so we went into the Columbus Hotel, and who do we see but our friend Bonnie. Well, we had about six or so beers each, and I think Ben had more; he was quite a drinker. Then we went to her place for dinner. It was about six in the evening when we started back to Haney. It is a long drive, so we said our goodbyes to Bonnie, and we were on our way.

I was driving and it started to get dark. As we were going along the highway between Prince George and Quesnel, we spotted a grocery store, and being out of cigarettes we decided to help ourselves. So we entered the store and took cigarettes, cash and something to eat. As I came out of the store I ran right into a German Shepherd dog. I figured he was going to attack me, but he just wagged his tail and sniffed me, so I gave him a piece of jerky. While he was eating the treat, we made it to our car and off we went.

We had the 1949 Ford painted black, and it was hard to see, which was just what we wanted. Murray took over driving and Ben was drinking his beer. I was happy to puff away on a cigarette. Whenever a police officer saw us and the car, he would pull us over, so we had to be careful. After a few hours we pulled into Spences Bridge and got more gas. We was taking the Fraser Canyon down to Haney and we were just outside Boston Bar when we saw a place we were interested in. We parked the car a little ways away from it, and as I said, the car was completely black so it was hard to see. We walked up to check out the place when a guy came from the back house with a rifle. Well, we all split up; Ben and I went towards the car, but Murray went the other way towards the highway and a tunnel. Ben and I heard two or three shots as they echoed off the inside of the Yale tunnel. I asked my brother later what happened, and he said, "I bolted from the place and ran through the tunnel when I heard the first shot and then the second until I came to the end of the tunnel. On the left I dove into some bushes and after that I heard nothing, so then I went down to where our car was parked." We left towards Yale and we never saw one RCMP car on the road.

Of course, we stopped at Yale, as we always did, and we had a beer and a cigarette even though it was four in the morning. I was happy my brother didn't get shot or go over the cliff.

It's a dangerous way to live. The three of us ended back in Haney, and I was happy to see my girlfriend Bernice Taylor. I would drive out to Silverdale and stay with her for a day or so.

One day the police showed up and charged all three of us guys with false pretense and using stolen credit cards. Murray got five months and I got the same, and Ben … I don't know what happened to him. I never saw him again till 1968. I went to Oakalla and ended up down at Westgate. One day I went to Warden's Court for refusing to work, and the warden gave me seven days in the Hole. As I was leaving, instead of having them put the cuffs on me and take me to the Hole, I ran down to where the tiers were and the metal trays were stacked. I started to throw them at the guards. Well, they finally cornered me and took me to the floor and handcuffed me. They then dragged me all the way to the Hole, which was under the old cow barn. It was a terrible place.

They put me in a cell, and I caused so much trouble that they took me to the hospital and I saw Doc Richman. I liked the doctor and he always treated me good. He gave me some pills and put me in the padded cell. The hospital was the old Young Offenders Unit and it was up in the main part of the prison where the gallows were. They hanged quite a few inmates up there in the early years, and Doc Richmond was the doctor that checked them after they were hanged.

South Wing was also death row, and I was in there along with Murray and Glen and my father. They had enough of me and sent me to the Criminally Insane Ward at Colony Farm. It was for people that were doing time and were mentally disturbed. I was fine but I wanted to put on an act to get good medication and good canteen etc. Well, once I got there, I didn't like it at all. I got to know this football player who played for the BC Lions. He was doing time for murder, but he heard voices and could become violent. He beat up a lot of male nurses. But they got him in time. When I used to catch the ball for him out in the yard he was six-foot-five and weighed two hundred and some odd pounds, but in time he was down to 120 pounds. They gave him shock treatment and what I heard was he just whittled away to nothing. I don't know what ever became of him. I will always remember him kicking the football; it went away up in the air and when it came down it was like a rocket. I tried to catch it every time, and he liked me for trying my best. Poor guy.

I finally told the head doctor that I was just putting on an act, and he said, "I figured as much" and put me down as a malingerer, meaning using mental illness as a crutch. He said, "I am sending you back to Oakalla, and don't try that again." I was lucky they didn't give me the shock treatment. I saw how they gave it; I watched a friend of mine get the treatment, and it was not a pretty thing to see. After he came out of the room he didn't know where he was or who he was. I don't know if they still give that treatment.

Anyway, I was shipped back to Oakalla. I had three weeks left of my time to go. I was in the hospital in Oakalla before they sent me to a unit, and I looked out the window and saw Glen and Murray walking from the main prison to Westgate. I yelled to them both and I was glad to see them even though it was at a distance. My girlfriend was writing to me while I was in.

I was released and went back home to Haney. the police were watching me; I guess they thought I was up to no good, which was the case some of the time. It was getting close to fall of 1965, and Murray was going around with Sandy and I was still with Bernice. I still have the letters she wrote me while I was in Oakalla. She was a very pretty girl, and her parents were very kind to me. I believe Glen was in the BC Pen at this time. It was his second time there and he told me when he was in the Pen that one day he was standing in the dome to get his medication and he heard someone behind him say hello. He turned around and our dad was standing there. He said a few things to Glen, like asked him how he was, and that was that. Glen didn't get along with our dad, who was doing two and a half years for what they called a "dirty spoon," meaning there were washings in the spoon after he got through fixing heroin.

The drug bulls kicked the door in just after my dad had finished fixing but he didn't wash the spoon out. So, he went to court and the judge gave him the two and a half years for the offence. Another time I was in the Hotel Strand with my dad, and I had asked him before why he put the dresser in front of the door when he was fixing. Well, I found out about a week later when we were in the Strand and he finished his business and washed out the spoon. In came the door and dresser and at first it surprised me; they didn't see my dad at first, so they grabbed me. How they did it in those days was they would grab you around the throat so you didn't swallow. A lot of guys kept a balloon in their mouth with the heroin in it. It could be dangerous, as I knew drug users who died from being strangled. Anyway, they didn't find anything, and they let my dad and I go.

I never used when I was in my teens, as my dad sold everything to get a high and I did not like the way he treated my mom, so I was against heroin. I used most of the so-called soft drugs and drank a bit. Getting back to Hastings Street, at one time it was a great place, with beautiful buildings and a lot of pubs and nightclubs. To see it now is just terrible. My dad and I were down at the Blue Eagle Café in the late fifties, and the Plaza Café was right beside it. In these two cafes, one could get just about anything as a lot of pushers hung out there. My dad knew most of them. I talked to guys years later and my dad was well liked. One day my dad and I were in the Plaza Café, and my dad said, "See that guy there?"

I said yes, and my dad said, "Do you recognize him?" I said no, I didn't think so, and when he told me who it was, I couldn't believe it. I had listened to his music when his band first came out. I won't name them. I asked my dad what he was doing there and my dad said, "He is looking to score, and he is a user." I couldn't believe it.

Over time I saw a few singers that would show up downtown. East Hastings was great in the fifties, and people looked out for one another. The Broadway Hotel was a good bar if you were looking for work such as logging; you just had to ask around and you could get hired on with some logging outfit. The trouble with scoring downtown was they had a drug squad that would scare the most hardened drug user. Across the street from the Plaza Café was an old building and the drug squad would be up there with binoculars and would see who was selling and who was buying. Then they would then rush into the café and bust whoever they could. I saw the drug squad jump a girl who had tried to swallow twenty-five caps in a balloon when she saw them coming. Well, the balloon got stuck in her throat and she choked to death. It didn't help that they had their hands around her throat. There were so many drug overdoses. A lot of people I knew went that way. Seeing as I never used, guys got me to hold onto their money because the drug squad would know they were selling and would confiscate all their money. The guys I was holding for knew I was honest and would never short them, and they would pay me for doing this. My reputation was important to me, and I was liked by many. My whole family was liked. If people were asked "Do you know the Storrings?" they would say we were solid people.

One night me and my two brothers were in Vancouver down at the Plaza Café and we saw a guy we knew who owed Glen some money. He gave Glen what he owed him, and I guess the drug squad was watching and thought Glen was getting drugs from the guy. The three of us got on a bus and went over the Granville Street Bridge, and as we were on our way over I thought I saw these two men in a car. As it turned out they were drug bulls and the four of them boarded the bus at a stop over the bridge. They all pretended to put money in the coin machine.

We were sitting about halfway down, so down they came. I was the first to get strangled then Murray, but they missed Glen as he sat in the back of the bus. The people on the bus didn't know what to think. When I saw them coming, I stiffened up so it wasn't so hard on my neck, as I had been through it before. They took us off the bus, searched us and started to lip off to us. Well, Glen didn't care for that and he told them he would take them all on. They thought better of that and told us to get lost so we went back to the café and told Wally what happened. He just said, "Right on, Glen."

We spent the night walking around and the police stopped us. You should have seen the money as well as pockets full of change. The cop said, "Now where did you get all this change? Let me guess, you were playing poker," and Murray said, "How did you know?"

The cop said, "Now, don't get smart with me. I know you, Storrings, and you are well known to us for your B&Es." They took us to the Vancouver Police Station and let us go in the morning. They kept the change as a few places had reported the B&Es but they couldn't prove anything. We went back to Haney and I broke up with Bernice.

My brothers and I had a nice Christmas at the Morse home and in come 1966. I got into trouble again and ended up in Chilliwack Camp. I think I was doing nine months. When Murray was out and I got out from the nine months, we went back and forth to Vancouver.

While I was in, Murray was living in Haney, and he bought a nice Pontiac ragtop, an American model. When I got out, we went to Vancouver in the car and one night we were driving around and decided to check this garage out. We had a flat tire and we didn't have a tire wrench. As we were looking around, a police car came flying up so we both hid under a parked car. We heard a cop say, "Come out of there," and he put the flashlight on us. Well, we had no choice but to come out. He said, "What are you doing?" and we said we were looking for a tire wrench as our tire was going flat. Lucky for us it was true. He checked our car out and frisked us and let us go. Somehow we got the tire fixed and went back to our hotel in Vancouver.

We were hanging around Van for a while and one day Murray and I got stoned on strong pills and we were drinking, A one-armed guy called Shorty turned us on to the pills, and they were bad. They were for bad nerves, something like Valium, but mixed with booze, they were not my thing. Anyway, I got the big idea to drive to Haney by myself. Well, I got to Port Moody and had to turn around and go back to Van. Close to Vancouver I smashed the car up; I ran right into a parked car. I got charged with undo care and attention, and I split my lip open. After getting out of the hospital I went and saw my brother at the hotel, and he wasn't too happy about his car getting wrecked. We never got it back—so much for that. And we lost all our belongings in the trunk. Crime was a way of life for me.

The New Fountain hotel was on Cordova Street, and it was famous in its day. I first went there around 1967 and I really liked the bar. There were all types in the place: miners, lawyers, drag queens, leather freaks, drug users, drug sellers, known singers—people from all walks of life. You see, in those days people looked out for each other, at least in the Fountain. There were other bars that were dangerous to go into.

I was sitting in the Fountain one day having a beer when the waiter threw this guy out. Well, he came back after a while with a pump shotgun and started shooting. People were hitting the floor, and I didn't even move, as I was taught not to show any kind of emotion. I think he was shot by police.

We stayed for a while and then went back to Haney as we always did; it was our safe place. One day Murray and I got some money from welfare and we went into Vancouver to live for a while. After we got into Vancouver on the bus we went up to Granville Street and got a room at the St. Helens, I believe. But we also drank in the Broadway Hotel down on Hastings. You could play pool there. It can be quite brutal on the streets with no money for food etc. but I went back to Haney and worked for farmers haying etc.

If I wasn't in jail, I was working in the sawmills. At times I would collect welfare even though I wasn't in foster homes anymore. I would supplement my income by doing crime. You might ask, How come you did so much time in the joints?" Well, you see, in those days one might get away with half a dozen things but when they catch you with one thing they knock you out of the ballpark, so to speak, and the sentences they gave out were big. You got life for heavy drug busts, seven years for breaking and entering etc.

I am writing this so people can get an idea of how it was in those days. I stayed by myself, and one day I just got sick of Vancouver and went back to Haney. Glen picked me up and we all went to work at the Peat Bog. It was coming into early '67 and there was an explosion of good bands such as Janis, Morrison and CCR. A lot of them were just starting out. It was a fun time and we all started buying record players and records. Woodstock was a big event too.

In 1967 I met Murray in Haney and we lived together in a little house in Pitt Meadows. Glen was there too, and we eventually split up but Murray and I stayed together. One day we thought we would go up to our grandmother's place for a while. Grandma always liked to see us. Murray and I stayed with her for about a week, and after a while we went to Hope and went over to the Super Value. We got some groceries for our grandmother, as she fed us while we were there. We put out our thumbs and got a ride in no time. It is fourteen or fifteen miles to Yale.

The guy that gave us a ride knew our grandmother, and he was just going to Texas Lake but that was okay. The lake had leeches or blood suckers, as they called them. There were quite a few in the lake in those days but it was a beautiful spot, just a grand place. Murray and I started to walk from there; it was about five miles to Yale. When Murray and I were ten or eleven we used to have rock fights up at Yale, and one day we were hiding in the bush throwing rocks at each other when I heard my grandmother calling, "Your mother is here." Well, we never did that again; one could lose an eye. It was really nice to see our mom.

Anyway, getting back to 1967. My grandmother was saying she would like to leave us a plot of land up across the highway and up on the mountain. She had five plots on the mountain in Yale. Well, my uncle was in the next room and could hear and suddenly he said we better leave and we could get a ride with his friend to Alberta, which we did. I loved my uncle, but he was just mad, I guess.

We never did get the property, which was our mother's share. Don't get me wrong, I love all my family members, and he gave us forty dollars for our trip as we had to have some money on us if we were going to Edmonton. So, we said goodbye to our grandmother, and we were on our way. I remember that a song come on the radio called "Hey Paula" by Paul and Paula. I always remember the song; I don't know why, other than it was a good song. It started to get dark, so the guy got a motel room and after having something to eat we went to sleep. In the morning he bought us breakfast, and we were on the road again. As we went further, we ran into a lot of snow, and when we got into Edmonton it was very cold.

We said goodbye to the guy that gave us a ride and thanked him. We went to the main street and boy was it cold; we could only walk a few blocks and our ears were burning so we would go into a store and warm up. We were looking for a girl we knew, but we couldn't find her. We thought we better go back to Haney or Vancouver as it was too darn cold for us in Edmonton. We got the bus to Kamloops, as that's all we could afford.

This was the end of '66 and going onto1967. We had enough money to get a room at the old Plaza Hotel and we were on the second floor. We went out to do what we do, and we got a case of beer, which was $2.52 a case. After a while this guy picked us up, and he had a 1957 Chevy two-door hard top. The front seats were one seat, not bucket seats, and I sat next to the driver and then Murray sat beside me. We were going down the Fraser Canyon and he said, "Would you two like a drink of wine?" and we said sure, okay. We started to think better of the idea when he started to weave all over the road and finally he said, "can one of you drive?"

I said, "I have been driving since I was ten years old," and he dropped us off in Yale. We made it to Chilliwack and then we got a room at a hotel and broke into five places. We made the mistake of throwing tags out the window onto a landing. We used our real names at the hotel, as we were not thinking of doing anything wrong at the time. The next morning, I went to the bus depot and all the people in there were talking about all the stores that had been broken into. They were saying there must have been a gang of people, and I asked for two tickets to Vancouver. They didn't even look at me twice.

I went back to where Murray was. We had all these black bags full of things. In those days you could smoke on the bus. People didn't look twice at us, as we always dressed well and were clean cut. On the bus in the 1960s there wasn't as much security on the bus as there is today. So away we went into Vancouver.

I always remember the old bus depot in Vancouver. As we pulled into the station, we thought we were in the clear, but little did we know they would be looking for us real soon. We got a room at the old Strand Hotel—it's still there, I believe. There was no bar, just rooms. We dressed up in some new clothes and I dyed my hair blonde. Murray didn't bother with his hair colour, but like I said, there were all kinds of people in the place. I knew a lot of people who drank in the hotels. After a couple of days we were in the hotel and I was standing near the cigarette machine drinking a beer. Murray was using the cigarette machine, and suddenly two detectives come up to him and say, "What is your name?"

Murray tried to give him a different name, but the detective said, "I know you're Murray Storrings. Put your hands behind your back," and he cuffed him and took him away. I thought *boy they didn't even look at me*. I guess it was because I dyed my hair and was a sharp-dressed man. I stayed around the hotel for a day and then I thought I had better go to the room. As I put my hand on the door knob and looked up I saw there was a light on in the room and I knew we didn't leave the light on. I thought *oh boy* and I started to walk away. Well, it was too late; I only got a few steps away and I heard "Stop right there."

I could have run, but it was too late. Two detectives grabbed me and said, "Dennis Storrings, you are under arrest," and they handcuffed me. One officer said, "You fooled me the first time with your blonde hair, but I got you now." They took me to the Vancouver Police Station and the next day they shipped me off to Oakalla. I always pleaded not guilty, even as a young kid. One thing I was happy about was I would get to see my brother again even if it was in prison.

Oakalla was an old prison built in 1914 but the prison down behind it was built in the late 1800s. I went into the old jail with my gang boss who was a guard in Oakalla. I was in the plumbing shop. They had a huge farm, also, with lots of animals.

As I was going into where they process you, I could hear someone say, "Storrings, how are you? Long time, no see." It was a guy I knew from HCI. Then a guard took me out of the cell, and I went up to the desk. If you had money, you could buy tobacco and papers etc. Then they took you in for a shower and sprayed you to make sure you didn't have anything like crabs or any other critters on you. Then you were given prison clothing and taken through the tunnel to another part of the prison I went up to the desk and asked the guard if I could get in the same cell as my brother, at this time they had two to a cell. When I started in the jails it was only one to a cell.

The guard said, "Sure, Storrings," and I went up to the third tier and there was my brother. I couldn't believe it. I threw my blankets on the top bunk and we had a smoke and talked. Murray said we were charged with five counts of breaking and entering and theft. He said he knew a lawyer who was very good; he was first in his class but he liked the booze a little too much.

Anyway, we had to go back and forth to Chilliwack, as in those days you had to show up once a week. We had to come through the tunnel again and put on our street clothes and then we were put in a big holding cell. When they called our names, they would yell, "The Two Storrings brothers," and a guard would open the big cell and we would go to the desk. There were two police officers from Chilliwack who cuffed us in front and took us up to the main gate and down the big granite stairs to a waiting police car. We got in the back and they drove up and out the old gate house and onto the highway in Burnaby then went east to Chilliwack. We never spoke to the officers on the ride to Chilliwack.

If the police didn't bother us, we wouldn't bother them, and this went on for months. You see, in those days the courts would not give you bail, or if they did it was so high you couldn't make it anyways. Our lawyer used to come out to the prisons and we would go over things. We got Larry, our lawyer, though Legal Aid. Murray would play poker and supplied us with tobacco and he still good at poker today, I think we waited for trial in the South Wing this time for almost a year.

After about six months of going back and forth to the courts in Chilliwack, one day we went for just a remand. We were down at the desk in Oakalla and the two officers that were there to pick us up started to get rough and handcuffed us behind our back. Well, we let them know we didn't like it. Even the old-time guards didn't like the way they were treating us, as we kept to ourselves and the old-time guards liked us. You see, being in a van handcuffed behind your back can be dangerous, as there was just a small wooden bench to sit on and when the cop went around corners you could get hurt flying all over the place. But we held on, and also the vent was open on the roof and pouring rain was getting us wet. They did it just to bug us and to make us plead guilty.

Anyway, we got to Chilliwack and into the jail and three officers started to push us around, which started and all-out fight. They didn't like that so they just stopped and put us in the cell block. They had it in for us. They had about three cells with double bunks, and we had to wait for the next morning to go to court. There was a big space to walk around after you were let out of your cell and there was a window with bars on it that caught our eye. Outside the window was an alley, and the idea turned into a thought as we turned it into a possibility. All we needed was a hacksaw blade….

So as the month went by, we met an ex-police officer who was in the west wing awaiting trial for bank robbery. They were on to him but had no evidence as of yet. One day he went to Vernon and robbed a bank. He had been a beat cop down on Hastings, and him and his partner used to walk the street on foot and arrest people who were breaking the law. He was a big man, about six foot three, two hundred and thirty pounds. He liked me and my brother, and I found him to be a likeable guy. A lot of guys thought they were going to beat him up, but he was a strong man and they left him alone. After the trouble with the police in Chilliwack, we got hold of an MLA and all the trouble stopped.

The Chilliwack ordeal, all three of us were transferred to the south wing where the gallows were and where guys went that were waiting to go to the Penitentiary. We waited for close to a year before we went to trial, but in the end we got off with time spent. My brother got out right away but I had to finish off a nine-month sentence relating to another charge. I said goodbye to my brother and I was sent back to the south wing and then sent to Westgate A. After I finished the nine months I went to live in Vancouver. I got a room at a hotel where the rooms were not that big but were fairly clean. It was going on to 1968 then and on Hastings Street there were quite a few clubs one could go to and have a good time. One such club was up a long flight of stairs, and a lot of people would go there after the bars would close. It had a juke box and you could bring in some booze but you had to be careful as it was against the law and they could arrest you for having booze in a public place.

So one night I was up at the club and the police patted me down and found a mickey of rye on me. Well, they took me away to the police station and the next morning I was in my cell and they called my name and said, "Someone paid your fine." The fine was fifty dollars, and I didn't have the money myself. It made me wonder who paid it. I walked out of the station and there was a friend, a little redhead girl I knew from Trail.

She said, "I paid your fine and don't worry about paying me back." I was twenty-three and she was twenty-one. I thanked her, and we went to the hotel for a drink. She was in Vancouver for a few months and was wearing a beautiful leopard-skin coat and she had beautiful red hair. She said her mom worked at Eaton's and her dad worked at the smelter in Trail. She was kind and I liked her. After some months went by, Linda and I moved in together.

She was working, and we got along good. I was working at the Palms Hotel on Hastings St. It had no bar, just rooms, and I was on the desk. When people wanted a room I would give them one and charge them. I think at the time a room was thirty-five dollars. I worked night shift and day shift. Linda and I met a couple; I will call them M.D. and P.B., and they were our drinking companions. Phil asked Linda and me if we wanted to go to Prince George with them, and we said sure. Phil had this other guy that had a car and was going there also.

It was snowing hard and we all got into the car and off we all went. As we went by my grandmother's place, I could see her sitting at her kitchen table as she always did. I was going to stop and say hello, but we had to get going and be on our way. It felt good to have my girl beside me and I was looking forward to our trip. We finally pulled into Quesnel and got a bite to eat, and then we started on the road from Quesnel to Prince George. It was dangerous, especially in the winter; a friend of mine lost his life on that highway, but we made it. We pulled into town and said goodbye to the guy that drove us. Linda and I got a room at a fairly good hotel, the Croft Hotel, and so did Phil and his woman. We got a badly needed rest and got up in the morning.

We stayed in Prince George for a few months, and while Linda was working one night, I met my dad. He was in a car with a friend of his. I came up to the car and said hello. Instead of saying, "Hello, Dennis," he said, "Do you have any money you can give me?" I had not seen my dad for twenty years and it upset me the way he acted. I knew what he wanted the money for, as he was using at the time. Little did I know I would never see him again, but Glen would run into him in the BC Penitentiary.

So anyway, Linda and I stayed in Prince George for a while longer, but our two friends went back to Vancouver. I was in the Canadian Hotel with my cousin Charlie and he started a fight with the waiter; well, instead of taking it to Charlie, the waiter knocked me out cold. That was the last time I drank with Charlie. He was wild, and always getting into fights.

Linda and I stayed in Prince George for a while longer and then we decided to go to Winnipeg. We took the bus there and got off at the station, and it was cold. Winnipeg is a nice city; we were down on Portage and Main, a well-known street. Linda and I went down to the old Winnipeg Hotel and got a room for a couple of days. We stayed in Winnipeg for a month or two. After that we left for Calgary, and I didn't mind it. I had been there in 1964. So, after a month we decided we would go to Trail, to stay at her Mom and Dad's, and I was there for about two weeks. I got a job working for the Town, cleaning the parks and the streets uptown. I was racking in the park one day when I saw this guy doing the same thing. I called to him, "Hey, Nelly," and he said, "Hello, Dennis." It was the guy from New Haven who put the cigarettes in my meal at suppertime while I was in the Hole. I never forgot that and I thanked him. About a week later I heard he was killed in a car crash and I felt bad.

I liked the old part of Trail. A lot of houses were built on the hill sides. One day Linda and I decided we were going back to Vancouver, so I quit my job and we said goodbye to her parents and got a ride to the Castlegar Airport. We got two tickets to Vancouver and off we went. I forget how long it took, but we finally got into Vancouver and we took a taxi to the hotel. As we walked in the door, we saw our friends and we got a great welcome.

Linda and I stayed in Vancouver for a few months and then she left to go to the States and years later seen her for the last time in Vancouver After a month or so I got charged with theft and got five months in Oakalla. I was sent to the trailers down by the cow barns, which was for inmates who were getting close to release. One night I did some drugs and overdosed and Murray called for help at the hospital. They came and pumped some stuff in me, and it brought me back and that was the last time I overdosed.

My brother moved back to Haney, and I stayed in Vancouver. I was living mostly on the street so I moved back to Haney. This was now 1970. After a while, Murray and I moved in together to one of the motels in uptown Haney, and one night I walked into the Haney Hotel and saw Gordy and his girlfriend. I had known her since she was eleven, and I knew all her family. She was a great person, or I should say *is* a great person as she is still doing well. Gordy was killed in a car crash.

I was charged with pot and sent to the Pen, and I went to RD, receiving and discharge, and made my way to the fish tier. New inmates coming in were put on a tier away from the other inmates. You had to watch out for guys who preyed on other inmates. The first day on the fish tier after coming back to my cell I found magazines and a few chocolate bars etc. I had heard of this before and was wise to it. What I did was I just left them there, and in a day or so they were gone. I never bothered with the gay crowd in the institutions.

I eventually moved to the B side of the east wing and went to work in the paint shop. Coming back from the shops you had to go through a metal detector in case you were carrying a shank, meaning a knife or worse. Murray would come in to visit the odd time.

After I was halfway into my two years; I went down to the gym to watch a movie. The funny thing is, I still remember the name of it: *Deliverance.* You see, in the gym there were chairs all set up in rows and about sixty inmates, for the tier I was on, and then the next night a different tier went and so on. Anyway, they turned the lights out and started the movie and after about thirty minutes we heard a commotion and the lights come on. You see there were guard towers in every corner of the gym, and the guards were armed with rifles. I looked over and there was a guy lying on the floor about forty to fifty feet from me, and he was twitching. I could see blood and gray brain matter all over and it was an awful sight. But the guards didn't see anything, so they turned the lights off again.

Well, the guy came over and wacked the guy again using a steel bar, and this time the guards saw what was going on and started to search everyone and send the searched ones back to their cells. As it turned out, it was a lover's quarrel. A big French guy and his partner were splitting up, and the big guy didn't want that to happen, so he decided to kill his partner. It was an awful sight. I saw a lot of that type of thing go on, and at close quarters sometime. The outcome of this tragedy was the big Frenchman was sent to the Hole and awaited trial for killing his lover, but before he could get to trial, he hung himself.

I didn't go to Matsqui this time. I stayed in the old penitentiary until I got out in '71. Getting out was always a wonderful feeling; it's hard to explain, but I will try. When you first start your sentence the time goes slow, but after you get a year or so in, you can start to see the light at the end of the tunnel. Some guys, when they get down to ninety days, mark the days off on the calendar. I did myself, and the night before you get out, the time goes slow. You hardly sleep, and when the morning comes, boy, it's a good feeling. They call you and you roll up your blankets and things and down to R and D you go. They give you your street clothes and the money you have saved. In this case I had $200. The guard opened the main gate and out I went. What a rush. I walked out to Columbia Street.

In the early days, they gave you a suit that was made in the penitentiary. I walked up Columbia Street to the bus depot or what I thought was the bus depot. I asked a cab driver where the depot was and, well, he looked at me strange and said, "Where have you been? They moved it about three miles down the road." I felt kind of stupid, but he asked me where I was going and I said to my hometown of Maple Ridge. Then I thought better of it, and I told the cab driver to take me over to the Turf Hotel in Newton.

I arrived at the Turf and paid the fare and gave him a tip. As I was getting out, he said, "How long did you do in the Pen?" and he laughed and said, "I have been there too." I thanked him and he said to have a good day and try to stay out of those places. I said

I would do my best. I went inside and got myself a nice cold beer. It sure tasted good. I phoned my friend MJ who I was in the pen with and who introduced me to the girl who was writing to me for the last two years. He showed up and we had a few beers and talked a bit. After that he drove me to the girl's apartment, and I said goodbye.

I rang the doorbell, but the girl wasn't there. The baby sitter said she was down at the Flamingo Hotel, so I phoned the bar and got a hold of my girl. She told me to take a cab to the Flamingo, so I did. I walked in and saw her and another girl sitting at a table, and when she saw me, she gave me a big hug and a kiss. We had a beer and then took a taxi to her apartment. the other girl came in also. They were sitting at the table and taking something out of a balloon. I knew right away what it was. It was heroin. They both did a hit and asked me if I wanted some, and I said no thanks. I was a user so I never could figure out why I said no. I guess I wanted to stay away from it all but things didn't go like I wanted them to go.

This was a turning point in my life of sadness, heartbreak and violence. I wish I could go back and change it, but I can't. At that time both my brothers were in Maple Ridge and staying out of trouble. I settled in and I got a job at a mill in Surrey, and things were going well until we started to use heroin and then things started to go downhill. I was charged with the robbery, and the judge gave me six years in the Pen. I went back to Oakalla for a few days, and then they shipped me over to the BC Pen. I was put on 4 B in the east wing. I was there for a month or so and they told me I was going to Matsqui Prison.

This part of the story is my favourite because it is when I met my dear wife. I got into Matsqui and was assigned to Unit 2. This was the middle part of 1973. I kept my old number, which was 5914. When Matsqui first opened in 1965, my dad was on the first load. I became cleaner on Unit 2. One day my friend said his wife worked at an old-age home and she was friends with this girl that worked there too. She asked this girl if she would be interested in coming into Matsqui and visiting a guy so she said okay. My friend gave me her name and I put her on my visiting list. After a week they okayed her; they had to check because if you had a criminal record you weren't allowed into the institution.

But Barb was a Christian girl and a good worker and came from a good family. She was twenty at the time, and I will always remember the day she came into the visiting area. I couldn't believe how beautiful she was. I was ten years older than her. My friend and I were called down to the visiting area and in came his wife and Barb, and we were introduced. It was quite crowded in the visiting area, and with me being shy and all the other visitors looking at the new girl, I didn't know what to say. Lucky for me, Barb said, "Would you like to go out in the yard?" Boy, was I happy she mention that to me .

Out in the yard there were tables and chairs and you could be alone, pretty well. We talked and got to feeling quite well. Barb said she just got a nice car, a Nova, and after an hour the visits were over, and we went back inside. As we were saying goodbye, my friend said, "Oh come on, give her a kiss," so I did and she had kisses sweeter than wine. I felt so good, and she asked me if I wanted her to come back in the afternoon. This was the morning visit.

My friend and I walked back to the units and it felt like I was walking on a cloud. He said, "What do you think?" and I could hardly talk. I said, I have never felt so good." And he said that was good. I thank my friend's wife so much for introducing me to my wife.

As the months went by and turned into a couple of years, we were in love and saw each other just about every other day with her coming in to visit me. We joined the Christian group and later the Exceptional Children's group who looked after developmentally delayed children from Woodlands School. They would come into the institution three times a week. It was hard work, but we all liked the program, and we eventually were on the series *W-5* with the kids. It did me a world of good, and it made me come out of my shell. You had to be screened to get into the program, as they didn't want any bad inmates in the group.

I went in front of the parole board and was granted an escorted pass for eight hours so my wife and I went up to Yale to visit with my grandmother with a guard. My grandmother said to the guard, "Now let me make you a nice cup of tea and we can talk for a while." We asked the guard if we could walk down to the old cemetery, which was only five minutes away, and he hesitated. My grandmother said, "Oh, let the kids go for a bit so they can get a chance to be alone." Well, she gave him a nice piece of apple pie and a cup of tea and he said, "Okay, but don't be too long."

Off we went and spent some time together, but we were longer than we thought, and on our way back we saw him coming. I can't blame him, as it's his job to watch us. I guess he thought we took off, but we wouldn't have done that. Time was up so we said goodbye to my grandmother. The guards really liked her so he put a good report in for us. The next time we got an unescorted eight-hour pass. You see, you have to work your way up slowly and not get into any trouble and have a good work record.

In the visiting area there were a lot of things going on, such as drugs being brought into the institution. Sometimes I think there were more drugs inside the prison than on the street, as most of the big-time people were in the prison. Not really, but it's just an example.

The next time we went up for a two-day unescorted pass and were granted it. My wife picked me up at the gate house and off we went to Harrison Lake and set up a tent. We were very happy at this time in our lives. She had things already made, and we had a nice bite to eat and really enjoyed our two days. I was always sad when the pass was over and I had to go back inside, and it affected my wife also. But myself I stayed out of trouble and worked our way out. The next thing I did was to get out of the main prison and get transferred to a small prison in the small town of Agassiz.

I got the chance to go with a gang of inmates at the back of Pitt Lake and work for Forestry, thinning and spacing. We got paid three dollars an hour, and we worked two weeks and then would go back to the prison and go out on a pass, which was good. It was beautiful country up there. I was at a couple of camps over the year, and I saved money and bought a nice wedding ring for Barb; we were getting married when I was released. At one camp we had to fly in and the pilot had to fly over the runway to chase the bears off. Then we would land and go to our camp in a big van with a few benches in it. This was 1975.

A friend of mine worked with me thinning and spacing, as we had to work in twos for safety reasons. Well, on our time off we would get a canoe and go out on this man-made lake and we could see the tops of big trees just peeking on the top of the water; what a sight. There were bald eagles. It was just beautiful country. We finished there and went back to Agassiz prison camp and one day I was visiting with my girl and I needed to change my shirt as it was too hot out. I went into my unit and I heard some yelling and a scuffle. I looked out of my cell and I saw a guard fighting with a friend of mine who was trying to reach the washrooms to flush some drugs he had.

I yelled at the guard to leave him alone and this distracted the guard and my friend flushed the drugs. I never thought anything more of it, but little did I know I was in trouble. I changed my shirt and went back to my girl. A few days went by, and the day came for me to go out on a pass with my girl. I was called into the office and the head guard said, "You won't be going out on a pass, and you will be going to Warden's Court." I asked for what, and he said for interfering with an officer in the line of his duty.

Well, I got mad and said, "Take me back to Matsqui." I tried to change my mind and say forget it, but they said no, I was going back. So I packed up my stuff and down the road I went. I was handcuffed and put in the back seat, and there were two guards in the front. We arrived at Matsqui and I was put in the Hole. After a day or so I went in front of the warden of Agassiz and he gave me seven days in the Hole, but I could still get visits by phone and behind glass. My girl and I worked my way up again and they gave our passes back and transferred me back to Agassiz.

They sent me to work in the bush again, at Winslow Creek, which was also nice country. I would like to mention something that I liked just as much as the kids' group, and that is finding someone's dad or mother. One day a young guy came up to me and asked if I knew his dad. You see, he knew I had been in the joints. I said, "What is your dad's name?" and when he told me I just about fell over. I told the young guy that me and his dad used to hang around together in one of the prisons we were in over the years. He asked if I could find him and I said I would do my best. I knew where to go, and it took me a few days.

Once out of prison and in Vancouver I walked to the corner of Main and Hastings and I saw him doing what they call a cocaine dance. I talked to him and he said he would like to see his son. They finally got to see each other, and he got cleaned up. The boy said, "I can't thank you enough for finding my dad." I said, "That's okay, I was happy that it turned out for you both." But I have seen it time after time, and he could not shake that monkey off his back. He died of an overdose shortly after.

My release date was December 1977, and the night before went slow but before I knew it, I was out and free. We rented a nice little house out by Sylvester Road, past Mission going east. There was a church on the property, and I cleaned it and I did the grounds. We were married on the 17th of December and we stayed at the place for a year or so. Emilee was born on April 18, 1978. It was a delightful time. We enjoyed our stay at the house on Sylvester Road, but we moved closer to Abbotsford.

I started to do more stained glass in our new place, and it had a good workshop. I started to do craft fairs and private homes with windows etc. and I also did mall shows. We were enjoying our little girl. We moved a few times, eventually moving to a place in Abbotsford, and I met a friend I knew in the BC Pen and he asked if I wanted to move to Quesnel and open up a craft store. He was from Quesnel and he knew a woman who was into pottery and knew other artists who would like to put their work into the shop. This woman who did pottery gave me ten thousand dollars to buy glass supplies. Glass is very expensive, so the glass alone cost me five thousand for fifty sheets of assorted glass. I got other stained-glass items as well.

My wife and I talked about moving to Quesnel and she said it would be okay with her. So, we packed up and left. None of the glass broke, and little Emilee thought it was a great adventure. We arrived and rented a house. This was the end of 1979. We fixed up our place and I went and looked at the shop. It was quite spacious, so I unloaded all the stained-glass supplies and started to do glass work. Well, things went well for a while, but the other artist started to drink in the shop and was just wrecking things for others. It didn't work out, so I packed up my things and left. I stayed in Quesnel for a while doing other jobs, but my wife didn't like it there, so she took our daughter Emilee and went home to Abbotsford.

After a while she moved into an apartment, and I stayed up in Quesnel for a few months but then I moved back with my wife. It was a nice place, and it also had a good workshop to do my glass. I settled in and did my glass and did odd jobs. On the way down from Quesnel, I got a ride with a guy who had truck big enough to carry all my stained glass and other belongings. I started doing drugs again, and it wasn't fair to my wife. One night I met this guy I knew from inside, and we were drinking in the bar in Abbotsford. He had quite a bit of money and wanted to buy some pot but couldn't find any that night so I asked him if he wanted to stay at my place overnight and he said okay. I waited until he went to sleep and took a few dollars from him and left a whole lot. I had never done that, ever, as I lived by the strict code.

Anyway, I made him a coffee in the morning and drove him to his car, which was left uptown. I said goodbye and he told me after he got gas that he noticed some money missing. Well, I was on my way into Vancouver to get heroin, and that's what drove me to take the money. I had a good name, and this made me angry at myself. This guy was a real gangster, not like today. Anyway, I got some drugs and came home and my wife told me that he came by and was quite angry, so I phoned him but he wasn't home. Little did I know he was on his way to see me. I went to sleep and later on I heard a noise downstairs at my basement window. Well, I got up and opened the door and he pushed his way in and hit me on the side of my head with a baseball bat. I fought with him and then he gave me a two-handed swing with the bat and broke my left tibia. I never made a sound, and as he was leaving, he shoved the corner of the coffee table into my left tibia and I made a sound, as it hurt. Well, that seemed to satisfy him and he told me to pay back the money I took from him and that would be it. He couldn't figure out why I did that, as I had a good name. I never did that again.

I saw him again and he said, "No hard feelings as you paid in many ways for doing that." I paid all the money back and that was that. I had the cast on for a few months. I believe he passed away years later; this was 1982 and on November 20 Joel was born.

We were getting along, doing a lot of stained glass, and we were at this last place until April 1985 when I got charged for impaired driving and got three months. I served it at a place up by the Chilliwack River. I got out on a pass halfway through the sentence and everything seemed fine with my wife, so I took the bus home. When I walked to our apartment, I sensed something was wrong, as there was a For Rent sign on my lawn. I opened the door and my heart sank; there was nothing left in our apartment except my things, and I knew my wife was gone. I couldn't really blame her, as I was always going out and doing drugs and not really looking out for the family.

So eventually I got a hold of her and she said, "I have had enough, and I am leaving you," so that was that. After a while I found a place in Abbotsford, a nice basement suite, and I stayed there until 1989. After that I got the chance to go up to my Uncle Walter's in Yale, and I stayed at his place for two years. My uncle and I worked on the old cemetery for a year and a half. After that I moved to Hope and stayed at my aunt's trailer for quite awhile. My brother Murray asked me if I wanted to move to Grand Forks with him and his wife, and I have been up in Grand Forks for eleven years now. I have stayed out of trouble for twenty years. I saw my daughter and her mother two years ago at Murray's in Osoyoos and spent some time with her, which was nice. My daughter Emilee is doing great. She is studying mental issues and going to school and maintains a 93.5% average. My son Joel is doing as well as can be expected.

My daughter Emilee.

Emilee Storrings

One of the reasons we wrote this book is that if just one person reads this and goes down a different path than I did, I will be happy.

Emilee, my daughter.

Prison Talk, by Dennis Storrings

Here are a few incidents of the brutality that can happen in some of the jails I was inside of. There were real cold-blooded murders. One case that always stuck in my mind hurt because I knew the fella well. W.F. was a great guy, and I first met him in Haney Correctional Institution in around 1960. He was a good fighter and used his boots as weapons. He wasn't that big, but he was wiry. After Haney I lost track of him but saw him again in Vancouver in 1968. I didn't use heroin at that time, but he did. Me and a friend of mine ran into W.F. one night. We was in his car and he said we needed some money. He probably needed it more because he was junk sick, meaning he hadn't had a fix for quite a while and was going through withdrawal. Anyway, he wanted me and my friend to rob Johnston's Motors, so he handed my friend a 45 handgun and off we went to do the score. W.F. and his girlfriend stayed in the car, and I thought that was kind of strange. As we got to the score, things didn't go right. For one thing, the guy at the outside booth thought something didn't look right. We were asking him for change for a twenty-dollar bill and he wouldn't open the door and get on the phone.

So, we took off and went back to the car. W.F. didn't like that, so he drove to a connection and the three of us went into a rooming house, knocked on the door and it opened. I recognized the guy from the joint and there were two other guys in the room, who I also recognized. I thought W.F. was just going to score a cap of junk from them but he pulled out the 45 and robbed them of the heroin. Well, I didn't want no part of it, as I lived by the code and you didn't do things like that. Luckily the three guys didn't recognize me, so I took off.

I didn't see W.F. for a few years but had heard through the grapevine that he was pistol-whipping guys and robbing them, which was not good. I was in the BC Pen in '70 or '71 when W.F. came in. I could tell he was nervous, and I didn't talk to him even though we were friends, because if you talked to a guy that was marked as a rip-off, you could wreck your reputation and get what he was going to get. Well, one day W.F. came down from the fourth tier with just a mattress cover on him instead of his joint clothing. He went to pick up his tray but instead of doing that he stuck his head into the big vat of milk and they took him to the Hole. I knew what he was doing; he was putting on the bug act, meaning he was insane.

Well, that didn't work, and after some time in the Hole he came back to the population. One day he was in his cell up on 4 B and a few inmates went up there who had a grudge against him, and somehow they got his cell open. W.F. knew what was coming and he had his shank ready. They rushed in and the stabbing started. I give him this, he fought for his life and got a few of them, but it was to no avail. I heard they stabbed him thirty times.

They had to watch out for the bulls, as they didn't want to get caught. So, after they were done, they all scattered and W.F. crawled all the way down to the dome floor four tiers down. He died on the dome floor, and nobody was ever convicted for the brutal crime.

I would just like to say that in those days, you never talked about another inmate because you could get into real trouble. That's why even today I still don't like to mention guys' names. R.I.P., W.F.

Another time, this guy who was a skinner, meaning a rapist, was on the fourth tier. They usually keep them in protective custody, but somehow, he stayed in the general population. Well, when the inmates found out they were mad that a skinner was on their tier. So, one day they were ready to get this guy. The cells were open, and they sprayed him with lighter fluid and set him on fire. He come out of his cell to get away. Being careful to not get burned, they threw him over the tier and he went four tiers down to the concrete floor. Well, there was blood all over and he split his head open; what a mess. He died there or shortly after. No one was ever convicted for that, either. In those days there was no wire mesh; there were just railings.

Another time, one day in BC Pen there was a guy who I will call Skip. Well, he decided he wanted to get high, so he went up to the fourth tier, the highest, and then he climbed up higher on some wire meshing. You could say he was up five tiers now, and he jumped straight onto the marble dome feet first. It drove everything up to his insides and he bit his tongue partly off. The strange thing was that he lived and when asked why he did it, he said he wanted to get high from painkillers from the doctors. I could never get his reasoning; I guess he thought he was either going to die or get high. Strange.

I wrote a poem once about W.F.:

I once knew a fella named Wayne,
He was wild but not insane.
He got used to taking what he desired
but paying he quite refrained.
Well, Wayne went too far
treating the boys he knew with blows
and never accepted the blame.
Caught by the law,
he ended up with some of the boys I will not name.
Well, he tried his best to sidestep and dodge,
but the only thing left was to appear insane.
I see him come from the top tier

and spring into a vat of milk
like a swimmer riddled with pain.
But one day his luck run out.
Thirty holes in him, no doubt.
That's the fella named Wayne ....

Murray is on the right. Behind him is Dennis. In the back row beside Dennis is Glen.
Next to Murray in front is Sharon, standing, and her brother sitting.
1950 at the Bourelle foster home on 17th Ave. in Haney.

BC Penitentiary in New Westminster BC where brothers Glen and Dennis, and Douglas Storrings (our Father) were incarcerated in the 1960s (Photo taken by Donald Waite)

Oakalla Prison Farm in Burnaby BC where the Storrings brothers were all incarcerated for long periods of time doing time and waiting trial, on the right of the photo was west wing(waiting Trial unit) and the left side was east wing(sentence was up to two years less a day) in the middle was south wing waiting to go to the Penitentiary and at times waiting trial which all three of us were housed waiting trial (death row was below our tier on two left ,it had a small yard to exercise and play cards .
(photo was taken by Donald Waite of Maple Ridge BC

AUTHORS' COMMENTS

The story in this book was not written to offend anyone but to tell the truth as much as possible and to tell our family's life story.

The story of us three brothers was in the making for several years, as the three of us got access to our CFD files from Victoria, which has helped us write a more complete picture of our lives combined with our memories of what happened to us in foster care and later in life.

We would like to dedicate this book to all the children that went though a similar process in the ministry. We hope this story will help them in their lives. They are not alone, as we often thought we were in our young lives growing up foster care the way it was then.

Also, we dedicate this to our wives and children who will read this book and realize why we were like we were and see what we went though as small children.

We also wish to say that we still love our lovely mother who had struggles in her life, as we did. She didn't survive, but we did, and we wonder how we did.

Special thanks to Eleanor Brooks and Don Waite. I'd also like to thank the staff at FriesenPress with special thanks to our editor, and Holly for all the help she gave when we were having problems with our story. Without their help this may not have progressed the way it did so quickly, and to the other people involved with inspiring us to write this book, we thank you all. Also, a special thanks to all the social workers and foster parents who tried to help us as much as they could. We thank you.

Authors Footnotes: A question we have often thought is why the Canadian Government chooses to apologize to certain groups of people who have being victimized but never have we heard any apologises to our Foster Children who have been Victims of the Foster care and still carry the scars of the abuse that we endured in the system for many years and still do. I am sending The Prime Minster Justin Trudeau a copy of our book so he can read first hand on how Canadian children are affected by the care in foster homes and still are today.

When the we request our CFD -files that show us what our lives were like from infant to later years in the foster care system we are handed our files and we are on our own to read what is in the files but there is no help if we find files that are to much for a person to handle ,and I have found there is no support groups for over 21 years old its like were on our own with no help and in our files it states these three boys need psychological help but none was ever offered or given .

CPSIA information can be obtained
at www.ICGtesting.com
Printed in the USA
BVHW012104240123
656673BV00006B/1

9 781525 558696